Modern Game Animati

Design Advanced Animation Pipelines and Motion Systems with OpenGL and Vulkan

Jose Gobert

Copyright

Table of Contents

Preface

This book was written for programmers who are serious about building **real-time animation systems** in modern C++ and want to implement them in **professional game development pipelines**. Whether you're an **intermediate to advanced C++ developer**, a **game engine architect**, or a **technical animator** looking to understand how animation works under the hood, this book is designed to equip you with the **concepts, code, and techniques** needed to create animation systems from scratch that are **performant, flexible, and production-ready**.

Who This Book Is For

This book assumes you already have a working knowledge of modern C++—ideally C++17 or newer—and a basic understanding of rendering concepts. If you've worked with C++ in graphics programming, game loops, simulation, or engine design, you're well-positioned to get the most value out of this material. The content is especially suited for:

Developers building custom **game engines** or modifying existing ones.

C++ programmers integrating animation into OpenGL/Vulkan-based applications.

Graphics and rendering engineers needing robust animation support.

Technical animators interested in engine-side implementation details.

Even if you're not a game developer by trade, if you're working with real-time graphics, this book will give you solid insight into how complex animations can be structured, optimized, and rendered efficiently using C++.

What You'll Gain

By the end of this book, you'll be able to:

Implement a full skeletal animation system using keyframes, interpolation, skinning, and joint hierarchies.

Write animation blending logic to combine multiple animations smoothly (e.g., idle + aiming).

Integrate inverse kinematics (IK) into gameplay logic, allowing characters to reach or place their limbs accurately.

Render animated models in both OpenGL and Vulkan, using GPU skinning techniques.

Build your own animation tools and formats, or integrate with asset pipelines via Assimp.

Optimize for **performance, memory efficiency, and modularity**, ensuring the animation system works well in both single-player and large-scale environments.

Throughout the book, all concepts are grounded in **real-world usage**. You won't just learn the theory—you'll implement, test, and profile systems that are ready to plug into a modern game loop.

Tools and Technologies Used

The book makes use of **widely adopted, production-grade tools and standards** to ensure the concepts are transferable to your projects. These include:

C++17/20: Used throughout the code to take advantage of modern features like `std::variant`, ranges, and structured bindings. We'll follow clean, modular C++ architecture.

OpenGL 4.6: A well-known graphics API used for teaching GPU skinning and shader animation techniques. Its wide adoption makes it a great place to learn.

Vulkan 1.3: For advanced rendering examples, you'll see how to structure descriptor sets and command buffers for animated models in Vulkan.

GLSL: OpenGL Shading Language for writing vertex shaders that handle animation on the GPU.

GLM: A mathematics library tailored for graphics applications. It supports vectors, matrices, and quaternions used in animation pipelines.

Assimp (Open Asset Import Library): Used for importing animation data such as bone hierarchies, skeletal poses, and keyframes from common formats like FBX and COLLADA.

ImGui: Immediate-mode GUI for building real-time debug and visualization tools. Useful for viewing skeletons, joint transforms, and animation states during runtime.

We avoid relying on proprietary engines or toolkits, so you'll have complete control and visibility into how everything works—making the knowledge applicable across any platform or project.

Acknowledgments

To everyone building custom game engines and real-time graphics systems from the ground up: your commitment to solving hard problems with clean code inspired the approach and depth of this book.

Special thanks to the contributors of open-source libraries like Assimp, GLM, and Dear ImGui. These tools power the low-level development many of us rely on but rarely get the recognition they deserve.

Lastly, to the developers and technical artists who keep asking, "how does this work under the hood?"—this book is a direct response to that question. May it give you the tools and confidence to build your own animation systems from the ground up.

Chapter 1: Understanding Real-Time Game Animation

Building animations for real-time applications like video games is very different from animating for movies or pre-rendered scenes. When you're working on games, you're not just creating motion—you're building **systems** that respond to player input, synchronize with physics, and stay performant under tight timing constraints. This chapter lays the foundation you need before writing a single line of C++ animation code. We'll start by defining how game animation differs from other forms of animation, then cover the core types you'll encounter, the real-time constraints you'll face, and the essential concepts you must understand before building your own animation system.

1.1 Animation in Games vs. Film

When you hear the word "animation," your first mental picture might be a beautifully choreographed character in a Pixar film, or a cinematic cutscene with smooth transitions and expressive motion. These animations are polished, artistic, and emotionally engaging. But when it comes to video games— especially real-time games—the goals and constraints are very different. Here, animation is not just about aesthetics; it's about interactivity, responsiveness, and performance. This difference changes everything—from how animations are created, to how they're stored, and especially how they're played back.

In film production, the animation is part of a linear storytelling process. Animators manually keyframe every major movement, every subtle eye twitch or hand motion, and then render each frame using sophisticated software with no constraint on time. Rendering a single frame can take several minutes or even hours. There's room to simulate highly detailed lighting, sub-surface scattering, motion blur, and hair dynamics because the result is not expected to update in real time. Once it's rendered, it's baked into the final output and doesn't need to change again.

In contrast, real-time games are constantly in motion, driven by player input, AI, physics, and random events in the simulation. Every animation must respond on-the-fly to what the player is doing. If the player changes direction, aims a weapon, presses jump, or gets hit by an enemy, the animation system must blend into the appropriate state—**within milliseconds**. There is no pre-rendering. Everything is computed on the spot, each frame, every frame. This real-time demand shapes how game animation systems are built.

For instance, in a third-person action game, let's say your player character is walking forward and then starts sprinting. In a film, you could blend those two motions by hand and render the transition once. But in a game, you must write logic that blends between the walking animation and the sprinting animation dynamically, at runtime, using parameters like speed and player input. The transition must look natural whether it starts from the beginning of the walk cycle, the middle, or even at the moment of foot impact. This means you're not just animating once—you're building **systems that evaluate poses, blend between animations, and react to real-time state changes**.

Let's make that more concrete. In a film pipeline, animators might keyframe a 300-frame sequence of a character drawing a sword, starting from an idle stance. That sequence is authored specifically for a cinematic shot. But in a game, the player might draw a sword from any state: idle, running, crouching, or even midair. The animation system must account for all of these possibilities by either:

blending from the current pose into the draw-sword animation, or

providing multiple context-sensitive variants of that action, and selecting the right one at runtime.

This is why game animation is so tightly coupled with **state machines**, **animation blending systems**, and sometimes even **behavior trees** or **gameplay logic layers**. Animations are often split into shorter clips: idle, step, start run, loop run, stop run, turn left, turn right, aim, shoot, reload. These pieces are reassembled dynamically based on what's happening in the game.

From a programming perspective, one of the biggest differences is the way we think about **timing and resources**. In film, a rig with hundreds of bones is normal—even desirable—because it gives animators fine control. But in real-time games, you're often limited to 64 or 128 bones per character due to performance constraints on the GPU. These bone transforms must be computed on the CPU or GPU and updated every frame. If you're animating

50 characters on screen, that's potentially thousands of matrices flying around every frame.

Let's say you're using GPU skinning, a common technique for real-time animation. You need to upload a palette of bone matrices each frame to a uniform buffer or a texture. Each matrix is 16 floats (64 bytes), and if you have 100 bones per character and 40 characters on screen, that's 256 KB of data per frame, just for animation matrices. That kind of memory bandwidth adds up fast, especially when you're also dealing with physics, lighting, and AI. And you still haven't rendered a single pixel yet.

There's also the challenge of animation **precision and memory storage**. In a film, every frame is keyframed or interpolated at 24 or 30 frames per second, and there's no issue storing that on disk. In games, animation data is compressed aggressively—using techniques like quaternion compression, delta encoding, or fixed-rate sampling—to reduce runtime memory usage. Instead of storing every bone transform for every frame, game engines often store key poses and interpolate between them at runtime using techniques like linear interpolation (LERP) for positions and spherical linear interpolation (SLERP) for rotations.

For example, a walk cycle might only have 10–15 keyframes over one second. Your animation system must fill in the rest using interpolation. And this interpolation must be accurate and fast. Here's a simplified version of how you might interpolate two quaternions for a bone rotation in C++ using GLM:

```
glm::quat interpolatedRotation =
glm::slerp(startRotation, endRotation, t);
```

Where t is a value between 0 and 1 representing the normalized time between keyframes. This needs to run for every animated bone, for every character, each frame. You can't afford unnecessary allocations, cache misses, or floating-point precision errors.

Now let's also consider interaction. In a film, the animation is linear and fixed. In games, it's player-driven. If a player presses a button to interrupt an animation—say, canceling a reload to dodge—you need to handle that transition cleanly. This leads to complex state management and animation graphs, where the game logic and animation logic must communicate seamlessly.

These are the kinds of details that make game animation programming not only challenging but deeply rewarding. You're not just visualizing motion—you're building **the systems that breathe life into characters in real time**, systems that must perform well, feel responsive, and never break immersion.

By understanding these fundamental differences between film and game animation, you'll appreciate why the structure, format, and logic of game animation systems must be so meticulously engineered. From this point forward, every technique we'll explore will take these real-time demands into account.

1.2 Types of Game Animations

When building a game animation system, one of the first decisions you'll make is what *type* of animation you need for a given character, object, or scenario. This choice isn't just about artistic style—it's deeply tied to how your game logic works, how your characters interact with the environment, and how your rendering and physics systems are structured. Most real-time games use a combination of several animation techniques working together, each with its own data format, runtime behavior, and performance cost. Understanding how and when to use each one is essential to writing efficient, scalable animation code.

Let's start with **skeletal animation**, the most widely used type in modern 3D games. It allows you to animate complex meshes—like humanoid characters or animals—by associating them with an internal skeleton. Each bone in the skeleton represents a joint or limb and has a local transform: position, rotation, and sometimes scale. These bones are connected hierarchically, so that when a parent bone moves (like the shoulder), its children (like the elbow and wrist) move with it. The character mesh itself is bound to this skeleton through a process called **skinning**, where each vertex is influenced by one or more bones. The weights define how much influence each bone has on the final position of a vertex.

This method is highly flexible. You can reuse the same skeleton with different meshes, and you can apply multiple animations—like walking, aiming, or crouching—at the same time through blending. Here's a minimal example of how you might represent a bone transform and a skinning calculation in C++ using GLM:

```cpp
struct Bone {
    int parentIndex;
    glm::vec3 localPosition;
    glm::quat localRotation;
    glm::mat4 localMatrix;
    glm::mat4 globalMatrix;
};

glm::vec3 ApplySkinning(
    glm::vec3 originalPosition,
    const glm::mat4 boneMatrices[4],
    const float weights[4]
) {
    glm::vec4 skinned = glm::vec4(0.0f);
    for (int i = 0; i < 4; ++i) {
        skinned += weights[i] * (boneMatrices[i] *
glm::vec4(originalPosition, 1.0f));
    }
    return glm::vec3(skinned);
}
```

In a real engine, this skinning calculation is usually moved to the GPU for performance reasons, and the bone matrices are uploaded each frame to a shader. But the conceptual structure remains the same.

Skeletal animation is used heavily in most genres—whether you're animating characters in an action RPG, creatures in a survival game, or robotic arms in a sci-fi puzzle game. Its hierarchical nature also makes it ideal for integrating with physics engines for ragdolls, or layering procedural movement like weapon sway or head tracking.

Now let's talk about **morph target animation**, also known as **blend shapes**. This technique is often used when skeletal animation isn't enough—specifically when you need detailed surface deformation that bones can't easily replicate. Facial animation is the most common example. While a skeleton can rotate a jaw or eyelid, it can't express subtle lip curls, cheek puffing, or eyebrow lifts with convincing realism. Instead, artists sculpt multiple versions of the same mesh, each representing a different "target" pose. At runtime, you interpolate between these targets based on input parameters, like emotion level or phoneme being spoken.

Technically, this means you're storing multiple versions of vertex positions (and sometimes normals), and blending them per-vertex. This can be expensive if not optimized carefully, especially on the GPU. You also need a data structure to hold the delta offsets and blend weights. Here's a conceptual example of morph target blending in C++:

```cpp
glm::vec3 ApplyMorphTargets(
    const glm::vec3& base,
    const glm::vec3* targets,
    const float* weights,
    int numTargets
) {
    glm::vec3 final = base;
    for (int i = 0; i < numTargets; ++i) {
        final += targets[i] * weights[i];
    }
    return final;
}
```

This function would typically be run per-vertex in a vertex shader or compute shader. Performance becomes a consideration quickly, especially if you're supporting 4–8 simultaneous blend shapes across hundreds of vertices. In many games, morph targets are limited to a few key expressions or phonemes and updated only on important characters (like protagonists or NPCs during dialogue scenes). This allows you to balance fidelity with budget.

The third category is **procedural animation**, and this is where you stop relying entirely on baked data and start generating motion dynamically, often through code. Procedural animation is especially useful for things that need to react to the environment in real-time, or that vary so much that hand-animating them becomes impractical.

For example, consider a procedural head-look system. Instead of keyframing a "look left" or "look right" animation, you compute the head bone's target rotation based on the position of an object or the camera. This can be updated every frame and blended with other animations. Or imagine a tentacle that reaches toward the player—its motion can be driven by inverse kinematics or even a spring-damped system based on distance and momentum.

Another example is foot placement on uneven terrain. Rather than playing a generic walk animation and letting the feet clip through the ground, you can raycast beneath each foot to find the surface and adjust the leg joints accordingly. This requires real-time IK (Inverse Kinematics), but it creates a more believable interaction with the game world.

Procedural techniques can also be layered on top of existing skeletal animations. For example, after playing a base run animation, you might add a slight tilt to the torso when turning, or apply a camera shake when landing. These effects are often simple math functions that modify bone transforms after the base pose has been calculated.

To support procedural animation, your engine architecture must allow pose overrides. Typically, you evaluate a base pose from keyframe animation, then apply procedural changes before skinning. This is commonly done by operating directly on the pose data (bone transforms) before it's sent to the GPU.

From a code perspective, you might write a function like this:

```cpp
void ApplyLookAt(
    Bone& head,
    const glm::vec3& headPosition,
    const glm::vec3& targetPosition
) {
    glm::vec3 forward =
glm::normalize(targetPosition - headPosition);
    glm::quat targetRotation =
glm::rotation(glm::vec3(0, 0, 1), forward);
    head.localRotation =
glm::mix(head.localRotation, targetRotation, 0.1f);
    // Smooth blend
}
```

This kind of code lets your characters react to the player, follow enemies, or dynamically change posture without needing an animator to manually keyframe every possible case. It's powerful, flexible, and increasingly common in modern animation systems.

What's important to understand is that these three techniques—skeletal, morph, and procedural—are not mutually exclusive. They often work together in the same character. A combat character might use skeletal animation for movement, morph targets for facial expressions, and procedural animation to adjust for camera-facing poses or terrain slopes.

Each type brings unique strengths, and each comes with trade-offs in terms of data complexity, runtime cost, and authoring requirements. A robust animation system needs to support all three cleanly, and expose hooks for gameplay programmers, animators, and AI systems to work together fluidly.

As we build out our system, we'll ensure that it's modular enough to support all these animation types. You'll see how to structure your pose evaluation logic, how to design data formats for keyframes and morphs, and how to keep things performant with real-time constraints in mind. But before we get to any of that, we need to address the one constraint that drives everything in real-time animation: performance.

1.3 Real-Time Performance Considerations

When working with animation in a real-time game environment, you're not just concerned with making things look good. You also have to make sure your system performs well under tight time constraints. Every animation you play, every bone you transform, and every vertex you skin contributes to your frame budget. And unlike offline rendering, you don't get the luxury of waiting. You have a fixed time window—usually **16.67 milliseconds** per frame at 60 FPS— and you must fit everything inside it: logic, physics, AI, rendering, audio, and of course, animation.

To build a practical and scalable animation system, you must treat performance as a first-class design requirement. This means understanding the cost of every operation, choosing efficient data structures, and deciding which tasks are handled by the CPU and which are offloaded to the GPU. It also means thinking about how your animation logic fits into the overall engine lifecycle.

Let's begin by looking at one of the most fundamental trade-offs you'll face: **CPU vs GPU animation processing**. When you're evaluating animations on the CPU, you have full control and visibility. You can cache results, modify poses with gameplay logic, apply procedural effects, or serialize pose data for networking or debugging. This is why many engines perform pose evaluation and blending on the CPU. However, the CPU becomes a bottleneck quickly when you start animating dozens of characters—especially in open-world or crowd-based games. Each character might have 60–100 bones, and you're performing matrix interpolation, hierarchy traversal, and skinning calculations per bone, per frame. That adds up fast.

Let's do a rough back-of-the-envelope calculation. Suppose you're animating 50 characters with 80 bones each. If each bone requires a matrix multiplication and interpolation between keyframes, you're doing around **4,000 matrix calculations per frame**, just for pose evaluation. And if you apply CPU skinning (transforming vertices on the CPU instead of in shaders), then you're also transforming **tens of thousands of vertices** every frame. That's unsustainable on modern CPUs, especially when you factor in everything else going on.

Here's a simplified example of pose evaluation per bone:

```
glm::mat4 InterpolatePose(const glm::mat4& start,
const glm::mat4& end, float t) {
    // This is a placeholder. Real systems often
interpolate position and rotation separately
    return glm::mix(start, end, t);
}
```

Now imagine calling this for every bone in every animated character. It gets expensive fast. To avoid this bottleneck, many engines perform **GPU skinning**, where only the bone matrices are computed on the CPU and then uploaded to the GPU as a matrix palette. The actual vertex transformation happens in the vertex shader, which can process thousands of vertices in parallel.

Here's a minimal example of what that shader might look like in GLSL:

```
uniform mat4 u_BoneMatrices[100]; // bone matrix
palette
in vec4 a_BoneIDs;
in vec4 a_Weights;

void main() {
```

```glsl
    mat4 skinMatrix =
        a_Weights.x *
u_BoneMatrices[int(a_BoneIDs.x)] +
        a_Weights.y *
u_BoneMatrices[int(a_BoneIDs.y)] +
        a_Weights.z *
u_BoneMatrices[int(a_BoneIDs.z)] +
        a_Weights.w *
u_BoneMatrices[int(a_BoneIDs.w)];

    vec4 skinnedPos = skinMatrix * vec4(a_Position,
1.0);
    gl_Position = u_ViewProjection * u_Model *
skinnedPos;
}
```

This lets the GPU handle thousands of vertices concurrently, but you still have to manage **bone matrix upload**. If each character uses 80 bones, and each matrix is 64 bytes (4x4 floats), that's 5 KB per character per frame. With 50 characters, that's **250 KB of matrix data per frame**. That might seem small in modern terms, but it must be transferred to GPU memory every single frame. If your render pipeline is not efficient—or if you don't batch these updates correctly—you'll quickly hit performance limits.

Besides raw computation, another performance consideration is **data layout**. Animation data is read frequently and in tight loops, so how you store it matters. Structuring keyframes, bone transforms, and weights in a way that is cache-friendly will significantly reduce CPU stalls and memory latency. This is especially important on consoles, mobile devices, or lower-end PCs.

Let's say you have an array of Keyframe structs, each containing a timestamp, a quaternion for rotation, and a vector for position. If these are laid out poorly, your CPU might be jumping around in memory every time it processes a frame. But if you separate the data into **Structure of Arrays (SoA)** form— storing all timestamps together, all positions together, etc.—you can vectorize operations and get better performance from your hardware's prefetchers.

Here's an example of what poor layout (AoS – Array of Structs) looks like:

```cpp
struct Keyframe {
    float time;
```

```
    glm::quat rotation;
    glm::vec3 position;
};

std::vector<Keyframe> keyframes; // Bad for large-
scale evaluation
```

And here's a better layout using SoA:

```
struct KeyframeData {
    std::vector<float> times;
    std::vector<glm::quat> rotations;
    std::vector<glm::vec3> positions;
};
```

This lets you iterate over each property in tight, predictable loops—making it easier to parallelize and cache.

Another challenge in real-time animation is **blending**. It's not enough to just play one animation at a time. In practice, a character is usually blending between multiple clips—walking while turning, crouching while aiming, jumping while holding a rifle. Each blend operation requires additional interpolation and weight normalization. In systems where multiple blend layers are evaluated (e.g., upper body vs lower body), the cost scales further. The blend tree must be traversed, each node evaluated, and the resulting poses composited.

You'll also need to consider **Level of Detail (LOD)** in animation. Just like with rendering, not every character needs full fidelity if they're far away from the camera. You might update animations at a lower frequency (e.g., every 3rd frame), reduce the number of bones, or switch to a simplified animation entirely. Some engines even use baked vertex animations for background characters—trading flexibility for performance.

A practical example: suppose your player is surrounded by a crowd of NPCs in a city. Only a few of them are close enough to matter. You can update those with full skeletal animation and GPU skinning. The rest can use simplified logic or looping animations with no interaction. This allows you to scale to hundreds of characters without breaking your budget.

Finally, **threading and job systems** can help spread the workload. Many modern engines (like Unity's DOTS or Unreal's Task Graph) execute animation updates across multiple threads. This means you can evaluate bone poses in parallel, as long as they don't depend on each other. Designing your animation system to be thread-safe and data-oriented from the start will help you get better scalability across CPU cores.

All of this—CPU vs GPU cost, memory layout, threading, LOD—must be designed carefully to avoid bottlenecks. Animation might only be one part of your engine, but it can quickly dominate your performance budget if not architected properly.

1.4 Core Concepts: Transforms, Joints, and Skinning

Before you can animate a character in real-time, you need a strong foundation in the basic building blocks of skeletal animation. At the core of every animation system are **transforms**, **joints**, and **skinning**—the pillars that drive mesh deformation and make your characters appear to move with purpose and fluidity. These aren't abstract concepts. They directly affect how your engine processes animation data, how you structure bone hierarchies, how GPU shaders compute vertex positions, and how your gameplay systems interact with character poses.

Let's start with the most fundamental structure: the **transform**. In animation, a transform typically consists of a **position**, a **rotation**, and sometimes a **scale**. These components together define how a bone or object is oriented in space. In C++, this is often represented with a 4x4 matrix (`glm::mat4`), or more efficiently with separate `glm::vec3` for position, `glm::quat` for rotation, and `glm::vec3` for scale. This separation allows for more intuitive manipulation, such as interpolating only the rotation using quaternion slerp or blending position vectors linearly.

In skeletal animation, every joint has a local transform that defines its position **relative to its parent**. When you walk up the chain of bones, each child inherits the transform of its parent. So, moving the shoulder affects the elbow, which in turn affects the wrist and the fingers. This hierarchy of transformations is what gives skeletal animation its expressive power.

Here's a simple C++ structure for representing a local bone transform:

```cpp
struct Transform {
    glm::vec3 position;
    glm::quat rotation;
    glm::vec3 scale;

    glm::mat4 ToMatrix() const {
        glm::mat4 translate =
glm::translate(glm::mat4(1.0f), position);
        glm::mat4 rotate = glm::toMat4(rotation);
        glm::mat4 scaleMat =
glm::scale(glm::mat4(1.0f), scale);
        return translate * rotate * scaleMat;
    }
};
```

This allows you to generate a matrix for a bone at runtime, which you can then combine with its parent's transform to produce a global matrix. This process is known as **forward kinematics**—you start from the root of the skeleton (usually the hips or pelvis), and build up the global transforms by multiplying each bone's local transform with its parent's global transform.

To support a full skeleton, you'll use a structure that maintains a list of bones and their parent indices. For example:

```cpp
struct Bone {
    int parentIndex;
    Transform localTransform;
    glm::mat4 globalTransform;
};
```

Then you calculate the global transform for each bone in the skeleton like this:

```cpp
void ComputeGlobalTransforms(std::vector<Bone>&
bones) {
    for (size_t i = 0; i < bones.size(); ++i) {
        if (bones[i].parentIndex >= 0) {
            bones[i].globalTransform =
bones[bones[i].parentIndex].globalTransform *
bones[i].localTransform.ToMatrix();
        } else {
```

```
                bones[i].globalTransform =
bones[i].localTransform.ToMatrix();
        }
    }
}
```

This recursive accumulation allows the entire skeleton to update efficiently based on local changes, such as adjusting the spine or turning the neck, while preserving hierarchical relationships.

Once your skeleton is producing meaningful global bone transforms, the next step is **skinning**—the process of applying these transforms to deform the mesh. In real-time graphics, this is almost always done using **linear blend skinning**, sometimes referred to as **smooth skinning**. Each vertex in the mesh is influenced by a small number of bones (typically up to four), and each influence has a weight. These weights determine how much each bone affects the vertex's final position.

Let's say a vertex is influenced by the upper arm and the forearm bones. If the upper arm rotates, the vertex moves partially with it. If the forearm rotates, it also influences the same vertex. The final position is a weighted combination of both bone transformations applied to the vertex's original bind pose position.

In shader code (GLSL), this might look like:

```
mat4 skinMatrix =
    a_Weights.x * u_BoneMatrices[int(a_BoneIDs.x)]
+
    a_Weights.y * u_BoneMatrices[int(a_BoneIDs.y)]
+
    a_Weights.z * u_BoneMatrices[int(a_BoneIDs.z)]
+
    a_Weights.w * u_BoneMatrices[int(a_BoneIDs.w)];

vec4 skinnedPosition = skinMatrix *
vec4(in_Position, 1.0);
```

On the CPU side, you'd upload u_BoneMatrices every frame based on the current global transforms of each bone in your character's skeleton. These matrices are actually **final bone transforms**, which are computed by multiplying the global transform of the current pose by the **inverse bind pose matrix** of that bone. The bind pose is the skeleton's original rest state—the state it was in when the mesh was rigged. The inverse bind matrix brings the vertex into bone space, and the global transform moves it into animated space.

Here's how that might look in C++:

```cpp
for (int i = 0; i < boneCount; ++i) {
    finalBoneMatrices[i] = globalPose[i] *
inverseBindPose[i];
}
```

These final matrices are what you use to drive GPU skinning.

Now let's think practically. Suppose you're animating a humanoid character with 72 bones. For each bone, you have a `Transform` struct and a 4x4 matrix. That's a significant chunk of memory and computation, especially if you're animating 50 characters per frame. So, your update step must be as efficient as possible. This is where SIMD-friendly math libraries like GLM or DirectXMath come into play, and where job systems can parallelize bone transform calculations across multiple cores.

In a real-world production setting, these systems get even more complex. Animators author multiple animation clips (walk, run, aim), and your engine needs to blend between them. That blending happens in **pose space**, meaning you compute the transforms for each animation, interpolate them, and then skin the mesh using the result. This requires that your `Transform` struct support blending—linear for positions, spherical for rotations, and multiplicative or interpolated for scale.

For example, to blend two poses:

```cpp
Transform BlendTransforms(const Transform& a, const
Transform& b, float t) {
    Transform result;
    result.position = glm::mix(a.position,
b.position, t);
    result.rotation = glm::slerp(a.rotation,
b.rotation, t);
    result.scale = glm::mix(a.scale, b.scale, t);
    return result;
```

This function can be called per bone when blending between animations. The key is that all of this happens **before** the skinning step, so the resulting pose is fully composed when it reaches the GPU.

Everything in skeletal animation flows from these three pieces: transforms define the movement, joints create the hierarchy that drives complex relationships, and skinning binds it all to the mesh so it visually responds to that motion. You'll be building these structures into your animation system from the start, and they will form the backbone of every feature you implement—from walk cycles to IK, from blend trees to physics-driven ragdolls.

Chapter 2: C++ and Math Foundations for Animation

If you're serious about building a real-time animation system in C++, you'll need to be comfortable with the math that drives it. This chapter focuses on exactly that: the foundational math concepts and C++ data structures that support animation systems. We're not going to review math in an academic way—we're going to use it practically. Every concept you'll see here—vectors, matrices, quaternions, interpolation methods, and transformation hierarchies—is something you'll be writing and using directly in your animation code.

Before we start blending poses or uploading bone matrices to the GPU, you must understand how to represent motion, rotate objects smoothly, and keep track of parent-child relationships. You'll also need to structure animation data in a way that is efficient and easy to work with inside your C++ engine.

2.1 Essential Math for Animation

Before you can animate anything—whether it's a bone, a mesh, or a full character—you need to understand how motion is represented mathematically. In real-time 3D animation systems, three mathematical tools are used almost everywhere: **vectors**, **matrices**, and **quaternions**. These aren't just abstract math terms. They're the language your engine uses to calculate bone positions, interpolate poses, compute skinning, and drive visual effects. If you're building an animation system from scratch in C++, these are the constructs you'll work with every day.

Let's start with vectors. A **vector** in 3D graphics is typically used to represent a point in space, a direction, a velocity, or a scale. In C++ animation systems, you'll typically use `glm::vec3` or a similar structure to represent these values. A vector isn't tied to any position in space—it's just a direction and a magnitude. If you subtract one position vector from another, you get a direction vector. If you multiply a normalized direction vector by a scalar, you get a point offset in that direction.

In the context of animation, vectors are used everywhere: defining the position of a bone, the offset from one joint to another, the axis of rotation, or even the motion of a projectile. Here's a very basic example using GLM:

```
glm::vec3 start = glm::vec3(1.0f, 2.0f, 0.0f);

glm::vec3 end = glm::vec3(4.0f, 3.0f, 0.0f);

glm::vec3 direction = glm::normalize(end - start);
```

This simple operation defines a direction vector that points from `start` to `end`. This is exactly the kind of calculation you'll do when orienting a bone toward a target (like a head turning to face a player).

Next, let's discuss matrices. A **matrix** is a mathematical structure that lets you perform transformations—things like translation, rotation, scaling, and projection. In 3D graphics and animation, the most common type is a **4x4 matrix** (`glm::mat4`), which combines all three transformation types into a single structure. You use it to move objects in space, rotate them around an axis, or scale them uniformly or non-uniformly.

Each joint in your character's skeleton will use a matrix to represent its transformation in 3D space. For efficiency and clarity, it's common to decompose these transforms into their parts—position (`vec3`), rotation (`quat`), and scale (`vec3`)—and then rebuild the matrix when needed.

```
glm::mat4 modelMatrix =
glm::translate(glm::mat4(1.0f), position)

                    * glm::toMat4(rotation)

                    * glm::scale(glm::mat4(1.0f),
scale);
```

This operation is critical. It composes the transform that will later be applied to each bone and, eventually, each vertex of the skinned mesh.

Let's move on to **quaternions**, which are used for representing rotation. You might be tempted to use Euler angles or rotation matrices, but they introduce several issues in animation. Euler angles suffer from **gimbal lock**, where you lose degrees of freedom during rotation. Rotation matrices, while mathematically robust, are bulky and don't interpolate well.

Quaternions avoid these issues. They allow you to represent smooth, continuous rotation, and—most importantly—they can be interpolated using **spherical linear interpolation** (SLERP), which is critical for blending animation keyframes.

Here's how you construct and use a quaternion in GLM:

```
glm::quat rotation =
glm::angleAxis(glm::radians(90.0f), glm::vec3(0, 1,
0)); // 90° around Y

glm::mat4 rotationMatrix = glm::toMat4(rotation);
```

This gives you a 90-degree rotation around the Y-axis, which you can then apply to a bone or object. If you're blending between two orientations—like transitioning from a walk to a run—quaternions make it possible to interpolate the rotation smoothly without artifacts:

```
glm::quat blended = glm::slerp(startRotation,
endRotation, t);
```

This line computes a new orientation that's t percent of the way between the start and end rotations. The value t ranges from 0.0 to 1.0. It's used in pose evaluation to generate smooth transitions between animation keyframes.

You'll often need to apply a quaternion to rotate a direction vector. This is a fundamental operation when adjusting forward directions, or applying bone orientation to a child transform:

```
glm::vec3 newDirection = rotation * glm::vec3(0, 0,
1); // rotate the forward vector
```

One thing that's worth noting is that quaternions must be **normalized** to work properly. This means their magnitude must equal 1.0, otherwise, you'll start getting incorrect results over time. Most libraries like GLM handle this internally, but it's a good habit to normalize after manual operations:

```
rotation = glm::normalize(rotation);
```

To give you a real-world example: when you're animating a character's arm swinging during a walk cycle, each bone in the arm hierarchy the shoulder, elbow, wrist—has its own rotation at each keyframe. To evaluate the pose at a specific time, you interpolate each bone's rotation using SLERP, apply that rotation using a quaternion, and then compose the result into a transformation matrix. This matrix gets passed to the GPU for skinning, which updates the character's mesh in the final rendered frame.

Here's a practical C++ structure that combines all of these concepts into a reusable `Transform` type:

```cpp
struct Transform {
    glm::vec3 position = glm::vec3(0.0f);
    glm::quat rotation = glm::quat(1.0f, 0.0f,
0.0f, 0.0f);
    glm::vec3 scale = glm::vec3(1.0f);

    glm::mat4 ToMatrix() const {
        glm::mat4 T =
glm::translate(glm::mat4(1.0f), position);
        glm::mat4 R = glm::toMat4(rotation);
        glm::mat4 S = glm::scale(glm::mat4(1.0f),
scale);
        return T * R * S;
    }
};
```

This structure is something you'll use frequently throughout your animation pipeline. Every pose you evaluate, every keyframe you sample, and every bone you animate will rely on this structure or something very close to it.

Mastering the use of vectors, matrices, and quaternions is non-negotiable in real-time animation. They're not just academic tools—they're the foundation of every pose your characters strike, every move they make, and every transition they undergo. Whether you're applying a simple rotation, blending between multiple animations, or building complex IK systems, these are the building blocks that keep everything consistent, performant, and expressive.

Now that you understand how to represent movement and orientation mathematically, we'll move on to **interpolation methods**—how to compute smooth transitions between poses and keyframes. This is where your transforms come to life over time.

2.2 Interpolation Methods (LERP, SLERP, Cubic)

In a real-time animation system, interpolation is what brings your data to life. Without interpolation, you'd be stuck snapping from one pose to another, and everything would look robotic or broken. Every frame of animation—whether it's part of a walk cycle, facial expression, or procedural blend—is a result of smoothly transitioning between two or more keyframes. This process needs to be efficient, predictable, and precise.

Let's start with the foundation: **LERP**, or Linear Interpolation. This is the simplest and most widely used interpolation method. You give it two values and a blend factor `t` between 0 and 1, and it returns a weighted average between them. In animation, `LERP` is commonly used for interpolating **positions** and **scales**, which are both linear quantities.

Here's the basic formula:

```
glm::vec3 Lerp(const glm::vec3& a, const glm::vec3&
b, float t) {
    return (1.0f - t) * a + t * b;
}
```

Or, using GLM directly:

```
glm::vec3 result = glm::mix(a, b, t); // glm::mix
performs a linear interpolation
```

You'll typically call this during pose evaluation. Let's say you're evaluating a walk animation. At time `t`, you determine that the character's root position is between keyframes 3 and 4. You interpolate between the two positions to get the in-between pose for that frame. This gives your animation its smooth motion without needing to keyframe every single moment.

But LERP only works well for linear values. When it comes to **rotation**, using LERP causes distortions and unnatural movement because it interpolates angles directly. This is where **SLERP** (Spherical Linear Interpolation) comes in. SLERP interpolates between two **quaternions**, which are the proper representation for rotations in 3D.

Here's how to perform a SLERP using GLM:

```
glm::quat blendedRotation =
glm::slerp(startRotation, endRotation, t);
```

This function rotates the orientation smoothly along the shortest arc between the two quaternions. The parameter t once again ranges from 0.0 to 1.0, and the result is always normalized (unit-length), which avoids distortions or scaling artifacts.

In a practical animation system, each bone has a rotation stored as a quaternion, and during pose sampling you perform a SLERP for each one. For example, to evaluate a pose between two animation keyframes:

```
Transform Interpolate(const Transform& a, const
Transform& b, float t) {
    Transform result;
    result.position = glm::mix(a.position,
b.position, t);
    result.rotation = glm::slerp(a.rotation,
b.rotation, t);
    result.scale = glm::mix(a.scale, b.scale, t);
    return result;
}
```

This pattern is used throughout animation pipelines, including pose blending, crossfades between states (walk to run), and additive layers.

Now let's take it a step further. When you're interpolating between **more than two keyframes**, especially over long timelines, linear and spherical interpolation alone aren't always enough. Animations can appear too stiff or too mechanical, because there's no acceleration or deceleration—it's just constant-speed blending from point A to point B.

To address this, we use **cubic interpolation**, specifically spline-based methods like **Catmull-Rom** or **Hermite splines**. These allow for smooth curves through multiple keyframes, and give you control over tangents to shape the motion more naturally. This is particularly useful in camera animation, facial motion, or soft organic movement where timing nuance matters.

Let's take Catmull-Rom as a concrete example. It allows you to interpolate a value through a set of points, ensuring the curve passes through each one smoothly. Here's a simplified implementation for position curves:

```
glm::vec3 CatmullRom(const glm::vec3& p0, const
glm::vec3& p1,
                     const glm::vec3& p2, const
glm::vec3& p3, float t) {
    float t2 = t * t;
    float t3 = t2 * t;

    return 0.5f * (
        (2.0f * p1) +
        (-p0 + p2) * t +
        (2.0f*p0 - 5.0f*p1 + 4.0f*p2 - p3) * t2 +
        (-p0 + 3.0f*p1 - 3.0f*p2 + p3) * t3
    );
}
```

You'll use this to interpolate a position between p1 and p2, given surrounding points p0 and p3. This allows your animation to move with better flow and transition characteristics than LERP.

While cubic interpolation is more computationally intensive, it's often used during **offline preprocessing** or in select systems where motion quality is prioritized over raw speed—for instance, cutscenes, camera systems, or cinematic sequences.

In real-time character animation, cubic interpolation is less common at runtime because of performance costs and memory layout complexity. But you'll still find it useful when baking high-quality movement data, generating smooth curve paths for vehicles or turrets, or managing character look-at behaviors with eased transitions.

One important consideration when using splines is tangent control. For Hermite splines, you must specify incoming and outgoing tangents manually or compute them from neighboring keyframes. This gives you fine control over how fast and in what direction motion begins and ends. It's more work, but for cases like eye blinking or lip sync, the payoff in realism is significant.

Let's recap the use case for each method through a practical lens:

You use **LERP** for positions and scale values because they are linear quantities.

You use **SLERP** for bone rotations because rotations are spherical in nature and must interpolate through space accurately.

You use **cubic interpolation** for multi-point sequences where smoothness and timing matter more than raw performance.

Each method serves a different role in your animation system, and knowing when and where to apply them is what separates a passable animation system from a professional one. These interpolation methods aren't just mathematical tools—they are the algorithms behind every pose blend, every head turn, every arm swing, and every believable transition in your characters.

2.3 Transform Hierarchies and Parent-Child Relationships

In any skeletal animation system, the concept of a **hierarchy** is not optional— it's fundamental. Bones in a skeleton aren't isolated entities. They are part of a connected structure where each bone's transformation depends on its **parent**. This relationship allows characters to move with realistic joint-based behavior. When you move the shoulder, the elbow follows. When the spine twists, the neck and head naturally rotate with it. This kind of motion is made possible by traversing and combining transforms through a **parent-child chain**.

To understand how this works in practice, you need to break down the difference between **local** and **global** transforms.

A **local transform** is the transformation of a bone relative to its parent. This includes its position (offset), rotation, and possibly scale. For example, a character's elbow might be 0.3 units away from the shoulder joint along the X-axis and rotated slightly forward. That transform is *relative* to the shoulder.

A **global transform**, on the other hand, is the transformation of the bone in world (or model) space. It is computed by **combining the local transform of the bone with the global transform of its parent**. This cumulative relationship forms a chain, starting from the root of the skeleton (typically the hips or pelvis) and flowing outward to the fingertips and toes.

Let's express that in code. First, you'll need a structure to represent each bone and its hierarchical connection:

```
struct Transform {
    glm::vec3 position;
    glm::quat rotation;
    glm::vec3 scale;

    glm::mat4 ToMatrix() const {
        glm::mat4 T =
glm::translate(glm::mat4(1.0f), position);
        glm::mat4 R = glm::toMat4(rotation);
        glm::mat4 S = glm::scale(glm::mat4(1.0f),
scale);
        return T * R * S;
    }
};

struct Bone {
    int parentIndex; // -1 for root
    Transform localTransform;
    glm::mat4 globalTransform;
};
```

Now, to evaluate a skeleton's pose for rendering or skinning, you must compute the **global transform** for each bone. This is typically done with a simple loop:

```
void ComputeGlobalTransforms(std::vector<Bone>&
bones) {
    for (size_t i = 0; i < bones.size(); ++i) {
        if (bones[i].parentIndex >= 0) {
            bones[i].globalTransform =
bones[bones[i].parentIndex].globalTransform *

bones[i].localTransform.ToMatrix();
```

```
        } else {
            bones[i].globalTransform =
bones[i].localTransform.ToMatrix();
        }
    }
}
```

This logic walks through each bone, checks if it has a parent, and if it does, multiplies its local matrix by its parent's global matrix. This multiplication is what propagates rotation and position through the skeleton. So when you rotate the pelvis of a character, it naturally causes the spine, chest, arms, and head to move as well.

Let's look at a real-world example: a humanoid character swinging a sword. When you apply a keyframe rotation to the shoulder bone, you're affecting its local transform. But the resulting motion—how the elbow, wrist, and hand follow through—is a result of hierarchical transformation. If you simply rotated the wrist without accounting for the upper bones, the arm would appear disconnected and broken. That's why maintaining and correctly evaluating the hierarchy is so important.

Another area where hierarchies matter is **inverse kinematics**. When solving for the position of a foot on uneven terrain, the IK solver adjusts the ankle, then propagates the result upward to the knee and hip. This only works because of the parent-child connections between bones.

Let's say you're blending between two animation clips: a walking cycle and a crouching pose. You evaluate both poses independently, each giving you a full set of local transforms. When blending, you interpolate each bone's local transform (position, rotation, scale) and then recalculate global transforms through the hierarchy.

```
Transform BlendTransforms(const Transform& a, const
Transform& b, float t) {
    Transform result;
    result.position = glm::mix(a.position,
b.position, t);
    result.rotation = glm::slerp(a.rotation,
b.rotation, t);
    result.scale = glm::mix(a.scale, b.scale, t);
    return result;
```

```
}
```

You apply this blend per bone, storing the result as a new pose. Then you run `ComputeGlobalTransforms()` again to get the final pose in model space. This ensures the character's joints maintain their correct relative positioning and move as a coherent whole.

Now, let's talk about performance. Evaluating these hierarchies can become expensive if you have many characters on screen. Each bone transform involves at least one matrix multiplication, and a typical character has between 40 to 80 bones. Multiply that by 50 characters, and you have thousands of operations per frame. This is why data layout matters. Bones should be stored in a flat array, and evaluated in topological order (parents before children), so that traversal is cache-friendly and parallelizable.

When integrating this into an ECS-based engine (Entity Component System), you can treat the skeleton as a single component and use a job system to parallelize hierarchy evaluation for multiple characters.

In some systems, especially those using dual quaternions or matrix palettes, you may precompute and cache inverse bind pose matrices. These matrices are used during GPU skinning to bring each vertex into bone space before applying animation.

```
glm::mat4 finalMatrix = globalTransform *
inverseBindPoseMatrix;
```

This result is what you upload to the GPU each frame. It allows your shader to correctly animate the mesh in real time.

To summarize practically: transform hierarchies allow motion to propagate naturally through bone chains. Without them, animated characters would not respond correctly to movement, rotations would not compound, and your animation system would fall apart during even basic actions like walking or turning.

Understanding this system deeply—how local transforms combine to produce global motion, how parenting influences pose calculation, and how data should be structured and evaluated—will prepare you to build everything from skeletal animation systems to IK chains and procedural motion overlays.

2.4 Structuring Animation Data in C++

Once you understand how transforms and hierarchies work in theory, the next essential step is building a practical, performant, and flexible structure in C++ to store and evaluate your animation data. This means designing the right data types for bones, tracks, keyframes, and poses, in a way that supports efficient runtime evaluation, memory access, blending, and playback. If you don't structure your animation data correctly, you'll either hit performance bottlenecks or create a system that's too rigid to extend when new features like additive blending, inverse kinematics, or event tracks are introduced.

Let's begin with the smallest piece of animation data: the **keyframe**. A keyframe represents the pose of a single bone at a specific point in time. It usually contains a position, a rotation, and a scale. These values are then interpolated at runtime to produce the final pose.

Here's a straightforward C++ struct for a keyframe:

```
struct Keyframe {
    float time;              // Time in seconds
    glm::vec3 position;      // Local position of
the bone
    glm::quat rotation;      // Local rotation as
a quaternion
    glm::vec3 scale;         // Local scale
};
```

You'll typically store multiple keyframes for each bone in an animation clip. These form a **track**, which is essentially an ordered list of keyframes associated with one specific bone. At runtime, your engine will interpolate between these keyframes to evaluate the current pose for that bone.

```
struct BoneTrack {
    std::vector<Keyframe> keyframes;
};
```

You'll then organize all the bone tracks under an **animation clip**, which represents one animation—for example, a walk cycle or an attack sequence.

```
struct AnimationClip {
    std::string name;
    float duration; // In seconds
```

```
    std::vector<BoneTrack> tracks;
};
```

The `tracks` array should be indexed in the same order as the bone array in your skeleton. That means if bone #3 in your skeleton is the right arm, then `tracks[3]` should contain all the keyframes for the right arm. This makes evaluation simpler and avoids expensive lookups during runtime.

When it's time to evaluate a pose at a given time `t`, you'll walk through each track, find the two keyframes surrounding `t`, interpolate between them, and store the result as a new `Transform`.

Here's what that looks like for a single track:

```
Transform SampleTrack(const BoneTrack& track, float
time) {
    if (track.keyframes.empty()) return {};

    const Keyframe* prev = nullptr;
    const Keyframe* next = nullptr;

    for (size_t i = 0; i < track.keyframes.size() -
1; ++i) {
        if (time >= track.keyframes[i].time && time
<= track.keyframes[i + 1].time) {
            prev = &track.keyframes[i];
            next = &track.keyframes[i + 1];
            break;
        }
    }

    if (!prev || !next) {
        return track.keyframes.back().time < time
            ?
Transform{track.keyframes.back().position,
track.keyframes.back().rotation,
track.keyframes.back().scale}
            :
Transform{track.keyframes.front().position,
track.keyframes.front().rotation,
track.keyframes.front().scale};
    }
```

```
    float t = (time - prev->time) / (next->time -
prev->time);

    return {
        glm::mix(prev->position, next->position,
t),
        glm::slerp(prev->rotation, next->rotation,
t),
        glm::mix(prev->scale, next->scale, t)
    };
}
```

This function gives you the interpolated transform for one bone. In practice, you'll call this function for each track in the animation clip and assemble the results into a full **pose**.

```
struct Pose {
    std::vector<Transform> localTransforms;
};
```

The `Pose` structure stores the local transform of each bone at a specific moment in time. Once you've built this pose, you then convert it into global space using the parent-child hierarchy logic we discussed earlier.

Now, let's talk about **memory layout and optimization**. When you start dealing with large characters or multiple animations, performance becomes a major concern. To reduce memory fragmentation and improve cache locality, you may want to avoid storing keyframes as arrays of structs. Instead, consider converting your animation data into a **Structure of Arrays (SoA)** format— one array for positions, one for rotations, one for scales, and one for timestamps.

This layout is more SIMD- and cache-friendly, especially during batched pose evaluations. Here's an example for one track:

```
struct SoAKeyframes {
    std::vector<float> times;
    std::vector<glm::vec3> positions;
    std::vector<glm::quat> rotations;
    std::vector<glm::vec3> scales;
};
```

At runtime, you'll interpolate the data from these separate arrays. It's slightly more complex to set up but pays off significantly when you're evaluating many characters or using a job system for animation updates.

Another optimization is **keyframe compression**. For instance, if a bone doesn't move during an animation, you don't need to store more than one keyframe. You can also quantize rotation quaternions using 16-bit float components, or sample the animation at a fixed rate (say 30 FPS) and store only delta frames.

In a production setting, you might preprocess your animation clips offline using a tool or script that converts them into binary blobs—stripped of redundant keys, aligned for SIMD access, and packed efficiently. Your engine then loads this binary data into memory directly, which minimizes startup time and runtime cost.

A fully baked animation system will also need additional data structures to support:

Playback state, which keeps track of current time, loop status, blend weight, etc.

Blend trees, which define how multiple animation clips are layered or blended.

Event tracks, for triggering footstep sounds, effects, or gameplay events.

Metadata, such as root motion vectors, bounding box extents, or tags like "idle," "upper body," or "mirrored."

But at the core of all of this is the structure we've just built: keyframes per bone, organized into tracks, grouped into animation clips, and evaluated into poses. If that structure is solid, the rest of the system becomes much easier to extend.

By structuring your animation data in C++ thoughtfully and carefully, you ensure that your characters move fluidly, your system runs efficiently, and your engine remains flexible as requirements grow.

Chapter 3: Designing a Modern Animation Pipeline

When you're building a real-time animation system, you're not just writing code that plays back keyframes. You're designing a full **pipeline**—a structured path that animation data travels from the artist's digital content creation (DCC) tool to your runtime engine. A well-designed pipeline makes your system predictable, performant, and maintainable, while also empowering animators and developers to work in parallel.

3.1 Offline vs Runtime Animation Responsibilities

A modern animation system in a real-time engine isn't just about getting bones to move—it's about dividing the work **strategically** between offline preprocessing and real-time evaluation. This division is crucial, especially when targeting 60 FPS or higher, because every millisecond matters. Animation systems, while essential for visual fidelity, must also respect strict performance budgets. And the best way to do that is to **offload as much work as possible to the offline stage**, where time and memory are virtually unlimited, and keep the runtime as lean as possible.

What Should Be Done Offline?

Offline animation processing happens before the game ever runs. This usually occurs during the asset build stage or within an editor tool. It's your opportunity to **optimize**, **compress**, and **prepare** the data in a way that makes runtime evaluation fast and predictable. Anything that can be computed ahead of time, *should* be.

1. Sampling Animation Curves into Keyframes

Animation in tools like Blender or Maya is often stored as F-curves—complex curves with tangents and easing baked into them. Evaluating these curves in real time would be too expensive. So, you sample them into discrete keyframes at a fixed rate (commonly 30 FPS). This produces evenly spaced data that's easy to interpolate with linear or spherical methods.

```
// Pseudo-process for offline sampling
```

```
for (float t = 0; t <= clipDuration; t += (1.0f /
30.0f)) {
    glm::vec3 pos = EvaluatePositionCurveAt(t);
    glm::quat rot = EvaluateRotationCurveAt(t);
    glm::vec3 scale = EvaluateScaleCurveAt(t);
    StoreKeyframe(t, pos, rot, scale);
}
```

2. Compressing Keyframe Data

Once you've sampled the curves, there's usually a lot of redundant data. For example, a hand may not move at all during an idle animation. Storing 30 identical keyframes is wasteful. During offline processing, you can remove redundant keys or quantize the values.

Rotation quaternions can be compressed from 32-bit floats to 16-bit floats.

Static bones (bones that don't animate in this clip) can be excluded entirely.

Threshold-based reduction can remove keyframes where the delta is below a certain margin.

3. Calculating Inverse Bind Pose Matrices

Each bone needs an **inverse bind pose matrix** to allow proper skinning. This is a static transform that maps the vertex from mesh space to bone space. You don't want to compute this at runtime. It's stable, so you compute and store it once offline and use it forever.

```
// At offline time, store this per bone

inverseBindPose =
glm::inverse(globalBindPoseMatrix);
```

4. Constructing Bone Index Maps

When loading animation data, bone names from the DCC tool must match the bone layout in your runtime skeleton. Offline processing is where you resolve these mappings and build fast index-based lookups so runtime code doesn't need to string-match anything.

5. Saving to a Compact Runtime Format

Finally, you serialize all of the processed data—bone hierarchies, keyframes, inverse bind matrices, metadata—into a compact binary file that your runtime engine can load quickly with minimal parsing. This file can be versioned, endian-safe, and memory-aligned for your platform.

What Must Be Done at Runtime?

Now let's focus on what actually has to run every frame. These are the operations that can't be precomputed because they depend on **player input, simulation state, or current playback time**. They're the core of your real-time animation system.

1. Evaluating Pose at a Given Time

At each frame, you need to determine what the skeleton looks like at a given timestamp. That means:

Finding which two keyframes surround the current time.

Interpolating between those keyframes.

Producing a full local-space transform for each bone.

```
Transform EvaluatePose(const BoneTrack& track,
float time) {
    const Keyframe* k0 = GetKeyBefore(track, time);
    const Keyframe* k1 = GetKeyAfter(track, time);
    float t = (time - k0->time) / (k1->time - k0-
>time);

    return {
        glm::mix(k0->position, k1->position, t),
        glm::slerp(k0->rotation, k1->rotation, t),
        glm::mix(k0->scale, k1->scale, t)
    };
}
```

You repeat this for every bone that is animated in the current clip.

2. Blending Between Multiple Poses

In most cases, a character isn't just playing a single clip. They're blending between idle and walk, overlaying an upper-body reload animation, or transitioning into a hit reaction. Runtime blending means interpolating two or more poses together and sometimes masking which bones are affected.

```
Transform Blend(const Transform& a, const
Transform& b, float weight) {
    return {
        glm::mix(a.position, b.position, weight),
        glm::slerp(a.rotation, b.rotation, weight),
        glm::mix(a.scale, b.scale, weight)
    };
}
```

You can also use **additive blending**—where a secondary pose offsets a base pose, typically used for things like breathing or aim offsets.

3. Evaluating Global Transforms (Hierarchy Traversal)

Once all local transforms are evaluated or blended, you must resolve each bone's **global transform** based on its parent. This is where parent-child relationships come into play.

```
void ComputeGlobalTransforms(const
std::vector<Bone>& bones, std::vector<Transform>&
local, std::vector<glm::mat4>& global) {
    for (int i = 0; i < bones.size(); ++i) {
        glm::mat4 localMatrix =
local[i].ToMatrix();
        if (bones[i].parentIndex >= 0) {
            global[i] =
global[bones[i].parentIndex] * localMatrix;
        } else {
            global[i] = localMatrix;
        }
    }
}
```

4. Uploading Final Bone Matrices to the GPU

The GPU needs a matrix palette per skinned mesh, which is a list of bone transforms to apply to each vertex. These matrices are computed by multiplying each global transform by its corresponding inverse bind pose.

```
for (int i = 0; i < boneCount; ++i) {
```

```
    finalMatrix[i] = globalTransform[i] *
inverseBindPose[i];
}
```

These matrices are uploaded to the GPU as a uniform buffer, texture, or SSBO, depending on your rendering backend.

5. Handling Events and State Transitions

Finally, the runtime system monitors playback for event markers—footstep triggers, attack frames, or audio sync points. It also manages animation state machines or blend trees to decide which clip to play and how to transition smoothly between them.

Practical Separation Benefits

To highlight how impactful this separation is, consider a game with 100 animated NPCs on screen. If your system tries to parse FBX files or decompress animation curves at runtime, your CPU will choke. But if you do all the preprocessing offline and hand the engine pre-sampled, compressed binary data, your runtime evaluation becomes a simple, predictable task that can be parallelized or even offloaded to a job system.

This model also improves **modularity**. Offline tools can be written in Python, C#, or even JavaScript, using bindings to libraries like Assimp or GLTF. Your runtime, on the other hand, can remain a clean, focused C++ implementation with no third-party dependencies—just reading raw structs from disk and evaluating math.

A well-architected animation system always makes this division of labor clear. Offline tools are allowed to be complex, heavyweight, and slow. Runtime code must be minimal, fast, and dependable.

3.2 Animation Asset Flow: From DCC Tools to Game Engine

To make an animation system work in a real-time engine, you need more than just good code. You need a reliable, automated **asset pipeline**—a process that takes animation data authored in tools like **Blender**, **Maya**, or **3ds Max**, processes it correctly, and transforms it into a format your engine can use efficiently. The more structured and predictable this pipeline is, the easier it becomes to support new characters, iterate on motion, and optimize performance.

Authoring Stage (Inside Blender or Maya)

The process begins with the **creation of a rigged model** and a set of animations. The animator defines a **skeleton**—a hierarchy of joints or bones—and attaches it to a mesh using skinning weights. This skeleton might include 60–100 bones for a typical humanoid character.

Animations are created as **clips** on a timeline. Each clip corresponds to a specific action or behavior: walking, running, jumping, attacking, breathing. Every joint is keyframed at various times to define how it should move. Animators may also add **animation events**—such as sound triggers, hit frames, or particle effects—as tagged markers on the timeline.

Once the character is fully rigged and animated, the entire package—mesh, bones, skin weights, and animations—is exported to a format like **FBX**, **GLTF**, or **Collada (.dae)**. This exported file contains all the raw animation data that your engine will later consume.

Importing Stage (Asset Processing Tool)

At this point, your engine must take that raw file and convert it into something usable. This is where an **importer tool** comes into play. Most engines don't parse FBX directly at runtime—it's far too heavy and complex. Instead, they use tools like **Assimp** (Open Asset Import Library) or GLTF SDK to load and extract the necessary data *offline*.

Here's a simplified example of loading an FBX using Assimp:

```
Assimp::Importer importer;
const aiScene* scene =
importer.ReadFile("character@walk.fbx",
    aiProcess_Triangulate |
aiProcess_LimitBoneWeights);

if (!scene || !scene->HasAnimations()) {
    std::cerr << "Failed to load animation
file.\n";
    return;
}
```

Once the file is loaded, you traverse the animation section:

```
aiAnimation* anim = scene->mAnimations[0];
for (unsigned int i = 0; i < anim->mNumChannels;
++i) {
    aiNodeAnim* channel = anim->mChannels[i];
    std::string boneName = channel-
>mNodeName.C_Str();

    // Extract position keyframes
    for (unsigned int j = 0; j < channel-
>mNumPositionKeys; ++j) {
        aiVectorKey key = channel-
>mPositionKeys[j];
        // Convert and store key.time and key.value
    }

    // Extract rotation keyframes
    for (unsigned int j = 0; j < channel-
>mNumRotationKeys; ++j) {
        aiQuatKey key = channel->mRotationKeys[j];
        // Convert and store key.time and key.value
    }

    // Scale keys (optional)
}
```

You also parse the **bone hierarchy** by traversing `scene->mRootNode`. Each node represents a transform in the hierarchy. You build a map of `boneName` → `parentIndex` and construct your own internal representation of the skeleton.

At this stage, you're working with high-level, float-precision data with no compression, no alignment, and often more detail than you actually need.

Processing and Optimization Stage (Offline Preprocessing)

Once you have the keyframes and skeleton, you begin optimizing the data for **runtime use**. This includes several steps:

Uniform sampling: Convert variable-rate keyframes into evenly spaced samples (e.g., every 1/30th of a second).

Keyframe reduction: Eliminate redundant keys that have negligible delta from their neighbors.

Quantization: Reduce floating point precision (e.g., use half-floats for positions or 16-bit normalized quaternions).

Inverse bind pose computation: Calculate and store per-bone matrices to use during skinning.

Remapping bone indices: Convert bone names to direct indices matching your runtime skeleton order.

Metadata attachment: Embed loop flags, tags, root motion tracks, and event markers.

Here's a pseudo C++ representation of a processed animation clip:

```cpp
struct CompressedKeyframe {
    uint16_t time16; // fixed time range
    glm::vec3 position; // quantized or half-
precision
    glm::quat rotation;
    glm::vec3 scale;
};

struct BoneTrack {
    std::vector<CompressedKeyframe> frames;
};

struct RuntimeAnimationClip {
    float duration;
    uint32_t numBones;
    std::vector<BoneTrack> tracks;
};
```

Once processed, this clip is saved into a **custom binary format**. This file will be read directly by your engine without further decoding or string parsing.

Runtime Loading and Evaluation Stage

At load time—whether at game start or level load—you read this binary file into memory. This is a fast operation, usually just a `fread()` and pointer fix-up. Your animation system now has everything it needs: precomputed bone maps, compressed keyframes, and metadata.

When the animation system plays the clip, it evaluates it as follows:

Sample pose at the current time for each track.

Blend with any other active clips or overlays.

Evaluate global transforms using the hierarchy.

Compute final matrices using inverse bind pose.

Upload matrices to GPU for skinning.

All of this happens efficiently because you've front-loaded the complexity. There's no FBX parsing, no name lookups, no real-time sampling of complex curves—just raw math over simplified structures.

End-to-End Trace Example

Let's say you want your character to play a "run" animation when moving.

An animator creates the animation in Blender and exports it as `hero@run.fbx`.

Your asset tool loads it with Assimp, extracts the skeleton and keyframes.

The data is compressed, sampled, and saved to `hero_run.animbin`.

At runtime, your engine loads `hero_run.animbin`, evaluates the current frame based on delta time, and outputs a pose.

The pose is converted into matrices and uploaded to the shader for GPU skinning.

The mesh deforms according to bone weights and is drawn to screen.

At every point in that flow, responsibilities are clear and predictable. Animators know their job ends at export. Tools handle data integrity and optimization. The engine stays fast and minimal.

Having a structured asset flow makes collaboration between technical and non-technical team members easier. It prevents bugs caused by mismatched bone names, undefined transforms, or misaligned skeletons. Most importantly, it ensures that animation quality doesn't come at the cost of runtime performance.

3.3 Custom File Formats vs Assimp Loader

When you're building an animation system, you'll need to load rigged meshes and animation data authored in external tools like Blender, Maya, or 3ds Max. Most of these tools export to common formats like FBX, GLTF, or Collada, and while those formats are rich and flexible, they are not designed with real-time performance in mind. The key question becomes: **should you rely on a general-purpose importer like Assimp**, or should you **design and maintain your own custom runtime format**?

The answer depends on where in the pipeline you're using each. Both Assimp and custom formats have important roles—but for very different phases. Let's explore these roles in depth and walk through the practical decisions involved in both.

What Assimp Does Well

Assimp (the Open Asset Import Library) is an incredibly useful tool for importing animation data from a wide range of file formats. It supports FBX, GLTF, DAE, and many others, and provides a unified data structure so you don't have to write a separate parser for each format.

Here's what makes Assimp suitable for the **offline processing stage**:

It understands and parses complex animation features like keyframes, node hierarchies, tangent curves, and even blend shapes.

It abstracts away format differences. Whether your artist gives you an FBX or a GLTF, Assimp presents you with a consistent interface.

It has bindings for C++, C#, and other languages, so you can integrate it into CLI tools, asset pipelines, or in-editor importers.

Let's walk through a quick C++ example of using Assimp to load an animation file:

```
Assimp::Importer importer;
const aiScene* scene =
importer.ReadFile("orc@attack.fbx",
```

```cpp
        aiProcess_Triangulate |
aiProcess_LimitBoneWeights |
aiProcess_JoinIdenticalVertices);

if (!scene || !scene->HasAnimations()) {
    std::cerr << "Animation file could not be
loaded.\n";
    return;
}

aiAnimation* animation = scene->mAnimations[0];
for (unsigned int i = 0; i < animation-
>mNumChannels; ++i) {
    aiNodeAnim* boneChannel = animation-
>mChannels[i];
    std::string boneName = boneChannel-
>mNodeName.C_Str();

    // Positions
    for (unsigned int j = 0; j < boneChannel-
>mNumPositionKeys; ++j) {
        aiVectorKey posKey = boneChannel-
>mPositionKeys[j];
        // Store time and position
    }

    // Rotations
    for (unsigned int j = 0; j < boneChannel-
>mNumRotationKeys; ++j) {
        aiQuatKey rotKey = boneChannel-
>mRotationKeys[j];
        // Store time and rotation
    }

    // Scales (optional)
}
```

This works well for **one-time import**, but it is not appropriate for real-time animation playback inside your engine.

Why You Shouldn't Use Assimp at Runtime

Assimp is designed to be a flexible and comprehensive import library—not a fast runtime solution. Its data structures are hierarchical, verbose, and include a lot of fields and metadata you don't need during frame-by-frame evaluation. More importantly, Assimp uses standard C++ memory management (with pointers and heap allocations), making it **cache-inefficient** and unsuitable for **multi-threaded or SIMD-optimized** workloads.

Using Assimp directly in your engine runtime leads to several serious issues:

Slow load times due to string-based node traversal and pointer chasing

Excessive memory use, including unused animation channels and duplicate transforms

Incompatibility with ECS or job systems, where data needs to be packed and contiguous

Debugging complexity, since you're tied to a third-party data model

For all of these reasons, you should extract only what you need from Assimp and convert it into a **custom runtime-friendly format**.

Designing a Custom Animation File Format

A custom format lets you store only the necessary data, in a compact, cache-friendly layout. Your file format should reflect how your engine evaluates animations:

Keyframes should be **sampled at fixed intervals** (e.g., 30 FPS).

All values should be stored as **binary blobs**, not JSON or XML.

Bone indices should be **pre-mapped** and aligned to your engine's internal skeleton layout.

Structures should be laid out for **fast streaming** and **sequential access**.

Here's a minimal custom format header definition in C++:

```cpp
struct AnimationHeader {
    uint32_t version;      // for format evolution
    float duration;        // seconds
    uint32_t numBones;
    uint32_t numFrames;
```

```
};

struct Keyframe {
    glm::vec3 position;
    glm::quat rotation;
    glm::vec3 scale;
};
```

Each bone will have its own track of keyframes. You can store the tracks in a flattened array, where each track has a known offset and stride. Or you can group all transforms per frame, depending on your engine's evaluation model.

The idea is to **write a post-processing tool** (CLI or editor-integrated) that loads an FBX or GLTF file with Assimp, then outputs a .animbin file in your custom format. This file is what the game loads—not the original FBX.

What Goes Into Your Custom File

Your format should include:

Header: version, clip duration, bone count, frame count, flags

Bone remapping table: mapping from source bone names to internal indices

Keyframe data: position, rotation, scale for each track

Optional metadata: events, loop flags, root motion vectors

Inverse bind pose matrices: if not stored separately in skeleton data

And it should be **binary**. Here's how you might write it out:

```
std::ofstream file("orc_attack.animbin",
std::ios::binary);

file.write(reinterpret_cast<const char*>(&header),
sizeof(AnimationHeader));

file.write(reinterpret_cast<const
char*>(boneRemap.data()), boneRemap.size() *
sizeof(uint16_t));
```

```
file.write(reinterpret_cast<const
char*>(keyframes.data()), keyframes.size() *
sizeof(Keyframe));

file.close();
```

When loading in your engine, this becomes:

```
std::ifstream file("orc_attack.animbin",
std::ios::binary);

file.read(reinterpret_cast<char*>(&header),
sizeof(AnimationHeader));

// load the rest...
```

This keeps your engine startup fast, minimizes memory usage, and makes it easier to support background streaming.

Real-World Example: How Unreal Engine Handles This

In Unreal Engine, artists import FBX files in the editor. The engine uses its own importer to extract the data, bakes the animation, and saves it into a `.uasset` file. This binary file contains compressed animation tracks, root motion data, and bone metadata. At runtime, only the `.uasset` is loaded—the FBX is discarded. This is the same model we've discussed here.

Summary: The Ideal Split

Responsibility	Assimp (Offline)	Custom (Runtime)	Format
Parsing FBX/GLTF	✅	❌	
Extracting bone hierarchies	✅	❌	
Evaluating tangents/curves	✅	❌	
Uniform sampling	✅	❌	
Keyframe compression	✅	❌	

Responsibility	Assimp (Offline)	Custom (Runtime)	Format
Binary serialization	☑	✖	
Fast loading and playback	✖	☑	
Low memory footprint	✖	☑	
SIMD/job-system friendly layout	✖	☑	

Use Assimp **once**, offline, to convert authored assets into a form your engine understands. Use your **own format** to load and play animation quickly and predictably every frame. This is the standard in almost all professional-grade engines—because it works.

3.4 Planning for Scalability and Modularity

As your animation system grows—supporting more characters, more behaviors, and more animation features—it becomes increasingly important to structure your code and data in a way that scales cleanly. Without that structure, you'll find yourself adding hacks to support upper-body blending, duplicating logic for each new feature, or fighting performance bottlenecks when your NPC count jumps from 5 to 50.

This section is about **planning with intention**. You're not just writing animation code—you're designing a **foundation** that can support new features like inverse kinematics, facial animation, layered blending, motion matching, and runtime retargeting without collapsing under its own complexity.

Separate Concerns Cleanly

The first principle is: **each part of your animation system should do one thing only and do it well**. That means animation clips should not know about skeletons. Skeletons should not know about meshes. Pose evaluators should not care about rendering. Blend trees should not handle playback state.

This kind of decoupling allows you to reuse systems in different contexts and test them independently.

For example, your core data types might look like this:

```cpp
struct Transform {
    glm::vec3 position;
    glm::quat rotation;
    glm::vec3 scale;

    glm::mat4 ToMatrix() const {
        return glm::translate(glm::mat4(1.0f),
position)
                * glm::toMat4(rotation)
                * glm::scale(glm::mat4(1.0f), scale);
    }
};

struct Pose {
    std::vector<Transform> localTransforms;
};

struct Skeleton {
    std::vector<std::string> boneNames;
    std::vector<int> parentIndices;
    std::vector<glm::mat4> inverseBindPoses;
};
```

Each piece is reusable and cleanly separated. `Pose` knows nothing about keyframes or clips—it's just a snapshot of local transforms. `Skeleton` provides hierarchy and bind-pose data. These two structs alone let you apply animation from any source—keyframes, procedural systems, or networked input.

Support Parallel Evaluation Early

Scalability means **parallelism**. Evaluating poses, blending them, and computing global transforms are all tasks that can be done per-character or per-bone, in parallel. But that only works if your data layout and code structure support it.

To prepare for this, structure your pose and clip data in **flat, contiguous arrays** that are safe for multithreading:

```cpp
std::vector<Transform> EvaluateClipAtTime(const
AnimationClip& clip, float time) {
    std::vector<Transform>
pose(clip.tracks.size());

    for (size_t i = 0; i < clip.tracks.size(); ++i)
{
        pose[i] = SampleTrack(clip.tracks[i],
time);
    }

    return pose;
}
```

Later, when using a job system or thread pool, this loop can be split into jobs by range (i = 0..15, 16..31, etc.). No mutexes, no shared pointers, just raw data and stateless evaluation.

Design Extensible Blending Systems

Blending is at the heart of modern animation. You're constantly combining poses: idle into walk, walk into jump, reload layered on top of aiming, and procedural noise layered on top of breathing.

A naive approach might hardcode these blends in gameplay logic. A scalable approach builds a **blend tree** system that evaluates a set of inputs and combines them dynamically. Blend trees are modular graphs where each node is either:

A leaf (clip sampler, procedural pose)

A blend operation (linear blend, additive blend, masked blend)

A transition or selector node

Each node implements a standard interface:

```cpp
class IBlendNode {
public:
    virtual Pose Evaluate(float deltaTime) = 0;
    virtual ~IBlendNode() {}
};
```

This allows nodes to be composed like a functional tree. For example:

```
auto walk = new ClipNode(walkClip);

auto aim = new AdditiveNode(aimOffsetClip, walk);

auto final = new LinearBlendNode(aim, idle,
blendWeight);
```

Now your engine's animation logic is just a matter of configuring nodes. This system can be reused across all characters, and new nodes—like IK solvers, motion warping, or physics-driven overrides—can be added without refactoring the entire system.

Component-Based Runtime Architecture

To keep animation flexible and integrated cleanly into the engine, use a **component-based runtime**. Each animated character has the following systems:

SkeletonComponent: Holds reference to skeleton asset, current pose, bone matrices.

AnimatorComponent: Holds current state machine or blend tree, playback timers, active clips.

SkinnedMeshComponent: Knows which mesh to draw and which bones affect which vertices.

Here's a conceptual update routine:

```
void UpdateAnimator(AnimatorComponent& anim, float
deltaTime) {

    Pose pose = anim.blendTree-
>Evaluate(deltaTime);

    ComputeGlobalTransforms(anim.skeleton, pose,
anim.globalMatrices);

}
```

This separation lets you reuse the animation system across different entities—player, NPC, enemy, animal—each with different logic but the same animation backend.

It also makes it easy to support **animation-only entities**, like dynamic environment props or animated UI, without pulling in unnecessary rendering or physics logic.

Expose Modularity to Tooling

Your pipeline is not just runtime—it includes tools. To support scalability in content creation, ensure your importers, exporters, and preview tools respect the same modular principles.

The **clip processing tool** shouldn't care what engine will use the output.

The **skeleton builder** should be a reusable tool for all characters.

Your **debug visualizers** should work with any animation source, not just keyframes.

Even at the CLI level, make each tool handle one job:

```
build_skeleton hero.fbx -o hero.skel

build_clip hero@walk.fbx -o hero_walk.animbin

preview_animation hero_walk.animbin hero.skel
```

This makes your build system composable and CI-friendly.

Design for Feature Growth

Finally, build your system with **hooks and extension points** for future growth. You might not need facial animation or runtime retargeting today, but you should avoid hardcoding decisions that make them impossible tomorrow.

Some forward-looking design decisions:

Don't assume each bone has only one transform per frame—support layered or masked poses.

Don't bake root motion into mesh vertices—store root motion as a separate track.

Don't tie bone indices to bone names—map bones at import, then use indices only.

Don't assume animations only affect skeletons—support morph targets or vertex caches as well.

A scalable and modular animation system is one where each part of the codebase knows its job, stays independent, and allows new systems to plug in without breaking existing ones. This isn't about over-engineering. It's about *deliberate design choices* that make room for your project's future.

Chapter 4: Importing Animation Assets with Assimp

When you're building a real-time animation system, the first step is getting usable animation data into your engine. Most of that data comes from digital content creation tools like Blender, Maya, or 3ds Max, and it's usually exported in standard formats like **FBX, GLTF**, or **Collada (.dae)**. But these formats are designed for maximum flexibility—not runtime performance.

This is where **Assimp (Open Asset Import Library)** comes in. Assimp acts as a bridge between high-level content creation and your low-level runtime engine. It supports over 50 different 3D file formats and gives you a consistent API to access mesh geometry, bone hierarchies, and animation tracks. But to use it effectively, you need to understand how Assimp organizes animation data—and how to convert that data into your own internal formats for evaluation and rendering.

4.1 Understanding Assimp's Animation Structures

To import animation data from formats like FBX, GLTF, or DAE into your engine, you need to understand how Assimp organizes that data internally. Assimp is not a runtime playback library—it's a **file format parser and abstraction layer**. Its role is to read complex files authored in digital content creation tools and expose their contents in a consistent C++ API. For animation data, this includes everything from skeleton hierarchies to keyframe-based motion curves.

Core Entry Point: aiScene

When you load a model or animation file with Assimp, you begin with the `aiScene` structure.

```
Assimp::Importer importer;

const aiScene* scene =
importer.ReadFile("orc@run.fbx",
```

```
      aiProcess_Triangulate |
aiProcess_JoinIdenticalVertices |
aiProcess_LimitBoneWeights);
```

If the `scene` pointer is non-null and `scene->HasAnimations()` returns true, then you know the file contains animation data. Now let's walk through how that animation data is organized.

aiAnimation: The Animation Clip

Each animation in the file is stored as an `aiAnimation*`. The scene may contain multiple clips (for example, idle, walk, run), accessible via `scene->mAnimations[i]`.

aiAnimation* clip = scene->mAnimations[0];

An `aiAnimation` structure contains:

`mDuration`: Length of the animation in **ticks**.

`mTicksPerSecond`: How many ticks equal one second (used to convert to real time).

`mChannels`: An array of `aiNodeAnim*` (one per bone).

`mNumChannels`: Number of channels.

You can calculate the animation's total length in seconds like this:

```
float durationSeconds = static_cast<float>(clip->mDuration);

if (clip->mTicksPerSecond > 0.0) {

    durationSeconds /= static_cast<float>(clip->mTicksPerSecond);

}
```

Each `aiAnimation` is essentially a clip made up of **animation channels**, where each channel represents a bone and holds its keyframes.

aiNodeAnim: A Bone's Animation Track

Each element of `clip->mChannels[i]` is an `aiNodeAnim*`. This represents the animation track for a specific bone or node in the hierarchy. It holds separate keyframe lists for position, rotation, and scale.

```
aiNodeAnim* channel = clip->mChannels[i];

std::string boneName = channel->mNodeName.C_Str();
```

An `aiNodeAnim` contains:

`mNodeName`: The name of the bone or transform node this animation affects.

`mNumPositionKeys`, `mPositionKeys`: Keyframes for position (`aiVectorKey`)

`mNumRotationKeys`, `mRotationKeys`: Keyframes for rotation (`aiQuatKey`)

`mNumScalingKeys`, `mScalingKeys`: Keyframes for scale (`aiVectorKey`)

These keyframe arrays are **not sampled uniformly**. This is important. You must assume each keyframe track is irregularly spaced, and their times are expressed in **ticks**, not seconds.

Let's extract the keys:

```
for (unsigned int i = 0; i < channel-
>mNumPositionKeys; ++i) {
    aiVectorKey key = channel->mPositionKeys[i];
    double tickTime = key.mTime;
    aiVector3D pos = key.mValue;
    glm::vec3 position(pos.x, pos.y, pos.z);
    float timeSec = static_cast<float>(tickTime /
clip->mTicksPerSecond);
    // Store (timeSec, position)
}
```

Repeat the same for `mRotationKeys` and `mScalingKeys`.

Transform Resolution Order

Each animation channel provides its position, rotation, and scale keys separately. You should evaluate and combine them in the correct transform order—scale → rotation → translation—just like in most game engines.

Assimp does **not** provide a combined transform per keyframe. That means you'll construct it manually using a helper like this:

```
glm::mat4 ToMatrix(const glm::vec3& position, const
glm::quat& rotation, const glm::vec3& scale) {
    glm::mat4 T = glm::translate(glm::mat4(1.0f),
position);
    glm::mat4 R = glm::toMat4(rotation);
    glm::mat4 S = glm::scale(glm::mat4(1.0f),
scale);
    return T * R * S;
}
```

When sampling poses at runtime, you'll interpolate each component individually and construct the transform using this order.

Linking Channels to Bones

You might be wondering: how do you connect an `aiNodeAnim` to a bone index in your skeleton?

The answer is through the bone name. The `mNodeName` of the channel must match the bone name in your skeleton.

During import, create a bone-name-to-index map:

```
std::unordered_map<std::string, int>
boneNameToIndex;

for (int i = 0; i < skeleton.bones.size(); ++i) {

    boneNameToIndex[skeleton.bones[i].name] = i;

}
```

Then, for each animation channel:

```
std::string boneName = channel->mNodeName.C_Str();
auto it = boneNameToIndex.find(boneName);
```

63

```
if (it != boneNameToIndex.end()) {
    int boneIndex = it->second;
    // Assign this track to tracks[boneIndex]
}
```

This ensures your animation tracks are stored in the same order as your skeleton, which is critical for efficient evaluation and GPU skinning.

Assimp's Limitations and Expectations

Before wrapping up this section, it's important to note some caveats when using Assimp for animation:

Bone names must match exactly. If the animation channel refers to a bone name not in your skeleton, you must ignore it—or raise a warning.

Some formats (like FBX) store root motion separately. You may want to extract that from the root node or handle it manually.

Scaling is optional. Many animators don't use scale in keyframes. If `mNumScalingKeys` is zero, default to `(1, 1, 1)`.

Ticks per second may be zero. If `clip->mTicksPerSecond == 0`, you must assume a default (usually 25.0 or 30.0 FPS) or base your timing on `mDuration` and desired sample rate.

Assimp gives you the raw ingredients—bone animation tracks, transforms, and metadata—but it's up to you to convert this into something clean and performant for your engine.

4.2 Reading Bone Hierarchies and Keyframes

One of the most fundamental steps in building an animation system is correctly reading and reconstructing the **bone hierarchy** from imported model data. Without an accurate hierarchy, transformations won't propagate through joints properly, and animations won't deform the mesh as intended. Equally important is extracting **keyframes** for each bone, which define how it moves over time. In this section, we'll focus on how to do both using Assimp.

We'll work step by step—starting with how bones are defined in Assimp, how they are structured in the node hierarchy, and how to collect and organize their animation keyframes for runtime evaluation.

Reconstructing the Bone Hierarchy from `aiNode`

Assimp represents the node hierarchy of a model using `aiNode`, starting at `scene->mRootNode`. This is not just for bones—it includes all scene nodes, including dummy nodes, sockets, and transform helpers. The actual bones used for skinning are typically a subset of this full hierarchy.

To reconstruct the hierarchy used for animation, you need to:

Traverse the `aiNode` tree.

Identify nodes whose names match bones (used in skinning or animation).

Record their parent-child relationships.

Let's define a simple `Bone` structure that you'll use internally:

```
struct Bone {
    std::string name;
    int parentIndex;                    // Index into
the bone array
    glm::mat4 localBindTransform;    // From node's
transformation
};
```

Now let's write the recursive function to build the skeleton:

```
int AddBoneRecursive(aiNode* node, int parentIndex,
std::vector<Bone>& bones,
std::unordered_map<std::string, int>& nameToIndex)
{
    Bone bone;
    bone.name = node->mName.C_Str();
    bone.parentIndex = parentIndex;
    bone.localBindTransform = ConvertMatrix(node-
>mTransformation); // aiMatrix4x4 → glm::mat4

    int currentIndex =
static_cast<int>(bones.size());
```

```
    bones.push_back(bone);
    nameToIndex[bone.name] = currentIndex;

    for (unsigned int i = 0; i < node-
>mNumChildren; ++i) {
        AddBoneRecursive(node->mChildren[i],
currentIndex, bones, nameToIndex);
    }

    return currentIndex;
}
```

Call this once at import:

```
std::vector<Bone> skeletonBones;

std::unordered_map<std::string, int>
boneNameToIndex;

AddBoneRecursive(scene->mRootNode, -1,
skeletonBones, boneNameToIndex);
```

This creates a flat array of bones with parent indices, which you'll use later to compute global transforms during pose evaluation.

Extracting Animation Keyframes from `aiNodeAnim`

Once the hierarchy is built, the next step is to collect **keyframe data per bone**. This data is found in the `aiAnimation` structure as `mChannels`, each of which is an `aiNodeAnim*`.

Each `aiNodeAnim` contains:

mNodeName: The name of the node it animates.

mPositionKeys: List of positions over time.

mRotationKeys: List of rotations over time.

mScalingKeys: List of scale values over time.

You want to organize this data into a runtime-friendly structure. Here's one that works well:

```cpp
struct Keyframe {
    float time;              // In seconds
    glm::vec3 position;
    glm::quat rotation;
    glm::vec3 scale;
};

struct BoneTrack {
    std::vector<Keyframe> keyframes;
};
```

Now let's loop through the animation channels and build tracks for bones you care about.

```cpp
std::vector<BoneTrack>
boneTracks(skeletonBones.size());

for (unsigned int i = 0; i < animation-
>mNumChannels; ++i) {
    aiNodeAnim* channel = animation->mChannels[i];
    std::string name = channel->mNodeName.C_Str();

    auto it = boneNameToIndex.find(name);
    if (it == boneNameToIndex.end()) {
        continue; // Animation for a node not in
our bone list
    }

    int boneIndex = it->second;
    BoneTrack& track = boneTracks[boneIndex];

    unsigned int maxKeyCount = std::max({
        channel->mNumPositionKeys,
        channel->mNumRotationKeys,
        channel->mNumScalingKeys
    });

    for (unsigned int k = 0; k < maxKeyCount; ++k)
{
        float time = 0.0f;
        glm::vec3 position(0.0f);
        glm::quat rotation(1.0f, 0.0f, 0.0f, 0.0f);
        glm::vec3 scale(1.0f);
```

```
        if (k < channel->mNumPositionKeys) {
            time = static_cast<float>(channel-
>mPositionKeys[k].mTime);
            auto v = channel-
>mPositionKeys[k].mValue;
            position = glm::vec3(v.x, v.y, v.z);
        }

        if (k < channel->mNumRotationKeys) {
            time = static_cast<float>(channel-
>mRotationKeys[k].mTime);
            auto q = channel-
>mRotationKeys[k].mValue;
            rotation = glm::quat(q.w, q.x, q.y,
q.z);
        }

        if (k < channel->mNumScalingKeys) {
            auto s = channel-
>mScalingKeys[k].mValue;
            scale = glm::vec3(s.x, s.y, s.z);
        }

        Keyframe key { time /
static_cast<float>(animation->mTicksPerSecond),
position, rotation, scale };
        track.keyframes.push_back(key);
    }
}
```

This gives you one `BoneTrack` per bone, each with a list of `Keyframe`s. You can now sample these tracks later using interpolation (LERP and SLERP) to build animated poses.

Handling Missing Key Types

In practice, many animations will omit scaling or even position keys for some bones. When that happens:

Missing position → use `(0,0,0)`

Missing rotation → use identity quaternion

Missing scale → use $(1,1,1)$

This ensures the transformation is well-defined even if certain tracks are sparse.

Linking to the Mesh Skinning Data

If you're also importing the mesh for skinning, the `aiMesh` structure contains bone weight data. Each bone there has:

A name (must match `aiNodeAnim`)

An offset matrix (the inverse bind pose)

A list of weighted vertices

This data must be merged with your skeleton to support GPU or CPU skinning. Here's how you might store inverse bind poses:

```
std::vector<glm::mat4>
inverseBindPoses(skeletonBones.size());

for (unsigned int i = 0; i < mesh->mNumBones; ++i)
{
    aiBone* bone = mesh->mBones[i];
    std::string name = bone->mName.C_Str();

    auto it = boneNameToIndex.find(name);
    if (it != boneNameToIndex.end()) {
        inverseBindPoses[it->second] =
ConvertMatrix(bone->mOffsetMatrix);
    }
}
```

These matrices will later be used to calculate final bone transforms like so:

```
glm::mat4 finalMatrix = globalPoseMatrix *
inverseBindPoseMatrix;
```

This is the matrix that will be passed to your skinning shader.

By correctly traversing the `aiNode` hierarchy and extracting animation keyframes from `aiNodeAnim`, you gain full control over both the **structure of the skeleton** and the **motion of its bones over time**. You now have everything you need to evaluate and blend poses at runtime, as well as to deform meshes accurately through skeletal animation.

4.3 Storing Skeleton and Animation Data Efficiently

Once you've parsed the bone hierarchy and extracted all relevant keyframes from Assimp, the next challenge is how to **store this data efficiently**—in memory and on disk. The goal here is not just correctness, but performance. You want a data layout that minimizes cache misses, supports SIMD and multi-threaded evaluation, and loads quickly at runtime without any need for re-parsing or allocations.

Structuring the Skeleton

Your skeleton must capture three essential pieces of information for each bone:

The bone's name (only during import—not needed at runtime)

The parent-child relationship (so you can reconstruct the global pose)

The inverse bind pose matrix (needed for skinning)

Here's a compact structure:

```
struct Skeleton {
    std::vector<int> parentIndices;        //
size = boneCount
    std::vector<glm::mat4> inverseBindPoses;  //
size = boneCount
};
```

This structure is designed for fast traversal. Each index in `parentIndices` corresponds to the same index in `inverseBindPoses`. You can compute global transforms using a flat loop:

```
void ComputeGlobalPose(const
std::vector<Transform>& local, const Skeleton&
skeleton, std::vector<glm::mat4>& global) {
    for (size_t i = 0; i <
skeleton.parentIndices.size(); ++i) {
        glm::mat4 localMat = local[i].ToMatrix();
```

```
        if (skeleton.parentIndices[i] >= 0) {
            global[i] =
global[skeleton.parentIndices[i]] * localMat;
        } else {
            global[i] = localMat;
        }
    }
}
```

There's no recursion here, just a flat for-loop that's easily parallelizable. If you need bone names for debugging or tooling, store them in a separate metadata structure that's stripped from the runtime asset.

Representing Animation Clips

Next, we want to store all sampled keyframes in a way that's predictable and cheap to evaluate. Instead of irregular, channel-separated keys like Assimp gives you, you'll use **uniformly sampled keyframes** per bone.

Let's define a simple runtime keyframe:

```
struct Keyframe {
    glm::vec3 position;
    glm::quat rotation;
    glm::vec3 scale;
};
```

Each bone will have one track:

```
struct BoneTrack {
    std::vector<Keyframe> keyframes;
};
```

And an animation clip holds the tracks for the entire skeleton:

```
struct AnimationClip {
    float duration;              // in seconds
    float frameRate;             // samples per
second
    std::vector<BoneTrack> tracks; // one per bone
};
```

This format gives you consistent indexing for every frame:

```
size_t frameIndex = static_cast<size_t>(time *
clip.frameRate);
Transform pose =
clip.tracks[boneIndex].keyframes[frameIndex];
```

No interpolation is needed if the data is dense enough (e.g., 30 or 60 FPS). If smoother motion is needed or storage space is a concern, you can use fewer keyframes and perform interpolation manually between two sampled frames.

Why Flat Arrays and Pre-Sampled Keys?

There are several performance reasons to use this structure:

Contiguous memory access: Linear access to arrays minimizes cache misses.

No dynamic lookups: Bone index directly maps to track index.

Fixed time steps: Frame-based evaluation avoids floating-point drift.

Job-system friendly: Sampling can be split across threads or vectorized.

When you want to support features like animation blending, LODs, or root motion extraction, this layout keeps logic simple and consistent.

Compact Disk Format for Animation Clips

To reduce memory and disk usage, you can serialize the clip into a custom binary format. Here's a basic layout:

```
struct AnimationHeader {
    uint32_t version;
    uint32_t numBones;
    uint32_t numFrames;
    float duration;
    float frameRate;
};
```

You follow this header with all the keyframe data in bone-major order (i.e., all frames for bone 0, then all frames for bone 1, etc.). This layout keeps I/O operations fast and enables memory-mapped reads.

Export code might look like this:

```cpp
std::ofstream out("orc_walk.animbin",
std::ios::binary);
AnimationHeader header = {1, boneCount, frameCount,
duration, 30.0f};
out.write(reinterpret_cast<const char*>(&header),
sizeof(header));

for (const BoneTrack& track : clip.tracks) {
    out.write(reinterpret_cast<const
char*>(track.keyframes.data()), sizeof(Keyframe) *
frameCount);
}
```

Loading is similarly straightforward:

```cpp
AnimationHeader header;
in.read(reinterpret_cast<char*>(&header),
sizeof(header));
clip.tracks.resize(header.numBones);

for (BoneTrack& track : clip.tracks) {
    track.keyframes.resize(header.numFrames);

in.read(reinterpret_cast<char*>(track.keyframes.dat
a()), sizeof(Keyframe) * header.numFrames);
}
```

This format is compact, fast, and tightly matches the runtime evaluation logic. If your engine supports streaming or progressive loading, this format also enables chunked reads.

Storing Compressed Keyframes

For even more efficiency, you can compress keyframe data:

Positions: Use 16-bit floats or encode into a bounding box range.

Rotations: Store quaternion x, y, z and reconstruct w on the fly.

Scales: Often constant—can be omitted per bone if not used.

You might define a packed keyframe like this:

```cpp
struct PackedKeyframe {
    uint16_t posX, posY, posZ;
```

```
    int16_t rotX, rotY, rotZ; // assume rotW is
reconstructed
};
```

Compression will vary depending on your needs, but the concept is the same: reduce per-frame data size while keeping it easy to decode at runtime.

Putting It Together at Runtime

At runtime, your evaluation pipeline looks like this:

Load skeleton and animation clip into memory.

For each frame:

Evaluate the current pose by sampling each bone's track.

Compute global transforms using parent indices.

Multiply by inverse bind pose to get final skinning matrices.

Upload bone matrices to the GPU.

Use these matrices in a vertex shader to deform the mesh.

This pipeline is simple, fast, and consistent for every character in your game. Whether you're animating a single player character or 100 NPCs, this structure supports scalable evaluation.

4.4 Preprocessing and Exporting Optimized Animation Formats

Now that you've parsed the animation data and organized it into a runtime-friendly structure, the final step in your asset pipeline is to **preprocess and export it into an optimized binary format**. This isn't just about getting it out of memory—it's about ensuring that when your game runs, animation data loads fast, consumes minimal memory, and supports efficient evaluation on CPU and GPU.

Goals of Preprocessing

Preprocessing is about preparing data so that it's:

Sampled at fixed intervals for predictable playback.

Reduced in size by removing redundant keyframes.

Aligned to your engine's expectations, such as frame counts, bone order, and matrix formats.

Stripped of unnecessary data, like unused bones, node names, or curve tangents.

Serialized into a binary format that is versioned, fast to load, and suitable for memory-mapped access.

The preprocessing stage is where you take full control over performance and data integrity.

Step 1: Resample to Fixed Frame Rate

Assimp keyframes are irregularly spaced, often using variable time deltas between keyframes. But for runtime playback, fixed-step sampling (e.g., 30 or 60 FPS) allows for direct indexing and avoids runtime time interpolation.

You start by choosing a **target frame rate**—usually 30.0f or 60.0f—and resample each track accordingly:

```
float frameRate = 30.0f;
float dt = 1.0f / frameRate;
int numFrames =
static_cast<int>(std::ceil(clip.duration *
frameRate));

for (int f = 0; f < numFrames; ++f) {
    float t = f * dt;
    for (int b = 0; b < boneCount; ++b) {
        Keyframe kf =
SampleBoneTrackAtTime(rawTracks[b], t);
        sampledTracks[b].keyframes.push_back(kf);
    }
}
```

This process results in a regular, evenly-spaced sequence of keyframes per bone, which is crucial for efficient evaluation.

Step 2: Eliminate Redundant Keyframes

Often, bones don't move at all in an animation—like a hand that remains still during an idle pose. Storing 300 identical keyframes for a static bone is wasteful.

You can compress tracks by removing keyframes where the delta from the previous frame is below a threshold:

```
bool IsRedundant(const Keyframe& a, const Keyframe&
b, float posEps, float rotEps) {
    return glm::length(a.position - b.position) <
posEps &&
         glm::angle(a.rotation, b.rotation) <
rotEps;
}
```

Walk through each track and remove keyframes that match the previous one within your precision tolerance. For bones that are completely static, consider marking them and skipping them entirely during runtime evaluation.

Step 3: Quantize Values (Optional Compression)

To save space, you can reduce the bit depth of keyframe data:

Positions: Store using 16-bit floats (FP16) or compress to bounding box.

Rotations: Store only the first 3 components of quaternion and reconstruct the 4th.

Scales: Often constant—omit if unused.

Here's a simple quantized keyframe struct:

```
struct QuantizedKeyframe {
    uint16_t pos[3]; // mapped into 16-bit range
    int16_t rot[3];  // rotW is reconstructed
};
```

During preprocessing, you encode the original values into this structure. During playback, you decode and reconstruct them.

If you do this, always save bounding box metadata (min/max per component) in the header so runtime decoding can remap values correctly.

Step 4: Export to a Versioned Binary Format

Design a compact binary format with clear sections and a version header. This allows future changes to remain backward compatible. A simple header might look like this:

```
struct AnimationHeader {
    uint32_t magic = 0x414E494D; // 'ANIM'
    uint32_t version = 1;
    float duration;
    float frameRate;
    uint32_t boneCount;
    uint32_t frameCount;
};
```

You then serialize each bone's track data in order:

```
std::ofstream out("orc_run.animbin",
std::ios::binary);
out.write(reinterpret_cast<const char*>(&header),
sizeof(header));

for (const BoneTrack& track : tracks) {
    out.write(reinterpret_cast<const
char*>(track.keyframes.data()), sizeof(Keyframe) *
frameCount);
}
```

This results in a flat file with:

A header

All keyframes, ordered by bone, then by frame

This layout is fast to stream and memory-map. There are no string lookups, no XML parsing, no JSON decoding—just binary data that your runtime can load and use immediately.

Step 5: Load and Use at Runtime

At runtime, you read the binary file directly into your animation system:

```
std::ifstream file("orc_run.animbin",
std::ios::binary);
AnimationHeader header;
```

```
file.read(reinterpret_cast<char*>(&header),
sizeof(header));

AnimationClip clip;
clip.duration = header.duration;
clip.frameRate = header.frameRate;
clip.tracks.resize(header.boneCount);

for (BoneTrack& track : clip.tracks) {
    track.keyframes.resize(header.frameCount);

file.read(reinterpret_cast<char*>(track.keyframes.d
ata()), sizeof(Keyframe) * header.frameCount);
}
```

Now your `clip` object is ready to evaluate at any time index using fixed frame indexing or interpolation.

Practical Debug Tip: Dump a Human-Readable Summary

During development, you may want to validate what's in your animation clips. You can write a debug dump tool:

```
void PrintAnimationClipSummary(const AnimationClip&
clip) {
    std::cout << "Duration: " << clip.duration << "
seconds\n";
    std::cout << "Frame rate: " << clip.frameRate
<< " FPS\n";
    std::cout << "Bones: " << clip.tracks.size() <<
"\n";
    std::cout << "Frames per track: " <<
clip.tracks[0].keyframes.size() << "\n";
}
```

This helps you verify that your exporter is working and the data makes sense before integrating into your rendering pipeline.

Organizing File Output

Store each character's assets in a consistent folder structure:

`/characters/orc/`

```
orc.skel               // Skeleton definition

orc_idle.animbin       // Idle animation

orc_walk.animbin       // Walk cycle

orc_attack.animbin     // Attack animation
```

This makes it easy for your engine or editor to load assets automatically and for animators to add new motions without touching code.

Preprocessing is where performance is won or lost. By baking animation data into a compact, fixed-frame, runtime-ready format, you avoid the overhead of parsing, conversion, or on-the-fly curve evaluation. Your animations load faster, play smoother, and scale better across complex characters and large scenes.

Chapter 5: Implementing Skeletal Animation Systems

At this point, you've imported animation data, parsed skeleton hierarchies, and serialized animation clips in a format your engine can load and evaluate efficiently. But there's still one more critical layer: applying those animations to characters on screen. This is where your **skeletal animation system** comes into play.

A skeletal animation system is responsible for combining animation data, evaluating poses, computing global bone transforms, and passing those transforms to the GPU for vertex skinning. In this chapter, we'll walk through the implementation of a full skeletal animation system—from data structures to shader interaction—so that your characters move correctly and efficiently every frame.

5.1 Skeleton Structures and Joint Definitions

In a skeletal animation system, the **skeleton** is the fundamental data structure that defines how a character moves. It's a collection of interconnected joints (or bones), organized in a hierarchy. Each joint affects part of the character's mesh, and movement flows from parent to child. To animate a mesh properly, your system must evaluate joint transforms every frame, propagate those changes through the hierarchy, and then use them to deform the geometry on the GPU.

At runtime, a skeleton is just data—specifically:

A list of joints (or bones), each with:

A local bind pose (its position, rotation, and scale in rest pose)

A reference to its parent

An inverse bind matrix (used to bring vertices into bone space for skinning)

The bones themselves are not responsible for motion. Instead, they define **how motion is propagated**.

Let's start by defining a basic `Transform` structure that represents the local transform of a bone:

```cpp
struct Transform {
    glm::vec3 position;
    glm::quat rotation;
    glm::vec3 scale;

    glm::mat4 ToMatrix() const {
        return glm::translate(glm::mat4(1.0f),
position)
                * glm::toMat4(rotation)
                * glm::scale(glm::mat4(1.0f), scale);
    }
};
```

This structure is used both at rest (bind pose) and during animation (current pose).

Defining the Joint Hierarchy

Each joint needs to know its parent in order to apply hierarchical transforms. We store this with an array of integers:

```cpp
std::vector<int> parentIndices; // parentIndices[i]
= index of parent of bone i
```

A value of -1 indicates that the bone is the **root** of the skeleton.

Here's how you define the overall Skeleton structure:

```cpp
struct Skeleton {
    std::vector<int> parentIndices;              //
For hierarchy evaluation
    std::vector<glm::mat4> inverseBindPoses;    //
Used in skinning
};
```

Each index in parentIndices corresponds to a bone. For example:

```
// Skeleton with 3 bones

// Root (index 0)

//  └── Spine (index 1)

//        └── Head (index 2)
```

```
parentIndices = [-1, 0, 1];
```

This compact format is critical for scalable pose evaluation—you'll use this when traversing bones in topological order during forward kinematics.

Bind Pose and Inverse Bind Matrices

The **bind pose** is the pose your skeleton is in when the mesh was skinned (typically in the modeling tool). It is usually represented as a set of local transforms (position, rotation, scale) for each joint.

To deform the mesh correctly at runtime, you need the **inverse bind matrix** for each bone. This matrix transforms vertices from model space into the bone's local space in the bind pose.

Here's how you compute it:

```
glm::mat4 globalBindTransform =
ComputeGlobalTransformFromHierarchy(...);

glm::mat4 inverseBindMatrix =
glm::inverse(globalBindTransform);
```

These matrices are usually computed offline and saved as part of your custom skeleton file.

Practical Skeleton Example

Let's say you have a skeleton with four bones:

Root

Spine

Left Arm

Right Arm

You might define it like this in code:

```
Skeleton skeleton;
skeleton.parentIndices = { -1, 0, 1, 1 };
```

```
skeleton.inverseBindPoses = {
    glm::inverse(rootBindMatrix),
    glm::inverse(spineBindMatrix),
    glm::inverse(leftArmBindMatrix),
    glm::inverse(rightArmBindMatrix)
};
```

At runtime, you evaluate the current pose as local `Transform` structs and compute the global matrices by applying them through the hierarchy.

Joint Naming and Debugging

Although names are not needed at runtime, they are useful during development, debugging, and editor tooling. You can store them separately:

std::vector<std::string> jointNames;

These names should be preserved when importing from Assimp or GLTF, but stripped out of final builds if performance or memory size is critical.

GPU Index Mapping

The final component of the skeleton is its mapping to the GPU. Each vertex in your mesh stores bone indices (usually 4) that reference this skeleton. These must match the index layout in `parentIndices` and `inverseBindPoses`.

If your animation data comes from different files or uses remapped bone indices, you need to ensure the mapping is resolved during preprocessing.

Summary of Skeleton Requirements

Minimal runtime memory: Store only what you need: parent indices, inverse bind matrices.

Fast traversal: Topologically sorted bones enable forward kinematics without recursion.

Consistent indexing: Bone indices in animation clips must match those in the skeleton.

GPU ready: Every bone index maps cleanly to a matrix in the skinning shader.

With this setup, you've defined the static structure needed to pose, animate, and skin any rigged character in real time.

5.2 Forward Kinematics and Bone Transform Propagation

Once you've structured your skeleton and populated it with local transforms per frame, the next step is to compute how each bone moves in world or model space. This is the process of **forward kinematics**—propagating transforms down a hierarchy from parent to child. Without it, bones would stay frozen at their rest pose, and animations wouldn't deform the character as expected.

At the core of forward kinematics is a very simple idea:

The **global transform** of a bone is the combination of its **local transform** and the **global transform of its parent**.

You start with the root bone, whose global transform is just its local transform. Then you walk down the skeleton hierarchy, combining each child's local transform with its parent's global transform. This gives you the position, rotation, and scale of every bone in model space.

This is why your skeleton must store `parentIndices[]`, and your pose must be an array of per-bone `Transform` objects. These relationships allow you to traverse the hierarchy and build a global matrix for each joint.

Data Structures Recap

Here's what you need before implementing forward kinematics:

```
struct Transform {
    glm::vec3 position;
    glm::quat rotation;
    glm::vec3 scale;

    glm::mat4 ToMatrix() const {
        return glm::translate(glm::mat4(1.0f),
position)
            * glm::toMat4(rotation)
            * glm::scale(glm::mat4(1.0f), scale);
    }
};
```

```
struct Skeleton {
    std::vector<int> parentIndices;          //
one per bone
    std::vector<glm::mat4> inverseBindPoses;   //
one per bone
};
```

At runtime, you evaluate a local pose per bone (from animation data), then compute its global transform.

Implementing the Global Transform Calculation

Here's the actual forward kinematics function:

```
void ComputeGlobalPose(const Skeleton& skeleton,
                       const
std::vector<Transform>& localPose,
                       std::vector<glm::mat4>&
globalPoseOut) {
    size_t boneCount =
skeleton.parentIndices.size();
    globalPoseOut.resize(boneCount);

    for (size_t i = 0; i < boneCount; ++i) {
        glm::mat4 localMat =
localPose[i].ToMatrix();
        int parentIndex =
skeleton.parentIndices[i];

        if (parentIndex >= 0) {
            globalPoseOut[i] =
globalPoseOut[parentIndex] * localMat;
        } else {
            globalPoseOut[i] = localMat;
        }
    }
}
```

This function assumes that bones are stored in **topological order**—meaning parents come before children. That's critical for a single-pass traversal without recursion.

If you load bones using a recursive Assimp import function that inserts parent bones before their children, you already satisfy this condition.

Real-World Example: Applying FK to a Walk Cycle

Suppose you load a walking animation and evaluate each bone's pose at $t = 1.0f$. The animation system provides you with a list of local `Transform`s for each bone. To prepare for skinning, you compute the global pose:

```
std::vector<glm::mat4> globalMatrices;

ComputeGlobalPose(skeleton, evaluatedPose,
globalMatrices);
```

Then, to prepare the final skinning matrices, you adjust for the bind pose:

```
std::vector<glm::mat4>
skinningMatrices(globalMatrices.size());
for (size_t i = 0; i < globalMatrices.size(); ++i)
{
    skinningMatrices[i] = globalMatrices[i] *
skeleton.inverseBindPoses[i];
}
```

These are the matrices you upload to the GPU. Each one transforms a vertex from bind pose space into the current animated pose.

Handling Optional Optimizations

If you're working in a game where many characters are animated simultaneously, you'll want to make this process faster and more parallel. Here are common optimization strategies:

1. Use SoA (Structure of Arrays) Format for Local Transforms

Instead of storing each transform as a `struct`, store arrays of positions, rotations, and scales separately. This makes SIMD processing easier.

2. Parallelize FK Traversal

Use a job system to break bones into chunks. Since each global matrix only depends on its parent, as long as you process in topological order, you can dispatch evaluation jobs safely in multiple threads.

3. Store Precomputed Bone Order

If you're importing skeletons offline, store a bone evaluation order array:

```
std::vector<int> boneEvaluationOrder;
```

This gives you strict control over traversal and avoids the need for runtime sorting.

Debugging Tip: Visualize Bone Positions

During development, draw a line from each bone to its parent using the `globalPose` array. It's one of the fastest ways to confirm that your hierarchy and transforms are working correctly.

```
for (size_t i = 0; i < globalPose.size(); ++i) {
    int parent = skeleton.parentIndices[i];
    if (parent >= 0) {
        glm::vec3 p1 = glm::vec3(globalPose[i][3]);
// current bone
        glm::vec3 p0 =
glm::vec3(globalPose[parent][3]);   // parent bone
        DrawDebugLine(p0, p1, Color::Yellow);
    }
}
```

If bones appear disconnected or offset strangely, it's usually due to a mismatch in the transform order (scale * rotation * translation), incorrect bind pose data, or non-uniform scaling.

Handling Special Cases

1. No Parent Bone

A root bone's global transform is equal to its local transform. That's handled in the `if (parentIndex >= 0)` check. You should ensure that your skeleton has at least one root (typically the pelvis or hips).

2. Zero Scale

While most bones retain a scale of (1,1,1), you should always handle scale explicitly. Some animation tools use scale to suppress movement (e.g., to cancel out facial motion on certain rigs). Always multiply scale during matrix construction, even if it's the identity.

3. Blend Space Evaluation

When blending two poses (e.g., walk and run), you compute a blended local transform per bone, then apply forward kinematics once:

```
Transform blended = BlendTransform(poseA[i],
poseB[i], weight);
```

Then feed that into your global transform function. Forward kinematics remains the same.

Forward kinematics is the backbone of skeletal animation. It's simple, fast, and scales well when bones are stored correctly. Once you've propagated the transforms from parent to child, your character has a complete model-space pose. From there, you can compute skinning matrices, send them to the GPU, and see your characters animate in real time.

5.3 GPU Skinning Fundamentals

Once you've evaluated your skeleton's pose and computed the bone matrices, the next step is **skinning**—the process of using those matrices to deform the character mesh. Skinning transforms each vertex based on the motion of the bones it's attached to. This operation happens every frame, for every animated character, and involves thousands (sometimes millions) of vertex updates per second. So it must be fast. That's why modern animation systems delegate skinning to the **GPU**.

GPU skinning—also called **hardware skinning**—means that the vertex shader applies bone transformations directly on the GPU. Instead of modifying vertices on the CPU and uploading them every frame, you leave the mesh static and let the GPU deform it dynamically using bone matrices.

Each vertex is influenced by 1–4 bones. Each bone contributes to the vertex's final position based on a weight.

Mathematically, the final position is computed like this:

```
skinnedPos =
```

```
(boneMatrixA * originalPos) * weightA +

(boneMatrixB * originalPos) * weightB +

(boneMatrixC * originalPos) * weightC +

(boneMatrixD * originalPos) * weightD;
```

Vertex Attributes for Skinning

Each vertex must store the following extra attributes:

Bone Indices: An `ivec4` specifying which bones influence this vertex.

Bone Weights: A `vec4` of corresponding weights (should sum to 1.0).

Bind Pose Position/Normal: Original vertex data, typically `vec3 position`, `vec3 normal`.

A common vertex structure looks like this in GLSL-compatible pseudocode:

```
layout(location = 0) in vec3 aPosition;

layout(location = 1) in vec3 aNormal;

layout(location = 2) in ivec4 aBoneIndices;

layout(location = 3) in vec4 aBoneWeights;
```

You should normalize the weights during asset import or in your preprocessing tool to ensure they always sum to 1.0.

Bone Matrix Palette (Uniform Buffer)

On the GPU, you maintain a **matrix palette**—an array of `mat4` transforms—one per bone. These matrices move vertices from their bind pose to their current animated pose.

To compute them on the CPU:

```
for (size_t i = 0; i < boneCount; ++i) {

    finalMatrix[i] = globalPose[i] *
inverseBindPose[i];

}
```

These matrices are uploaded to the GPU each frame as a uniform array:

```
uniform mat4 uBoneMatrices[MAX_BONES];
```

Each index in `aBoneIndices` maps to one matrix in this array.

If your engine supports many animated characters, you can use a **uniform buffer object (UBO)**, a **shader storage buffer (SSBO)**, or a **texture buffer** to store bone matrices more efficiently and bypass uniform limits.

Skinning in GLSL (Vertex Shader)

Here's a simplified GLSL example that performs linear blend skinning:

```glsl
uniform mat4 uBoneMatrices[MAX_BONES];

layout(location = 0) in vec3 aPosition;
layout(location = 1) in vec3 aNormal;
layout(location = 2) in ivec4 aBoneIndices;
layout(location = 3) in vec4 aBoneWeights;

uniform mat4 uModel;
uniform mat4 uViewProjection;

void main() {
    vec4 pos = vec4(aPosition, 1.0);
    mat4 skinMatrix =
        uBoneMatrices[aBoneIndices.x] *
aBoneWeights.x +
        uBoneMatrices[aBoneIndices.y] *
aBoneWeights.y +
        uBoneMatrices[aBoneIndices.z] *
aBoneWeights.z +
        uBoneMatrices[aBoneIndices.w] *
aBoneWeights.w;

    vec4 skinnedPosition = skinMatrix * pos;
    gl_Position = uViewProjection * uModel *
skinnedPosition;
}
```

Normals and tangents should also be skinned using the upper 3x3 part of the matrix or transformed using normal matrices derived from skinning matrices.

Performance Considerations

1. Limit Matrix Count Per Draw

Most GPUs have a limit on the number of uniform matrices you can bind at once. Keep skeletons within 64–128 bones per mesh when possible. If your characters have more, consider splitting the mesh into parts (e.g., upper body, lower body).

2. Upload Matrices Efficiently

Use `glBufferSubData` to update a UBO, or map the buffer directly if your platform supports it. Avoid allocating new buffers each frame.

```
glBindBuffer(GL_UNIFORM_BUFFER, ubo);

glBufferSubData(GL_UNIFORM_BUFFER, 0, matrixCount *
sizeof(glm::mat4), matrices);
```

3. Use Integer Indices

Avoid using floats for bone indices. Integer indexing ensures that GPUs use fast, correct lookups without rounding issues.

Skinning Artifacts and Quality Fixes

Elbow Collapse ("Candy Wrapper" Effect)

Linear blending of quaternions can cause joints to collapse or twist unnaturally. You can fix this with **dual quaternion skinning**, which blends rotations in a more robust way. However, this requires more complex math and custom GPU support.

Weight Normalization

Always normalize bone weights. Improper weights lead to deformation errors. You can normalize in the vertex shader (less optimal) or offline (preferred).

Per-Vertex vs Per-Bone Weights

Minimize the number of influencing bones per vertex. If possible, remap weights during import to reduce to 3 or even 2 per vertex using weight pruning.

Testing Your Skinning Implementation

To confirm your system is working correctly:

Play an animation and visually inspect deformation at joints.

Rotate a single bone (e.g., elbow) and ensure the vertices deform as expected.

Render bone debug lines and verify they match joint movement.

Zero out weights for a specific bone and verify that affected mesh regions disappear or flatten.

You can also write a visual test that compares GPU skinning output against CPU-evaluated vertex positions for the same pose.

GPU skinning is essential for real-time animation. It's fast, scalable, and flexible—but it requires clean integration between mesh data, skeleton definitions, animation evaluation, and shader logic.

By storing vertex weights and bone indices per vertex, computing final bone matrices on the CPU, and passing those to the GPU for per-vertex deformation, you achieve smooth, efficient animation at any scale—from single characters to entire crowds.

5.4 Bone Matrix Calculation and Uploading to Shaders

Everything in a skeletal animation pipeline builds toward one thing: computing a final matrix per bone that can be used in the GPU vertex shader to deform the character mesh. This final matrix, often called a **skinning matrix**, tells the GPU how to move a vertex based on the movement of its controlling bone. To get there, you'll take the evaluated pose, apply forward kinematics, combine each result with its corresponding inverse bind pose, and send the result to the GPU efficiently.

The goal is to deform the mesh using bone influence. Each vertex was originally bound to the mesh at the time of rigging, and at that time, each bone had a specific transform. As the skeleton animates, each bone gets a new global transform, and the difference between those two transforms is applied to vertices attached to that bone.

That difference is expressed with this formula:

```
finalMatrix = globalPoseMatrix *
inverseBindPoseMatrix;
```

So for every bone `i`, you calculate a matrix that:

Transforms the vertex from its bind pose into bone space (inverse bind).

Applies the current animation pose (global transform).

This combined matrix is what you'll use in the shader.

Input Data Recap

Before calculating these final matrices, you need:

`globalPose[i]`: A matrix representing the current pose of bone `i` in model space.

`inverseBindPose[i]`: A matrix that moves a vertex from model space into bone space in the bind pose.

`boneCount`: The number of bones in the skeleton (typically 20–100 for game characters).

You must compute and store one final `mat4` per bone, each frame.

Step-by-Step Bone Matrix Calculation

Here's the complete C++ function that calculates the matrices:

```cpp
void CalculateSkinningMatrices(const
std::vector<glm::mat4>& globalPose,
                               const
std::vector<glm::mat4>& inverseBindPose,

std::vector<glm::mat4>& outMatrices) {
    size_t boneCount = globalPose.size();
    outMatrices.resize(boneCount);

    for (size_t i = 0; i < boneCount; ++i) {
        outMatrices[i] = globalPose[i] *
inverseBindPose[i];
    }
```

```
}
```

This function should be called once per animated skeleton per frame, immediately after you compute global transforms via forward kinematics.

Allocating and Reusing Memory

For performance, don't allocate memory every frame. Instead, allocate once and reuse:

```
std::vector<glm::mat4> skinningMatrices;

skinningMatrices.reserve(maxBones);
```

Keep `outMatrices` in a per-character structure so you can upload them with minimal copy operations.

Uploading Matrices to the GPU (OpenGL)

You can use a **Uniform Buffer Object (UBO)** to send bone matrices to the shader. A UBO is a special buffer that stores uniform data in a structured layout accessible from GLSL.

1. Allocate a UBO

```
GLuint boneUBO;

glGenBuffers(1, &boneUBO);

glBindBuffer(GL_UNIFORM_BUFFER, boneUBO);

glBufferData(GL_UNIFORM_BUFFER, sizeof(glm::mat4) *
maxBones, nullptr, GL_DYNAMIC_DRAW);
```

2. Update UBO Per Frame

```
glBindBuffer(GL_UNIFORM_BUFFER, boneUBO);

glBufferSubData(GL_UNIFORM_BUFFER, 0,
sizeof(glm::mat4) * boneCount,
skinningMatrices.data());
```

3. Bind UBO to a Shader Binding Point

```
GLuint bindingPoint = 1; // must match
layout(binding = 1) in shader

glBindBufferBase(GL_UNIFORM_BUFFER, bindingPoint,
boneUBO);
```

4. In the Vertex Shader

```
layout(std140, binding = 1) uniform Bones {
    mat4 uBoneMatrices[MAX_BONES];
};
```

The shader can now access `uBoneMatrices[i]` directly using the bone indices per vertex.

Alternative: Using SSBO or Texture Buffers

For more complex scenes, or when you need more bones than uniforms allow, use a **Shader Storage Buffer Object (SSBO)** or a **texture buffer**. The logic stays the same—you just upload to a larger buffer and access it with flexible indexing.

Multi-Character Skinning

If your game features multiple animated characters on screen at once, each needs its own set of skinning matrices. You can:

Allocate one UBO per character.

Use a large SSBO and assign a character ID to each draw call.

Use instancing with texture buffer indexing if skinning data can be shared or interpolated.

In OpenGL or Vulkan, instancing combined with SSBO access lets you animate crowds efficiently.

Debugging Tip: Visualize Final Matrices

To verify your matrices are correct, render a debug skeleton using the same final matrices. You can draw lines from each bone to its parent:

```
for (size_t i = 0; i <
skeleton.parentIndices.size(); ++i) {
```

```
       int parent = skeleton.parentIndices[i];
       if (parent >= 0) {
           glm::vec3 p0 =
glm::vec3(skinningMatrices[parent][3]);
           glm::vec3 p1 =
glm::vec3(skinningMatrices[i][3]);
           DrawDebugLine(p0, p1, Color::Green);
       }
}
```

Incorrect positions usually indicate a bad inverse bind pose or matrix multiplication order.

Dealing with Coordinate System Differences

Some tools like Maya or Blender use different up axes or handedness (Y-up vs. Z-up, right-handed vs. left-handed). This affects your matrices.

Always ensure that:

Your skeleton's bind pose and mesh match the same coordinate space.

Your global matrices are computed using the same basis as the inverse bind pose.

You apply any import-specific corrections (e.g., flip Z axis) during the offline stage.

Final Integration

To use this in your rendering pipeline:

Load or generate inverse bind poses once per model.

Evaluate animation and compute global bone transforms each frame.

Calculate skinning matrices.

Upload them to the GPU.

Render the mesh using skinning-enabled vertex shaders.

Each character instance follows the same flow, with unique animation data and matrix buffers.

The calculation and uploading of bone matrices is the final bridge between your CPU-side animation system and the GPU's skinning shader. When done efficiently and correctly, this system enables dynamic, high-quality deformation for real-time characters—whether it's a lone hero, a background NPC, or a horde of monsters.

Chapter 6: Keyframe Animation and Blending

Now that your engine can evaluate skeletal poses and apply them to skinned meshes, the next level of realism and responsiveness comes from **blending** animations. Rarely does a character just play a single animation clip start-to-finish. They transition from idle to walk, overlay a reload on top of a run, or blend between several combat stances. This chapter is all about managing that complexity.

6.1 Sampling Animation at Arbitrary Time Points

In a real-time animation system, you don't just play clips from beginning to end like a static film. You need to evaluate them precisely at the current time—maybe 1.37 seconds into a walk cycle or 0.89 seconds into a reload animation. Since your animation clips are made of keyframes sampled at fixed intervals (usually 30 or 60 frames per second), this means you'll need to **interpolate** between two known keyframes that surround your current time.

Keyframes define how each bone moves over time. For any given frame of gameplay, your animation system needs to compute a **full pose**: the position, rotation, and scale of every bone.

But the current playback time rarely aligns perfectly with stored keyframe timestamps. So you have to find the two closest keyframes for each bone track, and interpolate between them. Do this for every bone, and you get the character's pose at that exact moment.

This is the foundation for smooth playback, blending, and advanced features like time-scaling or pose prediction.

The Input: Animation Tracks

Let's start with the structure you'll work with. Each animation clip stores a **track** per bone, and each track contains a list of time-stamped keyframes:

```
struct Keyframe {
    float time;              // in seconds
```

```
    glm::vec3 position;
    glm::quat rotation;
    glm::vec3 scale;
};

struct BoneTrack {
    std::vector<Keyframe> keyframes;
};
```

An animation clip is just a set of `BoneTracks`, one per bone.

```
struct AnimationClip {
    float duration;
    float frameRate;
    std::vector<BoneTrack> tracks; // one track per
bone
};
```

Step 1: Finding the Two Surrounding Keyframes

Let's say you're evaluating an animation clip at t = `1.17f` seconds. First, you need to find the two keyframes in each bone track such that:

keyframes[i].time <= t < keyframes[i+1].time

Here's a simple linear search:

```
int FindKeyframeIndex(const std::vector<Keyframe>&
keys, float t) {
    for (size_t i = 0; i < keys.size() - 1; ++i) {
        if (t < keys[i + 1].time)
            return static_cast<int>(i);
    }
    return static_cast<int>(keys.size() - 2); //
clamp to last interval
}
```

For short clips with 30–100 keyframes, this is fast enough. But if you have long or densely-sampled clips, consider binary search or caching the previous index.

Step 2: Interpolating the Pose

Once you've found `a = keys[i]` and `b = keys[i+1]`, you interpolate between them based on how far t falls between their timestamps.

float alpha = (t - a.time) / (b.time - a.time);

Then use:

glm::mix for position and scale (linear interpolation)

glm::slerp for rotation (spherical interpolation)

```
Transform Interpolate(const Keyframe& a, const
Keyframe& b, float t) {
    float alpha = (t - a.time) / (b.time - a.time);

    glm::vec3 pos = glm::mix(a.position,
b.position, alpha);
    glm::quat rot = glm::slerp(a.rotation,
b.rotation, alpha);
    glm::vec3 scl = glm::mix(a.scale, b.scale,
alpha);

    return { pos, rot, scl };
}
```

Never interpolate quaternions with `glm::mix`—it will cause snapping and rotational artifacts. Always use `glm::slerp`.

Step 3: Sampling the Whole Pose

Now apply this interpolation per bone. This function samples a full pose at time t:

```
std::vector<Transform> SampleAnimationAtTime(const
AnimationClip& clip, float t) {
    std::vector<Transform>
pose(clip.tracks.size());

    for (size_t i = 0; i < clip.tracks.size(); ++i)
{
        const BoneTrack& track = clip.tracks[i];

        if (track.keyframes.empty()) {
```

```
            pose[i] = {}; // default transform
            continue;
        }

        if (track.keyframes.size() == 1) {
            pose[i] = {
                track.keyframes[0].position,
                track.keyframes[0].rotation,
                track.keyframes[0].scale
            };
            continue;
        }

        int index =
FindKeyframeIndex(track.keyframes, t);
        pose[i] =
Interpolate(track.keyframes[index],
track.keyframes[index + 1], t);
    }

    return pose;
}
```

You'll call this function once per character per frame, per active animation clip.

Step 4: Looping and Clamping

Make sure t stays within clip bounds. For looping clips (like walk or idle), wrap time:

```
t = fmod(t, clip.duration);
```

For non-looping clips (like a punch or death), clamp:

```
t = std::min(t, clip.duration - epsilon);
```

Failing to handle this properly can cause out-of-bounds indexing or visual stuttering at the end of an animation.

Practical Debugging Exercise

Try sampling your walk animation at evenly spaced points and printing out the pelvis bone's Y position:

```
for (float t = 0; t < clip.duration; t += 0.1f) {
    auto pose = SampleAnimationAtTime(clip, t);
    std::cout << "t=" << t << ", pelvis.y=" <<
pose[pelvisIndex].position.y << "\n";
}
```

You should see a smooth vertical curve—indicating proper interpolation of footstep motion. If it snaps or flattens, your keyframe or interpolation logic likely has a bug.

Sampling is the building block for everything that follows—blending, state transitions, layering, procedural offsets. As long as your pose sampling is precise and reliable, you can confidently compose more complex animation behaviors without fearing inconsistencies.

6.2 Interpolating Rotations and Positions

In a skeletal animation system, accurate interpolation between keyframes is what makes motion appear fluid and believable. The way a hand moves from a lowered position to a salute, or how the chest subtly rotates during breathing—all of it depends on how well your engine can interpolate between two known poses. This section focuses on the technical precision required to interpolate **positions**, **rotations**, and **scales** properly, especially across time intervals.

Getting this right means that transitions between poses are free from jitter, snapping, and rotational anomalies. You'll implement the math for linear and spherical interpolation and examine the specific pitfalls you need to avoid when blending transforms.

Interpolating Positions and Scales

Both position and scale are represented by `glm::vec3` values. These are simple 3D vectors, and the interpolation here is **linear**.

You use `glm::mix`, which performs a linear interpolation:

```
glm::vec3 InterpolateVec3(const glm::vec3& a, const
glm::vec3& b, float alpha) {
```

```
        return glm::mix(a, b, alpha);
}
```

Here, `alpha` is a value between 0.0 and 1.0 that represents how far you are between the two keyframes. For instance, if `t` is halfway between `t0` and `t1`, then `alpha = 0.5`.

This works identically for both position and scale:

Position: ensures that the bone's translation moves along a straight path.

Scale: makes sure that gradual enlargements or shrinkage don't jump.

This form of interpolation is known as **LERP** (Linear Interpolation).

Interpolating Rotations: Why Slerp Matters

Rotation interpolation is far more delicate. Rotations are stored using **quaternions** (`glm::quat`), not Euler angles or matrices. Quaternions are ideal for representing rotation because they avoid gimbal lock, are compact, and can be smoothly interpolated.

You should never use `glm::mix` for quaternions. Instead, use `glm::slerp`:

```
glm::quat InterpolateQuat(const glm::quat& a, const
glm::quat& b, float alpha) {
        return glm::slerp(a, b, alpha);
}
```

Why?

`glm::slerp` (Spherical Linear Interpolation) ensures that the rotation travels along the shortest arc on a 4D hypersphere.

It provides constant angular velocity, which avoids visual jitter.

It avoids skewing and flipping that occur with naive interpolation.

When using `slerp`, the interpolated quaternion stays on the unit sphere, preserving its validity as a rotation.

Full Transform Interpolation Function

Combining all three components (position, rotation, scale), your final interpolation function for a keyframe pair looks like this:

```
Transform InterpolateTransform(const Keyframe& a,
const Keyframe& b, float t) {
    float alpha = (t - a.time) / (b.time - a.time);

    glm::vec3 position = glm::mix(a.position,
b.position, alpha);
    glm::quat rotation = glm::slerp(a.rotation,
b.rotation, alpha);
    glm::vec3 scale = glm::mix(a.scale, b.scale,
alpha);

    return { position, rotation, scale };
}
```

This will give you a smooth, artifact-free pose at any time between two keyframes.

Common Mistakes to Avoid

1. Interpolating Quaternions with LERP

You might be tempted to interpolate a quaternion with `glm::mix`—don't. It will create a path that is not a proper rotation, causing artifacts like limb flipping or joint collapse.

2. Failing to Normalize After Manual Blending

If you're performing manual operations like weighted blending of quaternions (e.g., for layered animation), always normalize:

```
glm::quat blended = glm::normalize(glm::slerp(a, b,
alpha));
```

3. Using Euler Angles Instead of Quaternions

Interpolating Euler angles (e.g., XYZ in degrees or radians) leads to gimbal lock, large swings, and inconsistent rotation paths. Always convert to quaternion first and interpolate in that space.

Real World Scenario: Blending Idle into Walk

Let's say you're transitioning from idle to walk over 0.5 seconds. The idle clip and walk clip each have bone tracks. For each bone, you sample from both clips at time `t`, then interpolate between those two poses with a blend factor `alpha = t / 0.5f`.

```
Transform idlePose =
InterpolateTransform(idleTrackA, idleTrackB,
idleTime);

Transform walkPose =
InterpolateTransform(walkTrackA, walkTrackB,
walkTime);

Transform blendedPose = {

    glm::mix(idlePose.position, walkPose.position,
alpha),

    glm::slerp(idlePose.rotation,
walkPose.rotation, alpha),

    glm::mix(idlePose.scale, walkPose.scale, alpha)

};
```

This lets you blend smoothly from idle to walk regardless of the bone count or frame rates of the source animations.

Test It: Visual Debugging for Interpolation

To verify that your interpolation works:

Play a looping idle animation and sample every 0.1s. Print the rotation of the pelvis bone.

Apply a visual debug system that draws bones using `glm::vec3(globalMatrix[i][3])` to verify their position over time.

Test extreme rotations (e.g., head turning 180°) to make sure the arc is smooth and doesn't snap.

Here's an example test output:

```
for (float t = 0; t < clip.duration; t += 0.05f) {
    auto pose = SampleAnimationAtTime(clip, t);
    glm::vec3 forward = pose[headIndex].rotation *
glm::vec3(0, 0, 1);
    std::cout << "Head forward at t=" << t << ": "
<< glm::to_string(forward) << "\n";
}
```

Interpolation is the mathematical backbone of animation. Whether you're sampling a single clip or blending multiple layers, doing it correctly—especially for rotation—is essential to producing realistic and stable motion.

You now have a precise, efficient, and reliable interpolation pipeline for every transform component. In the next section, we'll expand on this foundation by blending multiple animations together—both linearly and additively—and showing how to manage complex pose combinations dynamically.

6.3 Blending Multiple Animations

Blending animations is what allows characters to look alive and responsive in dynamic, non-scripted environments. It's how you go from just playing a walk animation to making the character turn their head while walking, wave while standing, or even recoil while reloading. These motions can't be stored in thousands of unique clips—they're built by **combining** animations.

This section is all about how to blend animations correctly. You'll learn how to implement **linear blending**, where two complete poses are interpolated over time (e.g., idle to walk), and **additive blending**, where secondary motion (like breathing or aiming) is layered over a base pose. Finally, we'll cover how to apply blending selectively to subsets of the skeleton to build **layered animation systems**.

Linear Blending: Smooth Transitions Between Full Poses

Linear blending is the simplest and most common form of animation blending. It involves interpolating two full poses bone-by-bone using a weight.

Let's say you want to blend between a walk and a run pose, with `weight = 0.0f` representing 100% walk and `1.0f` representing 100% run.

Here's the math:

```
Transform BlendLinear(const Transform& a, const
Transform& b, float weight) {
    return {
        glm::mix(a.position, b.position, weight),
        glm::slerp(a.rotation, b.rotation, weight),
        glm::mix(a.scale, b.scale, weight)
    };
}
```

Then you apply this across the entire pose:

```
std::vector<Transform> BlendPosesLinear(
    const std::vector<Transform>& poseA,
    const std::vector<Transform>& poseB,
    float weight) {

    size_t boneCount = poseA.size();
    std::vector<Transform> blendedPose(boneCount);

    for (size_t i = 0; i < boneCount; ++i) {
        blendedPose[i] = BlendLinear(poseA[i],
poseB[i], weight);
    }

    return blendedPose;
}
```

This technique is used for idle-to-walk transitions, walk-to-run blending, and shifting between stances like crouch or prone.

Example: Blending Run and Aim

In a third-person shooter, you may want to transition the upper body from a relaxed walk to an aiming stance.

```
float transitionProgress = elapsed / blendDuration;

std::vector<Transform> blended =
BlendPosesLinear(walkPose, aimPose,
transitionProgress);
```

Even with different animations, as long as they use the same skeleton, blending works correctly.

Additive Blending: Layering Offsets on a Base Pose

Additive blending is more powerful. Instead of interpolating from one pose to another, it applies **differences** (deltas) from a reference pose to a base pose.

Step 1: Compute the Additive Delta

You start by calculating how the additive pose deviates from a neutral or reference pose. This is typically done at import time or the first frame of the clip.

```
Transform MakeAdditiveDelta(const Transform&
reference, const Transform& current) {
    return {
        current.position - reference.position,
        glm::normalize(current.rotation *
glm::inverse(reference.rotation)),
        current.scale / reference.scale
    };
}
```

This gives you a **delta transform**: how much this pose moves the bone from the reference.

Step 2: Apply the Delta to the Base Pose

You then apply that delta to the currently playing animation:

```
Transform ApplyAdditive(const Transform& base,
const Transform& delta, float weight) {
    return {
        base.position + delta.position * weight,
        glm::slerp(base.rotation, base.rotation *
delta.rotation, weight),
        base.scale * glm::mix(glm::vec3(1.0f),
delta.scale, weight)
    };
}
```

The rotation part is key—you apply the delta as a relative quaternion and slerp the result.

Use Case: Breathing Animation

Suppose you want to add subtle breathing motion on top of idle.

The breathing clip is authored around the bind pose.

You sample the breathing pose at `t`, calculate the delta from the bind pose, and apply it to the idle pose with a small weight (e.g., `0.2f`).

```
Transform delta = MakeAdditiveDelta(bindPose[i],
breathingPose[i]);

blendedPose[i] = ApplyAdditive(idlePose[i], delta,
0.2f);
```

You apply this per bone, but typically only on upper-body bones like spine, chest, and shoulders.

Layered Blending: Mixing Different Poses Across the Skeleton

Layered blending allows you to apply different animations to different parts of the body simultaneously.

For example:

The lower body plays a walk or run cycle.

The upper body plays a reload or aim animation.

To do this, you define a **bone mask**—a set of bones that the upper layer should affect.

```
std::unordered_set<int> upperBodyBones = { spine1,
spine2, neck, shoulderL, shoulderR, armL, armR };
```

Then blend selectively:

```
Transform BlendLayered(const Transform& base, const
Transform& overlay, float weight, bool isMasked) {
    if (isMasked) {
        return BlendLinear(base, overlay, weight);
    }
    return base;
}
```

And apply to the whole pose:

```cpp
std::vector<Transform> BlendPosesLayered(
    const std::vector<Transform>& basePose,
    const std::vector<Transform>& overlayPose,
    const std::unordered_set<int>& maskedBones,
    float weight) {

    size_t boneCount = basePose.size();
    std::vector<Transform> result(boneCount);

    for (size_t i = 0; i < boneCount; ++i) {
        bool isMasked =
maskedBones.count(static_cast<int>(i)) > 0;
        result[i] = BlendLayered(basePose[i],
overlayPose[i], weight, isMasked);
    }

    return result;
}
```

This keeps the legs walking and the arms reloading at the same time, all without creating a separate walk+reload clip.

Performance Tip: Avoid Unnecessary Allocations

If you're doing multiple blends per frame, reuse output buffers instead of allocating new `std::vector<Transform>` each time. Use pre-sized arrays or a memory pool for large-scale character animation.

Debugging Tip: Visualize Layer Influence

To confirm your masking works:

Color bones by weight—red for fully influenced, green for none.

Show overlays in your editor to let animators tune blend masks interactively.

Print bone transforms before and after additive application to verify delta accuracy.

Blending animations—linearly, additively, and in layers—is what gives you control, reusability, and realism. Instead of creating thousands of unique animations, you create a handful of expressive motions and mix them at runtime.

This is the foundation for procedural animation systems, full-body controllers, and reactive character behaviors.

6.4 Creating and Managing Blend Trees

When you're working on a real-time animation system, managing transitions and combinations of animation clips manually gets unmanageable fast. Whether you're blending walk and run cycles, layering aiming on top of locomotion, or switching between idle states depending on weapon type, you need a structured way to control what clips are playing, how they blend, and when.

That's what a **blend tree** is for.

A blend tree is a composable runtime graph where each node samples and blends animations based on input parameters like speed, direction, or trigger events. It lets you declaratively organize and combine animation logic, allowing characters to smoothly react to dynamic gameplay without writing complex per-frame code.

Core Interface: IBlendNode

All blend tree nodes must implement a common interface. At runtime, each node is responsible for evaluating itself and returning a full character pose.

```
class IBlendNode {
public:
    virtual std::vector<Transform> Evaluate(float
deltaTime) = 0;
    virtual void SetWeight(float weight) {}
    virtual ~IBlendNode() {}
};
```

Every node takes in `deltaTime`, so it can advance its internal time if it's managing clip playback. You can extend the interface to include input parameters (e.g., movement speed, aiming flag) if needed.

Leaf Node: ClipNode

This is the lowest-level node. It plays a single animation clip and keeps track of time.

```cpp
class ClipNode : public IBlendNode {
public:
    AnimationClip* clip;
    float localTime = 0.0f;
    bool looping = true;

    ClipNode(AnimationClip* clip) : clip(clip) {}

    std::vector<Transform> Evaluate(float
deltaTime) override {
        localTime += deltaTime;
        if (looping) {
            localTime = fmod(localTime, clip-
>duration);
        } else {
            localTime = std::min(localTime, clip-
>duration);
        }
        return SampleAnimationAtTime(*clip,
localTime);
    }
};
```

This node does one thing: sample its clip at the current time and return the pose. You can reuse it in many higher-level nodes.

BlendNode: Interpolating Two Children

This node blends the output of two child nodes based on a weight. The weight should be in the range [0.0, 1.0].

```cpp
class BlendNode : public IBlendNode {
public:
    IBlendNode* a;
    IBlendNode* b;
    float weight;

    BlendNode(IBlendNode* a, IBlendNode* b, float
weight)
        : a(a), b(b), weight(weight) {}

    std::vector<Transform> Evaluate(float
deltaTime) override {
```

```cpp
        auto poseA = a->Evaluate(deltaTime);
        auto poseB = b->Evaluate(deltaTime);

        size_t boneCount = poseA.size();
        std::vector<Transform> result(boneCount);

        for (size_t i = 0; i < boneCount; ++i) {
            result[i] = {
                glm::mix(poseA[i].position,
poseB[i].position, weight),
                glm::slerp(poseA[i].rotation,
poseB[i].rotation, weight),
                glm::mix(poseA[i].scale,
poseB[i].scale, weight)
            };
        }

        return result;
    }

    void SetWeight(float newWeight) override {
        weight = glm::clamp(newWeight, 0.0f, 1.0f);
    }
};
```

This node is great for transitions: idle to walk, walk to run, or aiming in vs. out.

AdditiveNode: Layering Delta Motions

This node adds an animation (like breathing or recoil) on top of the base pose. The additive clip must be authored relative to a reference pose (usually bind pose or neutral stance).

```cpp
class AdditiveNode : public IBlendNode {
public:
    IBlendNode* base;
    IBlendNode* additive;
    std::vector<Transform> referencePose;
    float weight;
```

```cpp
    AdditiveNode(IBlendNode* base, IBlendNode*
additive, const std::vector<Transform>& reference,
float weight)
        : base(base), additive(additive),
referencePose(reference), weight(weight) {}

    std::vector<Transform> Evaluate(float
deltaTime) override {
        auto basePose = base->Evaluate(deltaTime);
        auto additivePose = additive-
>Evaluate(deltaTime);

        size_t boneCount = basePose.size();
        std::vector<Transform> result(boneCount);

        for (size_t i = 0; i < boneCount; ++i) {
            Transform delta = {
                additivePose[i].position -
referencePose[i].position,

glm::normalize(additivePose[i].rotation *
glm::inverse(referencePose[i].rotation)),
                additivePose[i].scale /
referencePose[i].scale
            };

            result[i] = {
                basePose[i].position +
delta.position * weight,
                glm::slerp(basePose[i].rotation,
basePose[i].rotation * delta.rotation, weight),
                basePose[i].scale *
glm::mix(glm::vec3(1.0f), delta.scale, weight)
            };
        }

        return result;
    }

    void SetWeight(float newWeight) override {
        weight = glm::clamp(newWeight, 0.0f, 1.0f);
    }
```

```
};
```

This node is ideal for layering secondary motions like breathing, flinching, or upper-body aiming.

SelectorNode: Conditional Playback

This node chooses between multiple child nodes based on input state. It's the bridge between gameplay logic and animation output.

```cpp
class SelectorNode : public IBlendNode {
public:
    std::function<int()> conditionFunc;
    std::vector<IBlendNode*> children;

    SelectorNode(const std::function<int()>&
selector) : conditionFunc(selector) {}

    std::vector<Transform> Evaluate(float
deltaTime) override {
        int index = conditionFunc();
        return children[index]-
>Evaluate(deltaTime);
    }

    void AddChild(IBlendNode* child) {
        children.push_back(child);
    }
};
```

Pass in a function like:

```cpp
int MovementStateSelector() {

    if (isSprinting) return 2;

    if (isWalking) return 1;

    return 0;

}
```

Then attach walk, run, and idle nodes to the selector. This keeps animation logic cleanly separated from control flow.

Example: Walk-Run Blend with Additive Breathing

You can build a blend tree that looks like this:

AdditiveNode (Breathing)

↑

BlendNode (walk ↔ run)

↑   ↑

ClipNode(walk)   ClipNode(run)

And set it up like this:

```
auto walk = new ClipNode(walkClip);

auto run  = new ClipNode(runClip);

auto breathe = new ClipNode(breathingClip);


auto locomotion = new BlendNode(walk, run, 0.0f);
// Set weight dynamically

auto fullMotion = new AdditiveNode(locomotion,
breathe, bindPose, 0.25f);
```

Call `fullMotion->Evaluate(deltaTime)` each frame, and feed the resulting pose to your skeleton pose system.

Managing Blend Tree Parameters

To control the tree at runtime:

Expose setters like `SetWeight()` for transition control.

Bind `conditionFunc` lambdas to gameplay state.

Cache previously evaluated nodes if they don't change.

Reuse blend trees across characters with shared skeletons.

Blend trees give your animation system structure, reusability, and adaptability. They allow you to build up complex behavior—such as walking while aiming, transitioning into reload, or layering reactive flinches—without tangled state machines or per-frame logic.

Chapter 7: Inverse Kinematics (IK) in Real-Time

So far, your animation system has worked primarily through **forward kinematics**—applying joint rotations from the root down through the skeleton to determine final bone positions. This approach works great for predefined motion like walk cycles or gestures authored in DCC tools. But what happens when a character's foot needs to align perfectly with uneven terrain? Or a hand must grab a door handle, or the eyes should track a moving object?

For that, you need **inverse kinematics (IK)**.

IK solves the opposite problem: you know where a bone should end up—like the position of a foot or hand—and you need to compute the joint rotations that get it there. This technique gives characters the ability to dynamically adapt their limbs to the environment in real time, without needing a dedicated animation for every situation.

7.1 Forward vs Inverse Kinematics

In any skeletal animation system, motion is defined and controlled through kinematics—either **forward** or **inverse**. Understanding the distinction between the two is not just theoretical; it has direct implications for how you structure your animation system, what kinds of gameplay interactions you can support, and how flexible your character behaviors become.

What is Forward Kinematics?

Forward Kinematics (FK) is the traditional, animation-authoring-friendly method used in most animation systems by default. In FK, the position and orientation of each joint in a bone chain are defined relative to its parent. You evaluate these transforms hierarchically—from the root of the skeleton to the end effector.

Each joint transform is represented as a local `Transform`, and its world-space or global transform is computed like this:

```
globalTransform[i] = globalTransform[parent[i]] *
localTransform[i];
```

This is a single-pass evaluation that starts at the root (which has no parent, or `parent[i] == -1`) and continues through the bone list.

Example: Animating an Arm Using FK

Let's say you have a simple arm structure:

Upper Arm (shoulder)

Forearm (elbow)

Hand (wrist)

Each joint has a rotation keyframe defined in your animation data. When you evaluate this animation at runtime:

You rotate the shoulder (upper arm).

The forearm inherits this rotation and applies its own.

The hand inherits both and applies its final local rotation.

The result is a fully articulated arm, animated according to the values authored in the animation clip. The motion flows **from the root to the tip**.

Strengths of FK

Fast and predictable evaluation.

Easy to author using keyframe tools (Maya, Blender).

Works well for full-body motion like walking, running, jumping.

Limitations of FK

You cannot control the final position of the end effector directly.

If you want a hand to touch a specific point in the world (e.g. a button, gun handle, or railing), you need to guess or animate it by hand.

Environment adaptation (like foot locking on slopes) is nearly impossible with FK alone.

What is Inverse Kinematics?

Inverse Kinematics (IK) solves the opposite problem. Instead of providing all the joint angles and asking, "Where will the hand end up?" you provide the **target position** for the hand and ask, **"What joint angles will place the hand there?"**

This reverses the flow of motion: it starts from the end effector and works backward to compute joint angles that satisfy the constraint.

Example: Reaching for a Target

Let's take that same arm chain:

Upper Arm

Forearm

Hand

Suppose you want the hand to reach out and touch a point at (3.2, 1.5, - 2.0) in world space. You don't know what the shoulder and elbow angles should be—you want the IK solver to compute those angles for you.

An IK algorithm, such as CCD (Cyclic Coordinate Descent) or FABRIK (Forward and Backward Reaching Inverse Kinematics), will adjust the joint rotations so that the hand (end effector) reaches the target position as closely as possible.

Strengths of IK

End-effector driven: perfect for aiming, grabbing, stepping, and tracking.

Makes characters reactive to the environment.

Can adapt pre-authored animations (e.g., walking) to match terrain or gameplay elements.

Limitations of IK

Computationally more expensive (usually iterative).

Less predictable motion if not constrained well.

Requires more care when blending or layering with FK animation.

Practical Comparison

Feature	Forward Kinematics	Inverse Kinematics
Direction of Evaluation	Root → Tip	Tip → Root
Input	Joint rotations	Target position
Output	End effector position	Joint angles
Use Case	Playing predefined animations	Dynamic interaction (reach, place foot)
Complexity	Very low	Medium to high
Typical Evaluation Method	Single pass (no iteration)	Iterative solvers (CCD, FABRIK, etc.)

When to Use FK vs IK

Both techniques have their place and are often **combined** within a single character rig.

Use FK when:

Playing standard animations from an authored clip (walking, attacking, emoting).

You want smooth, consistent motion exactly as authored.

Performance matters more than physical realism.

Use IK when:

You need real-time foot locking to uneven ground.

The hands must touch or align with world objects (handles, weapons, buttons).

You want reactive behavior—head tracking, aiming, procedural gestures.

A common pattern is to use **FK for the base motion** and **layer IK on top** for adjustments. For example:

Let the walk animation play via FK.

Use IK to correct the feet if the terrain is sloped.

Use another IK pass to rotate the head toward a nearby target.

Example: Combining FK and IK

Here's a simple workflow in code:

```
// 1. Evaluate walk cycle via FK

std::vector<Transform> pose =
SampleAnimationAtTime(walkClip, currentTime);


// 2. Compute global bone transforms

std::vector<glm::mat4> globalPose;

ComputeGlobalPose(skeleton, pose, globalPose);


// 3. Run IK on the foot chain to adjust to terrain

SolveIK_CCD(legBones, footTargetPosition, 10);


// 4. Overwrite affected bones with IK results

OverridePoseWithIK(pose, legBones);
```

This lets you retain the authored motion while correcting it in response to gameplay.

Forward kinematics gives you predictable playback from animation data. Inverse kinematics gives you adaptive control over final joint positioning. Neither is better than the other—they're tools that solve different problems. In a modern animation system, you almost always use both. FK runs the baseline animation, and IK makes it dynamic.

7.2 CCD and FABRIK Algorithms

Inverse kinematics becomes practical in real-time animation when it's backed by solvers that are simple, fast, and robust. Two of the most popular IK algorithms that meet these requirements are **Cyclic Coordinate Descent (CCD)** and **FABRIK (Forward And Backward Reaching Inverse Kinematics)**.

Cyclic Coordinate Descent (CCD)

CCD is an iterative solver that operates by rotating each joint in the chain one at a time to bring the end effector closer to the target. It does this from the last joint (closest to the end effector) up to the base joint, and repeats the process until the end effector reaches the target or a maximum number of iterations is reached.

Core Idea

Start from the joint just before the end effector.

At each joint:

Calculate the vector from the joint to the current end effector position.

Calculate the vector from the joint to the target position.

Find the shortest arc rotation that aligns the first vector with the second.

Rotate the joint by that amount.

Update the positions of all child joints.

Repeat the process until the end effector is close enough to the target.

CCD Solver in C++

Let's define a simple IK chain:

```
struct IKBone {
    glm::vec3 position;
    glm::quat rotation;
    float length;
};
```

We assume the chain is a flat list, where `chain[0]` is the root and `chain[n-1]` is the end effector.

Now here's the CCD solver:

```cpp
void SolveIK_CCD(std::vector<IKBone>& chain, const
glm::vec3& target, int iterations, float threshold
= 0.01f) {
    size_t boneCount = chain.size();
    if (boneCount < 2) return;

    for (int iter = 0; iter < iterations; ++iter) {
        for (int i = boneCount - 2; i >= 0; --i) {
            glm::vec3 jointPos = chain[i].position;
            glm::vec3 endPos =
chain.back().position;

            glm::vec3 toEnd = glm::normalize(endPos
- jointPos);
            glm::vec3 toTarget =
glm::normalize(target - jointPos);

            float dot = glm::dot(toEnd, toTarget);
            dot = glm::clamp(dot, -1.0f, 1.0f);
            float angle = acos(dot);
            if (angle < 1e-5f) continue;

            glm::vec3 axis = glm::cross(toEnd,
toTarget);
            if (glm::length2(axis) < 1e-6f)
continue;
            axis = glm::normalize(axis);

            glm::quat delta = glm::angleAxis(angle,
axis);
            chain[i].rotation = delta *
chain[i].rotation;

            // Forward update of child positions
            for (size_t j = i + 1; j < boneCount;
++j) {
```

```cpp
                glm::vec3 dir =
glm::normalize(chain[j].position - chain[j -
1].position);
                dir = chain[j - 1].rotation *
glm::vec3(0.0f, 0.0f, 1.0f);
                chain[j].position = chain[j -
1].position + dir * chain[j - 1].length;
            }

        if
(glm::distance(chain.back().position, target) <
threshold)
                return; // Close enough
        }
    }
}
```

This version is practical for arms, legs, tails, and even procedural chains like tentacles.

FABRIK (Forward And Backward Reaching IK)

FABRIK takes a different approach. Instead of adjusting angles, it manipulates joint **positions** directly, then derives rotations later. It alternates two passes:

Backward pass: Move from the end effector back to the root, adjusting each joint position so that it lies at the correct bone length from the next joint.

Forward pass: Move from root to end effector, again keeping correct bone lengths.

After several iterations, the chain converges, and you can reconstruct joint orientations from the new positions.

FABRIK Solver in C++

Define the chain again, focusing on position and length:

```cpp
struct IKNode {
    glm::vec3 position;
    float length;
};
```

FABRIK iteration looks like this:

```cpp
void SolveIK_FABRIK(std::vector<IKNode>& chain,
const glm::vec3& target, int iterations, float
threshold = 0.01f) {
    if (chain.size() < 2) return;

    glm::vec3 rootPos = chain[0].position;
    float totalLength = 0.0f;
    for (const auto& node : chain) totalLength +=
node.length;

    if (glm::distance(rootPos, target) >
totalLength) {
        // Unreachable target: stretch toward it
        for (size_t i = 1; i < chain.size(); ++i) {
            glm::vec3 dir = glm::normalize(target -
chain[i - 1].position);
            chain[i].position = chain[i -
1].position + dir * chain[i - 1].length;
        }
        return;
    }

    for (int iter = 0; iter < iterations; ++iter) {
        // Backward
        chain.back().position = target;
        for (int i = static_cast<int>(chain.size())
- 2; i >= 0; --i) {
            glm::vec3 dir =
glm::normalize(chain[i].position - chain[i +
1].position);
            chain[i].position = chain[i +
1].position + dir * chain[i].length;
        }

        // Forward
        chain[0].position = rootPos;
        for (size_t i = 1; i < chain.size(); ++i) {
            glm::vec3 dir =
glm::normalize(chain[i].position - chain[i -
1].position);
            chain[i].position = chain[i -
1].position + dir * chain[i - 1].length;
```

```
        }

        if (glm::distance(chain.back().position,
target) < threshold)
            break;
    }
}
```

After solving, you must compute rotations based on the direction between joints:

```
glm::quat ComputeBoneRotation(const glm::vec3&
from, const glm::vec3& to) {
    glm::vec3 forward = glm::normalize(to - from);
    return glm::rotation(glm::vec3(0, 0, 1),
forward);
}
```

Use this to update your skeleton's local rotation per bone if needed.

Comparison: CCD vs FABRIK

Feature	CCD	FABRIK
Solves via	Joint angles	Joint positions
Convergence	Slow for long chains	Fast and stable
Motion	Can be jerky	Smoother and more natural
Math	Requires axis-angle and quats	Pure vector math
Bones required	2 or more	2 or more
Target support	Good for precise end effector	Good for stretching/relaxing

Real-World Advice

Use **FABRIK** for legs and arms when smooth positioning is more important than perfect precision.

Use **CCD** when precision is needed, especially in short chains like elbows or wrists.

Always constrain joint angles if necessary (e.g., prevent elbows from bending backwards).

Run solvers in local or world space based on your engine architecture.

For runtime efficiency, use a small number of iterations (3–10) and early exit if the target is already reached.

Both CCD and FABRIK are viable for real-time applications. CCD gives you simplicity and rotational control, while FABRIK offers fast, elegant convergence with smoother results. A good animation system supports both and chooses the right one based on context. In the next section, you'll use these solvers to build practical systems for foot placement, aiming, and look-at control in gameplay.

7.3 Implementing IK Solvers in C++

To make inverse kinematics usable in your animation system, it's not enough to understand the theory—you need clean, real-time-capable C++ implementations. This section focuses on turning the IK concepts from the previous section into fully working code, with clear data structures and methods you can plug into your existing animation pipeline.

We'll implement both **CCD** and **FABRIK** solvers in C++, show how to integrate them with a skeleton structure, and give you debugging tips to ensure they're functioning properly. The focus is on solving 2D/3D chains of arbitrary length efficiently and accurately.

Foundation: The IK Chain Structure

An IK chain is just a list of bones where each one has:

A position in world space

A bone length

A rotation (typically used to apply to your actual skeleton)

A parent-child relationship that determines the direction of updates

We define a simple structure for each joint:

```
struct IKBone {
    glm::vec3 position;
    glm::quat rotation;
    float length;

    // Optional: store original bind pose data for
restoration
    glm::vec3 originalPosition;
    glm::quat originalRotation;
};
```

And the full IK chain is simply a list of these:

```
using IKChain = std::vector<IKBone>;
```

IK Solver: CCD Implementation in C++

Let's implement the CCD algorithm first. This version iteratively rotates joints from end-effector back to root.

```
void SolveIK_CCD(IKChain& chain, const glm::vec3&
target, int maxIterations = 10, float tolerance =
0.01f) {
    if (chain.size() < 2) return;

    for (int iter = 0; iter < maxIterations;
++iter) {
        // Start from second-to-last joint, move
backward
        for (int i = static_cast<int>(chain.size())
- 2; i >= 0; --i) {
            glm::vec3 jointPos = chain[i].position;
            glm::vec3 effectorPos =
chain.back().position;

            glm::vec3 toEffector =
glm::normalize(effectorPos - jointPos);
            glm::vec3 toTarget =
glm::normalize(target - jointPos);
```

```
                float angle =
acos(glm::clamp(glm::dot(toEffector, toTarget), -
1.0f, 1.0f));
                if (angle < 1e-5f) continue;

                glm::vec3 axis =
glm::normalize(glm::cross(toEffector, toTarget));
                if (glm::length2(axis) < 1e-6f)
continue;

                glm::quat rotationDelta =
glm::angleAxis(angle, axis);
                chain[i].rotation = rotationDelta *
chain[i].rotation;

                // Recalculate child positions based on
new rotations
                for (size_t j = i + 1; j <
chain.size(); ++j) {
                    glm::vec3 dir =
glm::normalize(chain[j].position - chain[j -
1].position);
                    dir = chain[j - 1].rotation *
glm::vec3(0, 0, 1); // forward axis
                    chain[j].position = chain[j -
1].position + dir * chain[j - 1].length;
                }
        }

        if (glm::distance(chain.back().position,
target) < tolerance)
            return; // done early
    }
}
```

This function updates the position and rotation of each joint. After solving, you'll usually feed the rotations into your skeleton pose structure.

IK Solver: FABRIK Implementation in C++

FABRIK works with joint positions first, then derives rotations from the updated bone directions.

```cpp
void SolveIK_FABRIK(IKChain& chain, const
glm::vec3& target, int maxIterations = 10, float
tolerance = 0.01f) {
    if (chain.size() < 2) return;

    glm::vec3 rootPos = chain[0].position;
    float totalLength = 0.0f;
    for (auto& bone : chain) totalLength +=
bone.length;

    if (glm::distance(rootPos, target) >
totalLength) {
        // Unreachable: stretch toward target
        for (size_t i = 1; i < chain.size(); ++i) {
            glm::vec3 dir = glm::normalize(target -
chain[i - 1].position);
            chain[i].position = chain[i -
1].position + dir * chain[i - 1].length;
        }
        return;
    }

    for (int iter = 0; iter < maxIterations;
++iter) {
        // Backward pass
        chain.back().position = target;
        for (int i = static_cast<int>(chain.size())
- 2; i >= 0; --i) {
            glm::vec3 dir =
glm::normalize(chain[i].position - chain[i +
1].position);
            chain[i].position = chain[i +
1].position + dir * chain[i].length;
        }

        // Forward pass
        chain[0].position = rootPos;
        for (size_t i = 1; i < chain.size(); ++i) {
            glm::vec3 dir =
glm::normalize(chain[i].position - chain[i -
1].position);
```

```
                chain[i].position = chain[i -
1].position + dir * chain[i - 1].length;
            }

            if (glm::distance(chain.back().position,
target) < tolerance)
                break;
        }

        // Compute new rotations
        for (size_t i = 0; i < chain.size() - 1; ++i) {
            glm::vec3 from = glm::vec3(0, 0, 1); //
forward
            glm::vec3 to = glm::normalize(chain[i +
1].position - chain[i].position);
            chain[i].rotation = glm::rotation(from,
to);
        }
}
```

FABRIK is smooth and stable, and it's usually preferred for full-body procedural effects like foot placement or tentacle control.

Integrating IK with a Skeleton Pose

Once you've solved an IK chain, you need to transfer its result back into your animation system. If your skeleton pose is represented as:

```
struct Pose {
    std::vector<glm::vec3> positions;
    std::vector<glm::quat> rotations;
};
```

You map the IKBone rotations and positions back into the pose using the bone indices.

```
void ApplyIKToPose(const IKChain& chain, const
std::vector<int>& boneIndices, Pose& pose) {
    for (size_t i = 0; i < chain.size(); ++i) {
        int boneIdx = boneIndices[i];
        pose.positions[boneIdx] =
chain[i].position;
```

132

```
        pose.rotations[boneIdx] =
chain[i].rotation;
    }
}
```

This lets you overlay IK solutions onto your regular animation output—either fully replacing or blending them depending on the use case.

Debugging and Visualization

IK problems often stem from incorrect input data or bone hierarchy mismatches. Use visual debugging to draw:

Bone lines (joint positions)

End effector vs target positions

Local axes or forward direction per joint

If you see sudden jumps or unnatural bends, it's usually due to incorrect local → world conversions, incorrect bone lengths, or unstable rotation interpolation.

Practical Exercise: IK-Driven Foot Placement

Here's a simple application of the FABRIK solver to solve for a character's foot to reach terrain:

```
glm::vec3 footTarget = RaycastGround(contactPoint);

IKChain legChain = BuildLegChain(skeleton, pose,
leftLegBones);

SolveIK_FABRIK(legChain, footTarget);

ApplyIKToPose(legChain, leftLegBones, pose);
```

This technique keeps the foot planted even when the character is walking on a slope or uneven rock.

You now have robust C++ implementations of both CCD and FABRIK solvers, ready to be used in your real-time engine. By encapsulating each solver, updating your pose structure after solving, and blending IK results into your final animation state, you gain full control over how characters respond to their world whether it's aligning with terrain, targeting, aiming, or gesturing.

7.4 Use Cases: Foot Placement, Look-at, Aiming

Inverse Kinematics is not just a theoretical feature—it solves real, tangible animation problems in interactive environments. Once you've built your IK solvers, the next step is applying them effectively. This section focuses on three high-impact use cases where IK enhances realism and interactivity: **foot placement**, **look-at control**, and **aiming**.

Each of these cases introduces unique technical demands, but they all follow the same principle—take the target position and solve the chain backward to determine joint rotations. We'll break down the logic, share practical examples, and show you exactly how to wire this into your character animation system.

Foot Placement on Uneven Terrain

Let's say your character is walking on an incline or climbing uneven rocks. Without IK, the feet follow the baked animation clip, which assumes a flat surface. The result is floating feet, feet clipping into geometry, or slipping that destroys immersion.

To solve this, we use IK to position each foot at the correct contact point on the terrain and orient it to match the surface normal.

Step-by-Step Approach

Detect the ground contact point
Use a downward raycast from the animated foot position to detect the exact surface location.

Build the IK chain for the leg
This usually includes the upper leg, lower leg, and foot bones (three segments).

Use FABRIK to solve

FABRIK is ideal here due to its smooth convergence and position-based nature.

Apply the solved pose back to the animation skeleton

This overrides the FK-computed pose for the leg, ensuring the foot is planted correctly.

C++ Snippet

```cpp
glm::vec3 footTarget =
RaycastGround(animFootPosition);

IKChain legChain = BuildLegChain(skeleton, pose,
leftLegBones);

SolveIK_FABRIK(legChain, footTarget);

ApplyIKToPose(legChain, leftLegBones, pose);
```

Foot Rotation Adjustment

To make the foot align with the terrain:

```cpp
glm::vec3 normal = GetSurfaceNormal(footTarget);

glm::quat align = glm::rotation(glm::vec3(0, 1, 0),
normal);

pose.rotations[footIndex] = align;
```

Blend this rotation smoothly with the animation rotation to prevent harsh snapping.

Look-at: Head or Eye Targeting

Characters often need to track objects, players, or enemies with their head or eyes. Instead of animating every possible direction, IK lets you procedurally rotate the head or neck bones toward a dynamic target.

Step-by-Step Approach

Identify bones in the chain
Typically neck, head, and optional eye bones.

Compute target direction
Convert the target into local space of each joint or compute a world-space direction vector.

Rotate the bones incrementally toward the target
You can use a simplified CCD or just angle clamping per bone.

Apply constraints
Limit how much the neck can turn horizontally or vertically to avoid unnatural twisting.

Simple Look-at Code

```
glm::vec3 targetDir = glm::normalize(target -
headPos);
glm::vec3 currentDir = headRotation * glm::vec3(0,
0, 1);
glm::quat lookAtRot = glm::rotation(currentDir,
targetDir);

// Clamp angle
float angle = glm::degrees(glm::angle(lookAtRot));
if (angle > 60.0f) {
    float t = 60.0f / angle;
    lookAtRot = glm::slerp(glm::quat(), lookAtRot,
t);
}

pose.rotations[headIndex] = lookAtRot *
pose.rotations[headIndex];
```

This keeps the motion realistic and avoids snapping.

Aiming: Aligning Weapon with Target

When a character needs to aim a gun, throw a projectile, or point a tool, the upper body must align with a world-space target. Aiming can be done purely with FK, but IK gives you much more accuracy and flexibility.

Typical Aiming Setup

A 3-bone chain: upper arm, forearm, and hand.

The weapon is typically attached to the hand bone.

Use IK to rotate the chain so the gun barrel points at the target.

Solver Considerations

CCD is often more precise here.

You must lock the elbow to a reasonable position, or define a plane in which the elbow should move.

Add constraints to prevent the shoulder from twisting unnaturally.

Implementation Snippet (CCD)

```
IKChain armChain = BuildArmChain(skeleton, pose,
rightArmBones);

glm::vec3 targetPoint = ComputeAimTarget(); //
world-space


SolveIK_CCD(armChain, targetPoint, 10);

ApplyIKToPose(armChain, rightArmBones, pose);
```

Optionally apply smoothing:

```
pose.rotations[shoulder] =
glm::slerp(pose.rotations[shoulder],
armChain[0].rotation, 0.2f);
```

Aligning Weapon Model

If your weapon model has a forward vector that doesn't align with the bone's default forward axis, compute an alignment offset and apply it during weapon attachment or solve.

Debugging Tips for All Use Cases

Draw joint positions and axes as colored lines.

Visualize the IK target point vs. current end-effector position.

Show constraints visually: rotation cones, angle arcs.

Use a real-time toggle to enable/disable IK for comparison.

Blending IK Output with Animation

You rarely want to 100% override the animation pose. Instead, interpolate:

```
pose.rotations[bone] =
glm::slerp(originalPose.rotations[bone],
ikPose.rotations[bone], weight);
```

Use weights based on:

Whether the foot is in the contact phase of a walk

Whether the player is actively aiming

How far off the current gaze is from the desired target

Foot locking, gaze tracking, and aiming are three of the most common real-time IK use cases—and all three dramatically enhance the believability and responsiveness of your character animations. By integrating CCD or FABRIK solvers into your engine and blending their results carefully into your pose system, you can give characters reactive, adaptive, and intelligent motion without relying on expensive or impractical hand-authored animation sets.

Chapter 8: Physics-Driven Animation and Ragdolls

So far, we've focused on animation systems where motion is controlled by data—keyframes, pose blending, IK solvers. But real-time characters don't exist in a vacuum. They collide with walls, respond to explosions, fall off ledges, or get knocked back. To handle these situations believably, you need to bring **physics** into the animation pipeline.

8.1 Integrating Physics with Animation

In traditional skeletal animation, characters move based on pose data—typically keyframes authored in a DCC tool like Blender or Maya. Every bone transform is explicitly defined or interpolated at runtime. This works well for predictable, controlled motion, but it falls short when real-world dynamics are required: characters falling down stairs, responding to explosions, balancing, or simply colliding naturally with the world.

Integrating **physics** into your animation system means adding a dynamic layer of realism. Rather than driving bones solely from animation data, you let physical forces influence how the skeleton behaves. This opens the door to features like ragdoll effects, dynamic hit reactions, soft-body jiggle (for things like backpacks or antennae), and even full-body physical control.

Key Concepts for Integration

Before jumping into implementation, let's define a few important terms:

Animation Pose: A per-frame hierarchy of local bone transforms.

Physics Rigid Body: A simulated object with mass, shape, and dynamic properties.

Constraint: A joint that restricts movement between rigid bodies (e.g. a hinge or ball socket).

Ragdoll Rig: A simplified physics representation of a character's skeleton using rigid bodies and constraints.

Modes of Integration

There are three general integration modes:

Animation-Driven with Physics Observers

Physics is passive: bones are animated, and physics bodies follow.

Used for attaching soft bodies or tracking animation-driven limbs.

Physics-Driven with Animation Observers

Physics controls movement, and animation visuals follow.

Used for ragdolls, collapsing characters, or physics-only props.

Blended Mode

Both systems influence the result with a weight factor.

Used for hit reactions, dynamic secondary motion, or transition states (e.g. from animation to full ragdoll).

Let's focus on building a system that can support all three.

Data Structure: Mapping Bones to Physics Proxies

You don't simulate every single bone. Instead, you choose a subset (spine, limbs, head) and create a simplified physics representation.

```
struct RagdollBone {
    int boneIndex; // Index in the animation
skeleton
    RigidBody* body; // Physics engine handle
    Constraint* joint; // Optional parent joint
    glm::vec3 offset; // Local offset from bone to
rigid body origin
};
```

The full ragdoll rig is just a list:

```
std::vector<RagdollBone> ragdoll;
```

This structure allows your animation system to query or update physics state per bone.

Animation to Physics: Driving the Simulation

To simulate secondary motion or partially animated characters, you can update the rigid bodies based on animation every frame.

```
for (const auto& rb : ragdoll) {
    glm::mat4 worldTransform =
ComputeBoneWorldMatrix(pose, rb.boneIndex);
    glm::vec3 position =
glm::vec3(worldTransform[3]);
    glm::quat rotation =
glm::quat_cast(worldTransform);

    rb.body->SetKinematicTarget(position,
rotation);
}
```

You usually want to:

Mark these rigid bodies as **kinematic** (not affected by forces).

Disable collisions between adjacent bones to avoid jittering.

Enable them to detect collisions with external objects (e.g. bullets, the environment).

Physics to Animation: Ragdoll Response

When physics takes over (e.g. during a fall or impact), the skeleton needs to follow the rigid bodies instead of the animation.

```
for (const auto& rb : ragdoll) {
    glm::vec3 position = rb.body-
>GetWorldPosition();
    glm::quat rotation = rb.body-
>GetWorldRotation();

    // Convert world transform back to local space
    int parent =
skeleton.GetParentIndex(rb.boneIndex);
    glm::mat4 parentTransform = (parent != -1) ?
globalPose[parent] : glm::mat4(1.0f);
    glm::mat4 invParent =
glm::inverse(parentTransform);
```

```
    glm::mat4 local = invParent *
glm::translate(glm::mat4(1.0f), position) *
glm::toMat4(rotation);
    pose.SetLocalTransform(rb.boneIndex, local);
}
```

This ensures the visual bones match the physics simulation in real time.

Blending Between Animation and Physics

Often you want a hybrid result. For example, the character is playing a death animation, but the upper body is influenced by a knockback. To do this, you blend the animation transform with the physics transform.

```
float weight = 0.6f; // 0 = full animation, 1 =
full physics

for (const auto& rb : ragdoll) {
    glm::vec3 animPos =
animPose.GetWorldPosition(rb.boneIndex);
    glm::quat animRot =
animPose.GetWorldRotation(rb.boneIndex);

    glm::vec3 physPos = rb.body-
>GetWorldPosition();
    glm::quat physRot = rb.body-
>GetWorldRotation();

    glm::vec3 finalPos = glm::mix(animPos, physPos,
weight);
    glm::quat finalRot = glm::slerp(animRot,
physRot, weight);

    pose.SetWorldTransform(rb.boneIndex, finalPos,
finalRot);
}
```

Blend weights can be controlled over time for smooth transitions (e.g. ragdoll-to-stand-up), or spatially (e.g. physics for upper body only).

Practical Use Case: Dynamic Backpacks or Accessories

Sometimes only one or two bones need physics. A good example is a dangling backpack, weapon sling, or tail.

Mark the relevant bones (e.g. "backpack_joint") as dynamic.

Set up a small chain of rigid bodies.

Let physics handle swing and collision.

Write back results to the animation pose.

This adds believable motion to props without baking any additional animation.

Practical Use Case: Hit Reactions

For reactive feedback to explosions, gunshots, or melee hits:

Keep the animation playing normally.

Temporarily enable physics for the impacted bone (e.g. spine).

Apply an impulse.

```
rb.body->ApplyImpulse(impactForce);

EnablePartialRagdoll(spineToHead);

BlendInPhysicsWeight(spineToHead, 0.4f);
```

This gives the appearance of dynamic reaction without needing full ragdoll.

Integration Checklist

To fully integrate physics with your animation system:

Maintain a clean mapping between bones and physics proxies.

Support kinematic and dynamic modes per bone.

Enable real-time blending between systems.

Use consistent local/global space conversions.

Ensure bones never "fight" each other between systems.

Integrating physics into animation gives you a new axis of believability. Characters react, fall, and interact with the environment in ways that authored animation alone cannot deliver. Whether you're implementing full ragdoll systems or subtle physics enhancements like reactive accessories or partial hit responses, this integration lays the foundation for lifelike motion that adapts to gameplay.

8.2 Skeleton-to-Rigid Body Mapping

To simulate characters physically—whether for ragdolls, hit reactions, or interactive body dynamics—you need to create a **physical representation of the character's skeleton**. This involves mapping bones to **rigid bodies** and connecting them using **constraints** that replicate joint behavior. The result is a ragdoll-like structure that behaves believably under simulation, respects anatomical limits, and can blend with animation data.

Most animation skeletons are too detailed and complex for direct physical simulation. They often include:

Extra bones for IK targets or facial rigging

Non-uniform scaling

Bones not aligned with typical joint axes

Irregular joint lengths or names

Instead, we construct a **physics proxy rig**. This is a simplified version of the skeleton, consisting of:

A limited set of bones (usually 12–16)

Rigid bodies with simple colliders (capsules or boxes)

Joint constraints with angular limits

One-to-one mapping to a subset of the animation skeleton

Step 1: Choose Target Bones

Identify the bones in your animation rig that will be represented physically. These typically include:

Pelvis (root of the ragdoll)

Spine (1–2 segments)

Head

Upper Arms, Lower Arms

Upper Legs, Lower Legs

This results in a clean hierarchy:

`pelvis`

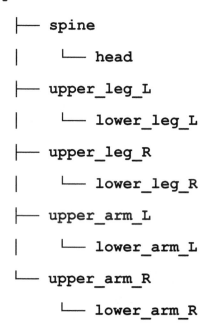

```
pelvis
├── spine
│       └── head
├── upper_leg_L
│       └── lower_leg_L
├── upper_leg_R
│       └── lower_leg_R
├── upper_arm_L
│       └── lower_arm_L
└── upper_arm_R
        └── lower_arm_R
```

Step 2: Create Rigid Bodies per Bone

Each mapped bone gets a rigid body. Capsule shapes are ideal for limbs and spines because they align with bone orientation and simplify collision resolution.

Here's a structure to represent the physics mapping:

```
struct RagdollPart {
    int boneIndex;            // Index into the animation skeleton
    RigidBody* body;          // Physics engine rigid body
    Collider* collider;       // Capsule or box collider
```

```
    glm::vec3 localOffset;            // Offset from
bone origin to physics shape origin
    float boneLength;                 // Used for
constraint setup and visualization
};
```

Rigid body initialization example:

```
RigidBody* CreateBoneRigidBody(const glm::vec3&
position, const glm::quat& rotation, float length)
{
    Collider* capsule = new CapsuleCollider(length
* 0.5f, radius);
    RigidBody* rb = new RigidBody();
    rb->SetCollider(capsule);
    rb->SetMass(length * 2.0f); // Heavier bones
have more resistance
    rb->SetTransform(position, rotation);
    return rb;
}
```

Each `RagdollPart` is stored in a collection:

std::vector<RagdollPart> ragdollParts;

You'll typically create these at character initialization or as part of a load-time asset.

Step 3: Set Up Bone Constraints

Once rigid bodies are created, you connect them using **joint constraints** that mimic human anatomy. For example:

Use **cone twist joints** for shoulders and hips (multi-axis limits)

Use **hinge joints** for elbows and knees (single-axis limits)

Joint creation example:

```
void ConnectWithConeTwist(RigidBody* parent,
RigidBody* child, const glm::vec3& pivotA, const
glm::vec3& pivotB, const JointLimits& limits) {
    Constraint* joint = new
ConeTwistConstraint(parent, child, pivotA, pivotB);
```

```
    joint->SetSwingLimit(limits.swing);
    joint->SetTwistLimit(limits.twistMin,
limits.twistMax);
    PhysicsWorld::AddConstraint(joint);
}
```

Typical joint angle limits:

Spine: ±30° twist, ±45° swing

Elbow: 0° to 135° flexion

Knee: 0° to 120° flexion

Neck: ±40° yaw, ±30° pitch

These constraints enforce anatomical realism and prevent collapsing or over-extension during simulation.

Step 4: Synchronize Physics to Skeleton at Runtime

When entering ragdoll mode or starting a simulation, you initialize the physics bodies to match the current animated pose.

```
for (auto& part : ragdollParts) {
    glm::mat4 worldMatrix =
GetBoneWorldTransform(pose, part.boneIndex);
    glm::vec3 position = glm::vec3(worldMatrix[3]);
    glm::quat rotation =
glm::quat_cast(worldMatrix);

    part.body->SetTransform(position, rotation);
}
```

This ensures a seamless transition into physics mode with no visual popping.

Step 5: Update Skeleton from Rigid Bodies (During Simulation)

In full ragdoll state, the animation system must follow the physics system.

```
for (auto& part : ragdollParts) {
    glm::vec3 pos = part.body->GetWorldPosition();
    glm::quat rot = part.body->GetWorldRotation();
```

```
    int parentIdx =
skeleton.GetParentIndex(part.boneIndex);
    glm::mat4 parentMatrix = (parentIdx != -1) ?
GetBoneWorldTransform(pose, parentIdx) :
glm::mat4(1.0f);
    glm::mat4 invParent =
glm::inverse(parentMatrix);

    glm::mat4 localMatrix = invParent *
glm::translate(glm::mat4(1.0f), pos) *
glm::toMat4(rot);
    pose.SetLocalTransform(part.boneIndex,
localMatrix);
}
```

This keeps your visuals tightly synchronized with simulation.

Testing and Validation Tips

Visualize the ragdoll structure using debug lines for bones, colliders, and joint constraints.

Drop the character from various heights and watch for collapsing limbs or jitter—this usually means constraint errors.

Log bone-to-physics transform mismatches during updates to catch drifting.

Create a separate test scene with a standalone ragdoll and trigger forces from different directions.

Practical Use Case: Full-Body Ragdoll on Death

Deactivate animation updates.

Enable dynamic simulation on all rigid bodies.

Apply impulse or velocity from the kill event.

Blend animation-to-ragdoll smoothly over 0.3–0.5 seconds.

This sequence creates a satisfying physical collapse that responds to player input (direction of impact, fall, etc.) with no canned death animations needed.

Conclusion

Creating a clean, efficient mapping between the animation skeleton and a physics proxy rig is the cornerstone of realistic physics-driven animation. By carefully choosing which bones to simulate, constructing rigid bodies that match proportions, applying appropriate constraints, and syncing data correctly at runtime, you build a stable, performant foundation for ragdolling, physical reactions, and dynamic motion blending.

8.3 Blending Between Animation and Physics

One of the most important features of a robust animation system is the ability to **blend smoothly between keyframe animation and physics simulation**. This blending is what makes ragdolls transition gracefully from animation-driven states, allows partial physical reactions like stagger or hit flinch, and enables procedural enhancements like dynamic foot locking or bouncing accessories.

Blending between animation and physics isn't just about switching control—it's about creating a coherent pose from **two sources of motion**, in a way that feels physically correct and visually seamless.

At any given frame, a bone can be influenced by:

An **animation pose**, derived from keyframes or blend trees.

A **physics pose**, derived from rigid body simulation (e.g., ragdoll).

Blending is about linearly or spherically interpolating between these two poses based on a **blend weight** w per bone or per body part.

w = 0.0 → fully animation-driven

w = 1.0 → fully physics-driven

0.0 < w < 1.0 → interpolated

This blending happens **per-frame, per-bone**, in world or local space.

Where to Perform the Blend

You can perform blending:

In **local bone space** (recommended when both animation and physics are aligned to the same parent transform)

In **world space** (required when skeleton and physics differ in hierarchy)

Either way, you must compute a consistent transform for each source.

The Blending Function

The most basic blend for a transform consists of:

Position: `glm::mix(animPos, physicsPos, w)`

Rotation: `glm::slerp(animRot, physicsRot, w)`

For a single bone:

```
Transform BlendTransform(const Transform& animT,
const Transform& physT, float w) {
    Transform result;
    result.position = glm::mix(animT.position,
physT.position, w);
    result.rotation = glm::slerp(animT.rotation,
physT.rotation, w);
    result.scale = glm::mix(animT.scale,
physT.scale, w); // usually uniform
    return result;
}
```

Applied in a loop:

```
for (int i = 0; i < pose.BoneCount(); ++i) {
    float blendWeight = GetPhysicsBlendWeight(i);
// per-bone control
    Transform anim = animPose.GetLocalTransform(i);
    Transform phys =
physicsPose.GetLocalTransform(i);
    Transform blended = BlendTransform(anim, phys,
blendWeight);
    finalPose.SetLocalTransform(i, blended);
}
```

Managing Blend Weights

There are different ways to determine how much physics affects each bone:

Global weight: All bones share the same `w` (e.g., transitioning from animation to full ragdoll).

Per-bone weight: Some bones have different `w` (e.g., physics on the upper body only).

Time-based weight: Weight increases/decreases over time (e.g., `w += delta * speed`).

Event-based triggers: Foot hits ground → `w` = `1` for foot bone, then fades out.

You can store weights in a separate array:

```
std::vector<float> physicsWeights; // per bone

void SetFullRagdollWeights(float w) {
    for (float& weight : physicsWeights)
        weight = w;
}
```

Or define masks for partial blending:

```
SetPartialRagdollWeights({spine, chest, neck,
head}, 0.5f);
```

Smooth Transitions (e.g., Into and Out of Ragdoll)

Let's say a character is shot and falls into a ragdoll. You want the blend to feel natural:

Animation → Physics (Fall)

```
float ragdollBlend = glm::clamp(currentTime /
entryDuration, 0.0f, 1.0f);
```

Start from `0.0` and reach `1.0` over `entryDuration`, typically 0.3 to 0.5 seconds.

Physics → Animation (Get Up)

Here, you reverse the process. The player presses a key to get up:

Freeze physics bones in their last state.

Choose a get-up animation (from face-up or face-down).

Blend from physics pose back into animation pose over time:

```
float recoveryBlend = glm::clamp(recoveryTime /
duration, 0.0f, 1.0f);

float physicsWeight = 1.0f - recoveryBlend;
```

When `physicsWeight` reaches 0.0, the animation system fully regains control.

Partial Ragdoll Example: Hit Reactions

A good example of partial blending is a hit reaction where the upper body goes limp while legs continue walking.

```
std::unordered_set<int> upperBodyBones = {spine,
chest, neck, head, shoulderL, shoulderR};

for (int i = 0; i < pose.BoneCount(); ++i) {
    float w = upperBodyBones.contains(i) ? 0.5f :
0.0f;
    physicsWeights[i] = w;
}
```

This lets physics simulate the flinch, but the legs continue animation-driven movement.

Optimizing the Blending Path

Blending every bone every frame can be expensive, especially in crowd simulations. Optimization strategies:

Skip blending for bones with `w == 0.0f`.

Use SIMD or parallel processing (e.g., multithreaded blend passes).

Avoid computing physics poses for bones that are 100% animation-driven.

Also, avoid interpolating transforms that are nearly equal to avoid float churn.

Common Pitfalls

Coordinate space mismatch: Always verify both poses are in the same space before blending.

Over-blending rotations: Slerp beyond 90° can interpolate the long way—ensure quaternions are in the same hemisphere.

Visual foot sliding: When blending ragdoll to stand-up, align foot positions first.

Snapping during transition: Never jump weights from $0 \to 1$. Use time-based ramping.

Debug Visualization Tips

Draw each bone's blend weight as a color (blue = animation, red = physics).

Render skeletons before and after blending for comparison.

Log blend weights per bone if transitions look incorrect.

The ability to blend between animation and physics allows for highly expressive, realistic, and reactive character motion. Whether you're easing into a ragdoll on death, applying secondary motion to a cape or tail, or managing subtle hit reactions, blending is the glue that binds physical simulation and animation control into one coherent output.

8.4 Realistic Hit Reactions and Death Animations

In modern games, players expect characters to react believably to physical events. When someone gets shot, hit with a melee weapon, or struck by an explosion, it's not enough to play a canned animation. The body should respond to the direction, force, and point of impact with motion that looks reactive, contextual, and grounded in physical reality. The same applies when a character dies—they shouldn't just slump in a generic way, but fall dynamically based on where and how they were hit.

Overview of the System

There are three key components:

Impact Detection: Where and how was the character hit?

Reaction Computation: What should move, and how much?

Animation/Physics Response: How is that movement executed—through animation, physics, or both?

You'll implement each of these with practical techniques, including partial ragdoll blending, impulse application, and procedural pose adjustment.

1. Detecting and Processing the Hit

Every reactive animation begins with an impact event. This can be from:

A projectile (hit scan or physical bullet)

A melee weapon

An explosion

Environmental collision (e.g. falling into a wall)

Each impact must report:

```
struct HitEvent {
    glm::vec3 point;          // world-space impact
point
    glm::vec3 normal;         // impact surface
normal
    glm::vec3 direction;      // direction of force
applied
    float magnitude;          // strength of impact
    int boneHit;              // closest bone index
    DamageType type;          // blunt, piercing,
explosive
};
```

This information is passed to your character's animation and physics system to decide how to respond.

2. Applying a Hit Reaction: Physics-Based Motion

Once the hit event is received, you can compute a reaction using physics impulses.

a. Partial Ragdoll on Upper Body

A common approach is to temporarily make part of the skeleton physics-driven:

```
EnablePhysicsBlend({ spine, chest, shoulderL,
shoulderR, neck, head }, 0.5f);
```

This enables blended motion between animation and physics on just the upper body.

b. Apply a Directional Impulse

Next, apply a directional force to simulate the blow:

```
glm::vec3 impulse = hit.direction * hit.magnitude;

if (RagdollPart* part =
GetRagdollPart(hit.boneHit)) {
    part->body->ApplyImpulse(impulse);
}
```

This causes the affected part of the skeleton to recoil naturally. For a headshot, the neck and head might whip backward; for a shoulder hit, the torso might twist.

c. Control the Blend Duration

The physics influence shouldn't stay forever. Use a timer or curve:

```
StartTimedBlend(upperBodyBones, startWeight = 0.5f,
fadeOutTime = 0.7f);
```

This lets the body react with a jolt and then smoothly return to animation.

3. Playing Procedural Flinch Animations (Optional)

Sometimes you want more control than pure physics allows, especially for subtle hits. Here, play a quick flinch or stagger animation **and** optionally enhance it with physics.

```
PlayFlinchAnimation("flinch_back");

if (IsCriticalHit(hit)) {
```

```
    EnablePhysicsBlend({ chest, head }, 0.3f);
    ApplyImpulseToBone(chest, hit.direction *
5.0f);
}
```

This lets you retain animator-authored intent while augmenting it with physically grounded motion.

4. Triggering Death and Full Ragdoll

When health reaches zero, you trigger a death response. This should involve full-body physics for maximum realism.

a. Transition to Ragdoll

Stop animation updates and enable full physics simulation:

```
DisablePoseUpdates();

EnableRagdollPhysics(); // sets all bones to
dynamic
```

b. Apply Death Impulse

Use hit direction and magnitude to create a meaningful fall:

```
glm::vec3 deathForce = hit.direction *
glm::max(hit.magnitude, 10.0f);

GetRagdollRoot()->ApplyImpulse(deathForce);
```

For explosive damage, apply a radial impulse outward from the explosion center.

c. Delay Cleanup

Keep the ragdoll alive for a few seconds before removing or replacing with a corpse mesh:

```
if (TimeSinceDeath > 10.0f) {
    RemoveRagdoll();
}
```

5. Optional: Blending From Ragdoll to Stand-Up

If your game allows characters to recover from knockdowns (e.g. a stunned state), you can blend back from ragdoll to animation:

Detect when ragdoll has settled (low velocity on all bodies).

Capture current ragdoll pose.

Match animation pose to ragdoll pose over time.

Fade animation back in as the character gets up.

```
StartStandUpAnimation(alignTo =
CurrentRagdollPose());

FadeOutPhysicsInfluence(duration = 0.8f);
```

This lets you recover smoothly without visible pops or sliding feet.

Debugging and Visual Checks

Draw force vectors at impact points for visual feedback.

Render per-bone physics weights as color gradients (0 = blue, 1 = red).

Log transition events to confirm blend start/end.

Play hits from various angles to test directionality.

These tools help ensure reactions behave consistently under different gameplay conditions.

Practical Example: Headshot Kill

Let's walk through a complete flow:

Bullet hits the head:

```
HitEvent headshot = {
    .point = hitPos,
    .normal = surfaceNormal,
    .direction = glm::normalize(hitPos -
shooterPos),
    .magnitude = 12.0f,
    .boneHit = headIndex,
    .type = DamageType::Piercing
```

```
};
```

Trigger full ragdoll:

```
TriggerDeathRagdoll(headshot);
```

Apply directional impulse:

```
ApplyImpulseToBone(headIndex, headshot.direction *
12.0f);
```

The character collapses backward from the headshot, with realistic joint motion and no need for pre-recorded death animations.

By combining animation blending, selective ragdoll activation, and physically reactive motion, you can build a hit response and death system that looks good in every situation—whether it's a minor punch or a lethal blow. Instead of relying on fixed animations, you're using physics to adapt to impact context in real time, ensuring your characters stay grounded in the environment and responsive to the world.

This technique enhances immersion dramatically and is one of the best examples of why hybrid systems—those that merge animation and simulation—are a powerful foundation for real-time character animation.

Chapter 9: Procedural and Runtime Animation Techniques

While keyframe animation, inverse kinematics, and physics-based ragdolls form the backbone of most real-time character systems, many of the most dynamic and convincing effects you see in modern games are achieved with **procedural techniques**. These techniques generate or modify motion at runtime, using math, player input, or physical context as input. They give your characters subtle breathing, reactive motion, dynamic posing, and nuanced transitions—all without needing to author additional animation assets.

9.1 Parametric Motion Generation

Parametric motion is the practice of generating character animation procedurally at runtime, using variables—called parameters—such as speed, direction, or state values. Instead of relying solely on pre-authored animation clips, you define formulas or logic that control the transformation of bones in real time. This approach offers highly responsive, adaptable motion that can handle a wide range of scenarios without requiring handcrafted content for each variation.

Generating Motion From Time and Speed

Let's begin with a foundational example: a simple procedural walk cycle based on step frequency and character velocity.

Step 1: Define Control Parameters

We'll use time and movement speed to drive a sine-wave oscillation that mimics leg motion.

```
float speed = GetCharacterSpeed();        // units
per second

float time = GetGlobalTime();             //
seconds

float stepFrequency = speed * 1.2f;       //
frequency increases with speed
```

You calculate the **phase** of the step, which progresses over time:

```
float phase = time * stepFrequency;          //
cycles per second
```

Step 2: Compute Joint Angles

For example, you can compute a leg swing angle based on sine and cosine:

```
float thighAngle = sin(phase) * 0.5f;          // swing
forward and backward

float kneeAngle  = abs(cos(phase)) * 0.8f; // bend
during lift, straighten when landing
```

Then apply these to the corresponding bones:

```
pose.SetLocalRotation(thighBone,
glm::angleAxis(thighAngle, glm::vec3(1, 0, 0)));

pose.SetLocalRotation(kneeBone,
glm::angleAxis(kneeAngle, glm::vec3(1, 0, 0)));
```

This produces a responsive, continuous walk animation that adapts directly to how fast the character is moving.

Alternating Left and Right Limbs

To support bipedal walking, you offset the phase for left and right legs:

```
float leftPhase = phase;

float rightPhase = phase + glm::pi<float>();


pose.SetLocalRotation(leftThigh,
glm::angleAxis(sin(leftPhase) * 0.5f, glm::vec3(1,
0, 0)));

pose.SetLocalRotation(rightThigh,
glm::angleAxis(sin(rightPhase) * 0.5f, glm::vec3(1,
0, 0)));
```

Knees follow a similar pattern using `cos()`:

```
pose.SetLocalRotation(leftKnee,
glm::angleAxis(abs(cos(leftPhase)) * 0.8f,
glm::vec3(1, 0, 0)));

pose.SetLocalRotation(rightKnee,
glm::angleAxis(abs(cos(rightPhase)) * 0.8f,
glm::vec3(1, 0, 0)));
```

This synchronizes alternating leg motion and allows for stride adjustments based on runtime speed.

Adding Torso and Arm Motion

For realism, you can procedurally swing the arms opposite the legs and add some torso twist:

```
float armSwing = sin(phase + glm::pi<float>()) *
0.4f;
pose.SetLocalRotation(leftArm,
glm::angleAxis(armSwing, glm::vec3(1, 0, 0)));
pose.SetLocalRotation(rightArm, glm::angleAxis(-
armSwing, glm::vec3(1, 0, 0)));

float spineTwist = sin(phase * 0.5f) * 0.1f;
pose.MultiplyLocalRotation(spine,
glm::angleAxis(spineTwist, glm::vec3(0, 1, 0)));
```

This brings the character to life without ever touching a keyframe animation.

Parametric Idle: Breathing and Sway

For idle poses, parametric motion helps break stillness with micro-animations that create a sense of life.

Breathing Simulation

Use a slow oscillation on the spine or chest to mimic inhalation and exhalation:

```
float breathingRate = isCalm ? 0.25f : 0.5f;
float offset = sin(time * breathingRate) * 0.01f;
```

```
pose.Translate(spineBone, glm::vec3(0.0f, offset,
0.0f));
```

This upward movement gives the appearance of the character taking in air.

Head Bobbing or Sway

You can apply similar functions to head or neck bones:

```
float sway = sin(time * 0.3f) * 0.02f;
pose.RotateLocal(neckBone, glm::angleAxis(sway,
glm::vec3(0, 0, 1)));
```

It's subtle, but helps prevent characters from feeling robotic when idle.

Modulating Parameters Dynamically

You can expose parameters like `step length`, `breath depth`, or `arm swing intensity` as inputs to AI or game state:

```
float breathIntensity = isInjured ? 0.03f : 0.01f;

float offset = sin(time * breathingRate) *
breathIntensity;

pose.Translate(spine, glm::vec3(0.0f, offset,
0.0f));
```
This allows a tired character to breathe more heavily, or a wounded one to show strain, all through math.

Combining Parametric Motion With Animation

You don't have to replace animation entirely. Often, the best results come from layering parametric motion **on top of** a keyframed base:

```
Transform animSpine =
basePose.GetLocalTransform(spineBone);

Transform parametricOffset =
ComputeBreathingTransform(time);

Transform finalSpine = CombineTransform(animSpine,
parametricOffset);
```

```
pose.SetLocalTransform(spineBone, finalSpine);
```

This adds realism without needing dozens of animation variants.

Exercise: Build a Runtime Walk Cycle

Create a small program with a pose system and bones for:

Left/Right thigh

Left/Right calf

Spine

Shoulders

Arms

Control a `speed` variable with input.

Generate `phase = time * speed * walkScale`.

Apply sinusoidal offsets to thighs, knees, arms, and spine.

Visualize the result with debug bones or a 3D model.

Parametric motion generation gives you scalable, reactive control over character animation. Instead of authoring dozens of animations to handle every variation in movement, you can describe motion with compact logic and math. Whether you're making a walking robot, a breathing NPC, or a procedural creature, parametric techniques help bring characters to life in a way that's efficient, expressive, and tightly integrated with gameplay state.

9.2 Animation Driven by Input and Physics

Traditional animation systems often operate in discrete states: you press a button, and the character transitions to a pre-authored animation. This works well for predefined, predictable behavior, but falls short when you need responsive, real-time motion that reflects subtle variations in player input or physical interactions with the environment.

Animation driven by input and physics fills that gap. Instead of switching between rigid clips, you synthesize or modify motion dynamically—adapting to analog stick directions, momentum, ground slope, or external forces. This leads to fluid, believable motion that stays in sync with gameplay.

1. Directly Mapping Input to Pose Modifiers

Rather than mapping input to a fixed animation, you can convert input values directly into pose adjustments.

Directional Leaning

One of the most common examples is upper-body leaning during movement. This gives players visual feedback that reflects inertia and turning direction.

```
glm::vec2 inputDir = GetLeftStickDirection(); // -1
to 1 for x and y

float forwardLean = glm::clamp(inputDir.y, -1.0f,
1.0f) * 0.25f;
float sidewaysLean = glm::clamp(inputDir.x, -1.0f,
1.0f) * 0.20f;

glm::quat leanRot = glm::angleAxis(forwardLean,
glm::vec3(1, 0, 0)) *
                        glm::angleAxis(-sidewaysLean,
glm::vec3(0, 0, 1));

pose.MultiplyLocalRotation(spineBone, leanRot);
```

Now the spine dynamically leans into movement, improving responsiveness and immersion.

2. Pose Offset Based on Physical Context

You can read physical data from the simulation and feed it into pose updates.

Hip Displacement from Velocity

Let's say you want to simulate weight shifting when the character is accelerating or decelerating:

```
glm::vec3 velocity = GetCharacterVelocity();
// world-space
glm::vec3 localVel = TransformToLocal(velocity);
// convert to character-local frame

glm::vec3 hipOffset = localVel * glm::vec3(0.01f,
0.005f, 0.01f); // scale X/Z only
pose.Translate(hipBone, hipOffset);
```

This creates subtle shifts in hip position that mimic momentum.

3. Head Stabilization with Camera Motion

When the camera is linked to the character (e.g. in first-person or over-the-shoulder), it helps to stabilize the head to reduce motion sickness and preserve aim.

```
glm::vec3 cameraVelocity = GetCameraVelocity();
float dampening = 0.08f;

glm::vec3 inverseOffset = -cameraVelocity *
dampening;
pose.Translate(neckBone, inverseOffset);
```

The head now offsets slightly in the opposite direction of camera shifts, making transitions smoother.

4. Weapon Aiming and Alignment

For aiming weapons or tools, it's critical that the character visually tracks the target direction. You can compute this from the input vector or target position.

```
glm::vec3 weaponPos =
GetBoneWorldPosition(handBone);
glm::vec3 aimTarget = GetAimingTargetWorldPos();

glm::vec3 aimDir = glm::normalize(aimTarget -
weaponPos);
glm::quat desiredRot = glm::rotation(glm::vec3(0,
0, 1), aimDir); // assume forward is +Z

pose.SetWorldRotation(handBone, desiredRot);
```

For smoother results, blend the rotation over time:

```
glm::quat currentRot =
pose.GetWorldRotation(handBone);

pose.SetWorldRotation(handBone,
glm::slerp(currentRot, desiredRot, 0.2f));
```

This supports responsive aiming, even when layered on top of locomotion.

5. Foot Locking and Terrain Adaptation

Physics and animation can interact directly when characters stand on uneven or moving ground.

Detect Surface Contact

Use a raycast from each foot bone to find terrain height:

```
glm::vec3 footWorldPos =
pose.GetWorldPosition(footBone);
RaycastResult hit =
PhysicsWorld::Raycast(footWorldPos + glm::vec3(0,
0.1f, 0), glm::vec3(0, -1, 0), 0.2f);

if (hit.hit) {
    glm::vec3 footTarget = hit.position;
    glm::vec3 normal = hit.normal;

    pose.SetWorldPosition(footBone, footTarget);
    glm::quat footAlign =
glm::rotation(glm::vec3(0, 1, 0), normal);
    pose.SetWorldRotation(footBone, footAlign);
}
```

Blend With FK Animation

If the foot is in contact, use a weight to blend physics-corrected pose with animation:

```
Transform animFoot =
animPose.GetWorldTransform(footBone);
Transform corrected =
ikPose.GetWorldTransform(footBone);
```

```
float blend = IsFootPlanted(footBone) ? 0.7f :
0.0f;
Transform final = LerpTransform(animFoot,
corrected, blend);
pose.SetWorldTransform(footBone, final);
```

This ensures feet stay planted convincingly without completely discarding the walk cycle.

6. Real-Time Procedural Adjustments

Sometimes, motion needs to reflect contextual conditions—without relying on authored content.

Recoil Response

When firing a weapon:

```
if (IsFiring()) {

    float recoilMagnitude = GetWeaponRecoilValue();

    glm::quat kick =
glm::angleAxis(recoilMagnitude, glm::vec3(1, 0,
0)); // pitch upward

    pose.MultiplyLocalRotation(spineBone, kick);

}
```

To avoid snap motion, apply a spring system to smooth return to neutral.

Dynamic Posture Adjustments

Crouching or squeezing through gaps may be driven by triggers instead of keyframe animations:

```
if (IsInTightSpace()) {
    pose.Translate(spineBone, glm::vec3(0, -0.15f,
0)); // lower posture
    pose.MultiplyLocalRotation(headBone,
glm::angleAxis(-0.1f, glm::vec3(1, 0, 0))); // look
down
```

```
}
```

This helps adapt full-body motion to unpredictable world geometry or player actions.

Combining Animation With Physics Jitter

In high-impact moments (explosions, heavy landings), add a physics-based noise or jitter layer on top of your pose:

```
float jitter = PerlinNoise1D(time * 30.0f) * 0.05f;
pose.RotateLocal(spineBone, glm::angleAxis(jitter,
glm::vec3(0, 0, 1)));
```

You can scale this based on impact magnitude or ground shake intensity.

Debugging and Control

When working with input- or physics-driven animation:

Visualize bones and target vectors for validation.

Log parameter values (speed, input direction, impact force) in the editor.

Use runtime toggles to disable components (e.g. physics override) for testing.

This helps isolate issues when behavior looks off or inconsistent.

By driving animation directly from input and physics, you remove latency between player action and character response. This creates a tight feedback loop where characters feel aware of their surroundings and connected to the controls. Whether it's leaning into motion, aligning a weapon, or recoiling from an explosion, these effects bridge the gap between animation fidelity and gameplay clarity.

The techniques in this section can be layered seamlessly over existing animation systems, giving you fine-grained control over realism, responsiveness, and reactivity—without ballooning the number of assets you need to author. Next, we'll go deeper into enhancing these effects using spring-damper systems and procedural noise to bring out lifelike motion even in passive states.

9.3 Spring-Damper Systems and Noise Functions

Procedural animation benefits greatly from physical models that can create natural, responsive motion without the need for complex simulation. One of the most effective and efficient tools in this area is the **spring-damper system**, which you can use to simulate delayed response, inertia, jiggling, or stabilizing behavior.

Combined with **noise functions**, especially Perlin or simplex noise, you can add irregular, organic variation to bone movement, eliminating artificial stillness in idle poses or creating effects like jitter, vibration, and randomness that enhance believability.

1. The Spring-Damper Model

A spring-damper system models a value that chases a target, influenced by tension (spring) and resistance (damping). It's governed by a second-order differential equation, but you can simulate it iteratively per frame.

Why Use It?

Head or camera stabilization

Weapon lag or sway

Jiggle bones

Tail or cloth root movement

Recovery from recoil or impact

Basic Structure

```
struct SpringState {
    glm::vec3 position;  // current spring value
    glm::vec3 velocity;  // current velocity
};
```

Update Function

```
void UpdateSpring(SpringState& spring, const
glm::vec3& target, float stiffness, float damping,
float deltaTime) {
    glm::vec3 displacement = target -
spring.position;
    glm::vec3 springForce = stiffness *
displacement;
    glm::vec3 dampingForce = -damping *
spring.velocity;

    glm::vec3 acceleration = springForce +
dampingForce;

    spring.velocity += acceleration * deltaTime;
    spring.position += spring.velocity * deltaTime;
}
```

This runs every frame. `stiffness` defines how fast the value catches up to the target. `damping` reduces oscillation and smooths the motion.

2. Using Springs in Character Animation

Let's apply it to a **weapon sway** effect:

Setup

```
SpringState weaponSpring;

weaponSpring.position = initialWeaponOffset;

weaponSpring.velocity = glm::vec3(0.0f);
```

Update

```
glm::vec3 targetOffset =
GetHandBoneWorldPosition();

UpdateSpring(weaponSpring, targetOffset, 220.0f,
24.0f, deltaTime);
```

```
pose.SetWorldPosition(weaponBone,
weaponSpring.position);
```

As the hand moves, the weapon follows with a slight delay and damping. This mimics inertia and gives the weapon a sense of weight.

Camera Head-Bob Stabilization

Apply the same logic to the neck or head bone:

```
SpringState neckSpring;

glm::vec3 spineAnchor =
pose.GetWorldPosition(spineBone);
UpdateSpring(neckSpring, spineAnchor + glm::vec3(0,
0.2f, 0), 100.0f, 20.0f, deltaTime);

pose.SetWorldPosition(neckBone,
neckSpring.position);
```

This stabilizes the head in response to body motion without resorting to full ragdoll simulation.

3. Bone-Level Jiggle or Drag

Simulate bone inertia for items like tails or antennas:

```
struct BoneSpring {
    glm::quat rotation;
    glm::vec3 angularVelocity;
};

void UpdateBoneSpring(BoneSpring& bone, glm::quat
targetRot, float stiffness, float damping, float
dt) {
    glm::quat deltaRot = targetRot *
glm::inverse(bone.rotation);
    glm::vec3 axis;
    float angle;
    glm::axisAngle(deltaRot, axis, angle); //
Decompose to axis-angle

    glm::vec3 torque = stiffness * axis * angle -
damping * bone.angularVelocity;
```

```
    glm::vec3 angularAccel = torque; // inertia = 1
for simplicity

    bone.angularVelocity += angularAccel * dt;
    glm::quat delta =
glm::angleAxis(glm::length(bone.angularVelocity) *
dt, glm::normalize(bone.angularVelocity));
    bone.rotation = delta * bone.rotation;
}
```

Apply this to spine or tail segments for lifelike lag and motion follow-through.

4. Introducing Noise for Lifelike Motion

Sometimes motion should vary irregularly—small, unnoticeable differences that make a character feel alive. This is where **noise functions** shine.

Perlin Noise Example

```
float noiseX = PerlinNoise1D(time * 0.5f) * 0.02f;

float noiseY = PerlinNoise1D((time + 10.0f) * 0.5f)
* 0.02f;



pose.Translate(spineBone, glm::vec3(noiseX, noiseY,
0.0f));
```

This mimics tiny postural shifts in an idle stance—subtle enough to seem natural, but enough to avoid the frozen mannequin effect.

Applying Noise to Breathing

Combine with sine wave breathing:

```
float breath = sin(time * 0.3f) * 0.01f;

float jitter = PerlinNoise1D(time * 1.2f) * 0.003f;



pose.Translate(spineBone, glm::vec3(0, breath +
jitter, 0));
```

Now each breath has slightly different timing and amplitude, which feels more human and less mechanical.

Combining Spring and Noise for Impact Reactions

You can apply both systems during intense gameplay sequences.

Hit Jitter

```
float shock = GetImpactForce();
float intensity = glm::clamp(shock / 10.0f, 0.0f,
1.0f);

float noiseZ = PerlinNoise1D(time * 20.0f) *
intensity * 0.05f;
pose.RotateLocal(spineBone, glm::angleAxis(noiseZ,
glm::vec3(0, 0, 1)));
```

This creates a quick jolt or vibration after receiving an impact, mimicking muscle tension or a stunned state.

Post-Hit Spring Recovery

Instead of snapping back to idle, use spring recovery to ease into the original pose:

```
UpdateSpring(spineSpring,
targetPose.GetWorldPosition(spineBone), 140.0f,
18.0f, deltaTime);

pose.SetWorldPosition(spineBone,
spineSpring.position);
```

Debugging Spring Behavior

To validate and tune your system:

Visualize vectors: draw current, target, and spring positions.

Plot curves: log position over time to ensure damping behaves correctly.

Clamp velocities: prevent excessive oscillation by limiting `velocity`.

Example:

```
spring.velocity = glm::clamp(spring.velocity, -
maxVel, maxVel);
```

Spring-damper systems and noise functions are the cornerstone of expressive, believable procedural animation. They're easy to integrate, highly tunable, and computationally cheap. Whether you're stabilizing a head, swaying a weapon, adding ambient motion to idle characters, or jiggling accessories like tails or antennae, these techniques add a layer of fluidity and realism that goes beyond what hand-authored animation alone can achieve.

9.4 Curve-Based Timing and Pose Modifiers

In procedural animation, precise timing is just as important as motion. Not all effects should be linear or constant—some actions need to ease in, peak, and ease out. Others should pulse, oscillate, or change speed dynamically over time. To handle these variations with precision and control, you use **curve-based systems**.

Curves are functions that define how a value changes over a normalized time interval—usually from 0.0 to 1.0. When applied to animation, they can control the intensity of a pose modification, drive blend weights, or orchestrate layered effects like breathing, leaning, or recoil recovery.

An animation curve is just a 1D function: given a time t, it returns a value. These values can represent anything—rotation multipliers, blending factors, offsets, intensities.

The most flexible implementation is a **keyframe-based curve** with interpolation.

```
struct CurveKey {
    float time;  // 0.0 to 1.0 normalized
    float value;
};

struct AnimationCurve {
    std::vector<CurveKey> keys;

    float Evaluate(float t) const {
        if (keys.empty()) return 0.0f;
```

```
            if (t <= keys.front().time) return
keys.front().value;
            if (t >= keys.back().time) return
keys.back().value;

            for (size_t i = 0; i < keys.size() - 1;
++i) {
                if (t >= keys[i].time && t <= keys[i +
1].time) {
                    float alpha = (t - keys[i].time) /
(keys[i + 1].time - keys[i].time);
                    return glm::mix(keys[i].value,
keys[i + 1].value, alpha);
                }
            }

            return keys.back().value;
    }
};
```

You can define custom curves as data or expose them to tools/editors for easy authoring.

Common Curves for Procedural Motion

Here are some standard shapes and how they're used:

Ease-In-Out: Starts slow, accelerates, then slows again. Great for natural motion.

Bell Curve: Peaking in the middle. Useful for flinches, aim offsets, or quick reactions.

Sinusoidal: Oscillating motion. Great for looping cycles or breathing.

Linear: Constant ramp up/down. Used for timing fades or ramps.

You can generate these programmatically if you don't want keyframes:

```
float EaseInOut(float t) {
    return t * t * (3.0f - 2.0f * t);
}
```

Applying Curves to Drive Pose Modifications

Curves are often used to modulate bone transforms over time. Let's look at practical examples.

Recoil Kickback Curve

You want a short upper-body kick when firing a weapon:

```
float t = timeSinceFire / recoilDuration;
float curveValue = recoilCurve.Evaluate(t); //
returns 0-1

float pitch = curveValue * maxRecoilAngle;
glm::quat recoilRot = glm::angleAxis(pitch,
glm::vec3(1, 0, 0));
pose.MultiplyLocalRotation(spineBone, recoilRot);
```

This creates a kick that rises and settles naturally without hardcoded timing logic.

Idle Sway Cycle

Combine a sine function with a curve to adjust frequency over time:

```
float swayFreq =
swayCurve.Evaluate(timeSinceIdleStart);

float swayValue = sin(globalTime * swayFreq) *
0.01f;

pose.Translate(spineBone, glm::vec3(swayValue,
0.0f, 0.0f));
```

This makes sway more or less intense based on how long the character has been idle.

Time-Normalized Events

Use curves to structure time-based animations, like a power-up or dodge pose.

Timed Action Modifier

```
struct TimedPoseModifier {
    AnimationCurve curve;
    float duration;
```

```
    float elapsed;

    float GetWeight() const {
        return curve.Evaluate(glm::clamp(elapsed /
duration, 0.0f, 1.0f));
    }
};
```

Apply it to control torso lean during a roll:

```
float lean = -rollModifier.GetWeight() *
maxRollAngle;

pose.MultiplyLocalRotation(spineBone,
glm::angleAxis(lean, glm::vec3(0, 0, 1)));
```

The pose automatically follows the curve over the course of the animation.

Dynamic Blend Weights with Curves

In animation layering systems, you often need to blend poses over time. Curves give you full control.

```
float blendWeight =
blendInCurve.Evaluate(elapsedTime /
fadeInDuration);

BlendPose(pose, targetPose, blendWeight);
```

If `blendInCurve` starts at 0 and ramps to 1 over 0.4 seconds, the system fades in smoothly.

This is useful for:

Transitioning into aim poses

Layering hit flinch over idle/walk

Phasing in breathing or posture correction

Curve-Controlled Positional Oscillation

Procedural breathing enhanced with curve-controlled amplitude:

```
float breathIntensity =
breathAmplitudeCurve.Evaluate(timeSinceStart);

float breath = sin(globalTime * 0.3f) *
breathIntensity;



pose.Translate(spineBone, glm::vec3(0, breath, 0));
```

Here, the intensity of the breath is not fixed—it can scale up or down over time or in response to stamina, injury, or emotional state.

Editor Integration for Curves

In most modern pipelines, curves are editable in tools. However, even without a UI, you can define common presets:

```
AnimationCurve CreateEaseInOut() {
    return {
        { {0.0f, 0.0f}, {0.5f, 0.75f}, {1.0f, 1.0f}
}
    };
}
```

Use JSON or scriptable assets to define curves externally so designers can tweak timing without changing code.

Exercises

Create a procedural aim pose that blends in based on time using a custom blend curve.

Build a hit reaction that uses a bell-shaped curve to rotate the head over 0.3s.

Use a sine wave plus an amplitude curve to animate tail wagging that intensifies over time.

Curve-based systems give you precise, expressive control over how procedural motion behaves over time. Whether you're easing into a weapon aim, timing a flinch, modulating idle breathing, or blending between states, curves let you define **how** something moves—not just **what** moves.

In procedural animation, curves act as your control surface. They give you the ability to shape motion profiles, trigger reactive adjustments, and balance physical accuracy with expressive stylization—all with consistent, predictable math that integrates seamlessly with your runtime logic.

Chapter 10: Rendering Skinned Meshes with OpenGL

Up to this point, we've focused on how to build animation data—how to represent skeletons, interpolate poses, apply IK, and manage physics interactions. But none of that comes to life without the final step: rendering your animated characters.

This chapter walks you through the exact process of rendering **skinned meshes**—models that deform based on skeletal animation—in **OpenGL**. You'll learn how to prepare mesh data, upload bone matrices, write vertex shaders for GPU skinning, optimize performance using uniform buffers, and debug animation issues visually. The techniques in this chapter are low-level but critical if you want full control over how your animation system reaches the screen.

10.1 Preparing Mesh and Bone Data for the GPU

Rendering animated characters in real time requires tightly coordinating your CPU-side animation system with your GPU rendering pipeline. When it comes to skeletal animation, this means preparing both your **mesh data** (with vertex-level bone influence) and your **bone transform data** (the animation results) in a format that the GPU can efficiently consume.

The Structure of a Skinned Mesh

A skinned mesh has more than just positions, normals, and UVs. Each vertex is also influenced by one or more **bones**, each of which affects the vertex based on a **weight**.

For OpenGL, you want each vertex to store:

`position`: the base vertex position

`normal`: for lighting

`uv`: for texturing

`boneIndices`: an array of up to 4 integers

`boneWeights`: corresponding weights for each bone index

Here's how to define this in C++:

```cpp
struct SkinnedVertex {
    glm::vec3 position;
    glm::vec3 normal;
    glm::vec2 uv;
    glm::uvec4 boneIndices;   // indices into the
bone matrix array
    glm::vec4 boneWeights;    // normalized to sum
to 1.0
};
```

This format supports **GPU skinning** where bone indices and weights are passed as vertex attributes into a vertex shader.

Generating Vertex Skinning Data from Importers

If you're using a library like Assimp to load your animated models, you'll typically access the bone weights per vertex through the mesh's bone list.

Assimp example:

```cpp
for (unsigned int b = 0; b < mesh->mNumBones; ++b)
{
    aiBone* bone = mesh->mBones[b];
    int boneIndex = GetOrCreateBoneIndex(bone-
>mName.C_Str());

    for (unsigned int w = 0; w < bone->mNumWeights;
++w) {
        int vertexID = bone->mWeights[w].mVertexId;
        float weight = bone->mWeights[w].mWeight;


AddBoneWeightToVertex(skinnedVertices[vertexID],
boneIndex, weight);
    }

    inverseBindMatrices[boneIndex] =
AssimpToGLM(bone->mOffsetMatrix);
}
```

The `AddBoneWeightToVertex()` function must enforce a maximum of 4 weights per vertex. You'll also want to **normalize the weights** so they sum to 1.0.

Bone Indexing and Bind Pose Matrices

You need to define a consistent **bone indexing scheme**—usually by assigning each bone a unique integer ID when loading the skeleton hierarchy.

Each bone must store its **inverse bind pose matrix**, which transforms vertices from mesh space into the bone's rest pose space.

When animating, you multiply the **animated transform** of the bone by this **inverse bind matrix** to get the final skinning matrix.

```
finalMatrix = animatedBoneTransform * inverseBindMatrix;
```

Store these in a per-mesh or shared skeleton structure:

```
std::vector<glm::mat4> inverseBindMatrices;

std::vector<std::string> boneNames;

std::unordered_map<std::string, int> boneIndexMap;
```

Uploading Vertex Data to OpenGL

Once you've created an array of `SkinnedVertex`, upload it as a VBO.

```
GLuint vertexBuffer;

glGenBuffers(1, &vertexBuffer);

glBindBuffer(GL_ARRAY_BUFFER, vertexBuffer);

glBufferData(GL_ARRAY_BUFFER, sizeof(SkinnedVertex)
* vertexCount, &skinnedVertices[0],
GL_STATIC_DRAW);
```

Now set up the vertex attributes in your VAO:

```
// Position
```

```cpp
glVertexAttribPointer(0, 3, GL_FLOAT, GL_FALSE,
sizeof(SkinnedVertex),
(void*)offsetof(SkinnedVertex, position));

glEnableVertexAttribArray(0);



// Normal

glVertexAttribPointer(1, 3, GL_FLOAT, GL_FALSE,
sizeof(SkinnedVertex),
(void*)offsetof(SkinnedVertex, normal));

glEnableVertexAttribArray(1);



// UV

glVertexAttribPointer(2, 2, GL_FLOAT, GL_FALSE,
sizeof(SkinnedVertex),
(void*)offsetof(SkinnedVertex, uv));

glEnableVertexAttribArray(2);



// Bone Indices (integer attribute)

glVertexAttribIPointer(4, 4, GL_UNSIGNED_INT,
sizeof(SkinnedVertex),
(void*)offsetof(SkinnedVertex, boneIndices));

glEnableVertexAttribArray(4);



// Bone Weights

glVertexAttribPointer(5, 4, GL_FLOAT, GL_FALSE,
sizeof(SkinnedVertex),
(void*)offsetof(SkinnedVertex, boneWeights));
```

```
glEnableVertexAttribArray(5);
```

Sending Bone Matrices to the GPU

Every frame, you compute the pose matrices for each bone:

```
for (int i = 0; i < boneCount; ++i) {
    finalBoneMatrices[i] = currentBoneTransforms[i]
* inverseBindMatrices[i];
}
```

These `finalBoneMatrices` are passed to the vertex shader as a uniform array or UBO (covered in 10.3). Each vertex references these matrices using its `boneIndices`.

For small skeletons (under ~50 bones), a uniform array works fine:

uniform mat4 u_BoneMatrices[100];

Common Pitfalls to Avoid

Weight normalization: Always normalize bone weights per vertex. Values should sum to 1.0.

Bone count limit: Stay under the uniform limit (`GL_MAX_VERTEX_UNIFORM_COMPONENTS`) unless you use UBOs.

Invalid indices: Make sure every bone used in the mesh is included in the bone matrix array.

Bind pose mismatch: Use the same bind pose used at authoring time for correct skinning.

Exercise: Load and Display a Skinned Mesh

Build a minimal loader and renderer:

Load a mesh with bones using Assimp.

For each vertex, extract bone indices and weights.

Create and upload a `SkinnedVertex[]` VBO.

Compute bind pose transforms for each bone.

Write a simple vertex shader that applies skinning using a uniform bone matrix array.

Visualize the animated character by updating bone matrices every frame.

Getting your mesh and bone data structured properly is the backbone of rendering animated characters with OpenGL. By packing bone indices and weights per vertex, computing inverse bind matrices, and preparing a consistent bone hierarchy, you set up everything the GPU needs for real-time deformation. This groundwork ensures your vertex shader can apply animation-driven skinning efficiently, frame after frame.

10.2 GLSL Shaders for Bone Skinning

Once your vertex data is correctly set up with bone indices and weights, and your animation system is generating the correct bone matrices per frame, the next step is getting your **vertex shader** to deform the mesh based on that skeletal data. This is where **GPU skinning** happens—in the GLSL shader program running per vertex.

Understanding the Skinning Math

Each vertex in a skinned mesh is influenced by up to 4 bones. Each bone contributes a weighted transformation to the final position of the vertex.

The formula per vertex is:

```
skinnedPosition =

    (boneMatrix0 * originalPosition) * weight0 +

    (boneMatrix1 * originalPosition) * weight1 +

    (boneMatrix2 * originalPosition) * weight2 +

    (boneMatrix3 * originalPosition) * weight3;
```

These bone matrices are computed per frame on the CPU and passed to the shader. Each bone matrix is:

```
finalBoneMatrix = currentAnimationTransform *
inverseBindPose
```

This transforms the vertex from **bind-pose model space** to **animated model space**.

Vertex Attributes Required

Each vertex provides:

`vec3 a_Position`: the base position

`vec3 a_Normal`: for lighting

`vec2 a_TexCoord`: for UV mapping

`uvec4 a_BoneIndices`: which 4 bones affect this vertex

`vec4 a_BoneWeights`: corresponding influence weights

You must declare these attributes with matching layout indices as in your VAO:

`layout(location = 0) in vec3 a_Position;`

`layout(location = 1) in vec3 a_Normal;`

`layout(location = 2) in vec2 a_TexCoord;`

`layout(location = 4) in uvec4 a_BoneIndices;`

`layout(location = 5) in vec4 a_BoneWeights;`

Notice that `a_BoneIndices` is declared as `uvec4`, not `ivec4`. OpenGL integer attributes must be treated as unsigned or signed explicitly.

Passing Bone Matrices to GLSL

If your skeleton has ≤ 100 bones, you can use a uniform array:

```
uniform mat4 u_BoneMatrices[100]; // 0-99 bone slots
```

Each matrix transforms a vertex according to that bone's animation state.

The CPU uploads the data with:

```
glUniformMatrix4fv(boneMatrixLocation, boneCount,
GL_FALSE, &boneMatrices[0][0]);
```

Vertex Shader Implementation

Here's a complete GLSL vertex shader for skinning:

```glsl
#version 330 core

layout(location = 0) in vec3 a_Position;
layout(location = 1) in vec3 a_Normal;
layout(location = 2) in vec2 a_TexCoord;
layout(location = 4) in uvec4 a_BoneIndices;
layout(location = 5) in vec4 a_BoneWeights;

uniform mat4 u_Model;
uniform mat4 u_ViewProjection;
uniform mat4 u_BoneMatrices[100];

out vec2 v_TexCoord;
out vec3 v_WorldNormal;

void main() {
    // Skinning matrix: weighted blend of bone
matrices
    mat4 skinMatrix =
        a_BoneWeights.x *
u_BoneMatrices[a_BoneIndices.x] +
        a_BoneWeights.y *
u_BoneMatrices[a_BoneIndices.y] +
        a_BoneWeights.z *
u_BoneMatrices[a_BoneIndices.z] +
        a_BoneWeights.w *
u_BoneMatrices[a_BoneIndices.w];

    // Transform position
    vec4 skinnedPosition = skinMatrix *
vec4(a_Position, 1.0);
    gl_Position = u_ViewProjection * u_Model *
skinnedPosition;

    // Transform normal (ignore scaling if not
uniform)
    vec3 skinnedNormal = mat3(skinMatrix) *
a_Normal;
    v_WorldNormal = mat3(u_Model) * skinnedNormal;
```

```
    v_TexCoord = a_TexCoord;
}
```

Things You Must Get Right

Normalize Bone Weights

On the CPU, weights must sum to 1.0. If not, vertices will stretch or collapse.

```
float total = w0 + w1 + w2 + w3;

if (total > 0.0f) {

    w0 /= total;

    w1 /= total;

    w2 /= total;

    w3 /= total;

}
```

Use Consistent Bone Indices

The GPU expects indices passed to match exactly the index of each matrix in u_BoneMatrices[]. Maintain a stable bone-to-index mapping when exporting from tools or loading from asset files.

Optimization Tips

Reorder vertices to group by bone influences and reduce redundant matrix loads.

Use UBOs if your skeleton has >100 bones or you want to batch multiple characters in a single draw call.

Use bone palette culling: if only a subset of bones affect a mesh (e.g., only upper body), you can upload fewer matrices per draw.

Debugging Tools

Visual Bone Influence

Use a debug shader that colors each vertex based on the most influential bone:

```
int dominant = 0;
float maxWeight = a_BoneWeights[0];
for (int i = 1; i < 4; ++i) {
    if (a_BoneWeights[i] > maxWeight) {
        maxWeight = a_BoneWeights[i];
        dominant = i;
    }
}

vec3 color = vec3(float(a_BoneIndices[dominant]) /
100.0, 0.5, 1.0);
```

This helps validate that weights and indices are correct.

Pose Test Shader

Write a test shader that applies only one bone's transform to all vertices to isolate specific joints:

```
mat4 skinMatrix = u_BoneMatrices[fixedBoneIndex];
```

You can then check visually whether that bone affects the correct region.

Exercise: Build a Simple Skinning Demo

Load a mesh and bind-pose skeleton.

Build a pose with animated bone matrices.

Pass bone matrices to the shader.

In the vertex shader, implement bone skinning.

Display the skinned mesh deforming in real time.

Try modifying the pose in code (e.g., rotate the spine bone over time) to see the results in the mesh.

The vertex shader is where skinning actually happens—where vertex positions and normals are transformed according to the active skeleton pose. By understanding and implementing bone skinning directly in GLSL, you gain full control over how character deformations are calculated and rendered. This not only gives you flexibility and performance, but also opens the door to custom effects like physics blending, procedural offsets, and GPU driven animation systems.

10.3 Efficient Uniform/UBO Management

When rendering animated characters with skeletal animation in OpenGL, one of the biggest bottlenecks—especially when rendering many characters—is the way you send **bone matrices** to the GPU every frame. If you rely on regular uniform arrays, you quickly hit the limits of what OpenGL allows, both in terms of size and performance. The solution is to use **Uniform Buffer Objects (UBOs)** to batch your bone matrix data in a scalable, GPU-friendly way.

The Problem With glUniform

The `glUniformMatrix4fv()` function is easy to use but inefficient at scale. Here's why:

You can only upload uniforms to the **currently active shader program**.

The maximum number of uniform components is **limited** (commonly 1024–2048 components per shader stage).

Uploading large arrays of matrices every frame with `glUniform*` incurs a CPU-GPU synchronization cost.

You can't share uniform data between draw calls or shader programs easily.

This becomes a problem fast if you're animating dozens of skeletons or using more than ~50 bones per character.

Enter Uniform Buffer Objects (UBOs)

UBOs allow you to store a block of uniform data (like bone matrices) in a dedicated GPU buffer. The benefits are:

Can be reused across shaders.

Can be updated dynamically or in bulk.

Bound by index rather than by name.

Can hold multiple skeletons' worth of data.

UBOs are managed like VBOs but are used for shader uniforms.

Declaring a UBO in GLSL

Here's what the shader side looks like:

```
layout(std140) uniform BoneBlock {

    mat4 u_BoneMatrices[100];

};
```

The layout `std140` guarantees a known alignment between CPU and GPU.

Each `mat4` in `std140` takes **4 * 4 * 4 = 64 bytes**, so 100 bones require 6.4 KB.

You bind this uniform block using a **binding point** (an integer):

```
layout(std140, binding = 0) uniform BoneBlock { ... };
```

Then on the CPU, you link this block to a buffer bound to binding point `0`.

Creating and Using a UBO in OpenGL

Step 1: Generate and allocate

```
GLuint boneUBO;
glGenBuffers(1, &boneUBO);
glBindBuffer(GL_UNIFORM_BUFFER, boneUBO);
glBufferData(GL_UNIFORM_BUFFER, sizeof(glm::mat4) *
100, nullptr, GL_DYNAMIC_DRAW);
```

Here we reserve space for 100 bone matrices.

Step 2: Bind it to a binding point

glBindBufferBase(GL_UNIFORM_BUFFER, 0, boneUBO);

This binds the buffer to binding point `0` (matching the shader).

Step 3: Upload bone matrix data

Every frame, you update the buffer with the current pose:

```
glBindBuffer(GL_UNIFORM_BUFFER, boneUBO);

void* ptr = glMapBuffer(GL_UNIFORM_BUFFER,
GL_WRITE_ONLY);

memcpy(ptr, &finalBoneMatrices[0],
sizeof(glm::mat4) * boneCount);

glUnmapBuffer(GL_UNIFORM_BUFFER);
```

You can also use `glBufferSubData`:

```
glBufferSubData(GL_UNIFORM_BUFFER, 0,
sizeof(glm::mat4) * boneCount,
&finalBoneMatrices[0]);
```

Use whichever method gives better performance on your hardware—`glMapBuffer` allows direct writing; `glBufferSubData` avoids synchronization overhead in some cases.

Sharing Bone Data Across Shaders

UBOs shine when you need the same uniform data in multiple shader programs (e.g., one for lit, one for depth pass).

Since you bind the UBO by index, you only need to **link the binding point once**:

```
GLuint index = glGetUniformBlockIndex(program,
"BoneBlock");
glUniformBlockBinding(program, index, 0); // match
binding point 0
```

Now all programs that use `BoneBlock` can access the same buffer.

Multiple Skeletons in a Single UBO

Let's say you want to render multiple animated characters using the same shader but with different bone matrices. You can store multiple **bone matrices blocks** in a single large UBO, then bind only the relevant range per draw.

```
constexpr int maxBonesPerSkeleton = 100;
```

```
constexpr int maxSkeletons = 64;


GLuint multiSkeletonUBO;

glGenBuffers(1, &multiSkeletonUBO);

glBindBuffer(GL_UNIFORM_BUFFER, multiSkeletonUBO);

glBufferData(GL_UNIFORM_BUFFER, maxSkeletons *
maxBonesPerSkeleton * sizeof(glm::mat4), nullptr,
GL_DYNAMIC_DRAW);
```

Bind a range for character i

```
int skeletonIndex = i;

glBindBufferRange(GL_UNIFORM_BUFFER, 0,
multiSkeletonUBO,

    skeletonIndex * maxBonesPerSkeleton *
sizeof(glm::mat4),

    maxBonesPerSkeleton * sizeof(glm::mat4));
```

Then update that range:

```
glBufferSubData(GL_UNIFORM_BUFFER,

    skeletonIndex * maxBonesPerSkeleton *
sizeof(glm::mat4),

    boneCount * sizeof(glm::mat4),

    &finalBoneMatrices[0]);
```

This allows efficient batching across many skinned instances.

Layout and Alignment Rules (std140)

When writing data to a UBO, the structure must match GPU layout
expectations. In std140:

`mat4` = 64 bytes (aligned to 16-byte boundaries)

No padding is needed between consecutive `mat4` entries

Arrays of `mat4` are tightly packed

That's why uploading an array of `glm::mat4` using `sizeof(glm::mat4) * count` is always safe.

Practical Tips

Always call `glBindBufferBase()` before rendering if you change the buffer.

If you use multiple UBOs, assign each a unique binding point and don't exceed `GL_MAX_UNIFORM_BUFFER_BINDINGS`.

Avoid updating the entire UBO if only a subset of matrices change—use `glBufferSubData` with offset.

For best performance, try to allocate the UBO once and reuse it across frames.

Exercise: Batch Animate Multiple Characters

Allocate a single UBO for 64 skeletons.

Write code to upload each character's bone matrices into a different block in the UBO.

Before each draw call, use `glBindBufferRange` to bind the relevant slice.

Use the same shader for all characters without modifying uniforms per draw.

Uniform Buffer Objects are essential for scaling your animation system. They let you avoid the overhead of per-shader `glUniform` calls, bypass uniform size limits, and enable modern batching strategies. With correct alignment, layout, and memory management, you can update hundreds of characters per frame with minimal overhead, keeping your animation pipeline GPU-friendly and future-proof.

10.4 Visual Debugging of Animation States

Even if your skeletal animation system is mathematically correct and your GPU skinning pipeline is logically sound, things can still go wrong in subtle—or spectacular—ways. Limbs might twist uncontrollably, vertices might collapse or explode, and characters might deform in ways that break immersion. Debugging these issues blindly is frustrating and inefficient. That's why building **visual debugging tools** into your engine is essential.

Drawing the Skeleton

Start by rendering your skeleton as a hierarchy of lines or gizmos. This lets you confirm that joint transforms are correct, bone parenting is functioning, and the animation data is being interpreted properly.

Step 1: Traverse the Skeleton

Use a recursive or flat loop to process the global transform of each joint in your animation system:

```
void DrawSkeleton(const std::vector<Bone>& bones,
const std::vector<glm::mat4>& globalTransforms) {
    for (size_t i = 0; i < bones.size(); ++i) {
        int parent = bones[i].parentIndex;
        if (parent >= 0) {
            glm::vec3 a =
glm::vec3(globalTransforms[parent][3]);
            glm::vec3 b =
glm::vec3(globalTransforms[i][3]);
            DrawLine(a, b, glm::vec3(0.8f, 0.2f,
0.2f)); // red lines
        }
    }
}
```

Draw this after skinning, every frame. It should match the character's animation pose exactly.

Step 2: Highlight Specific Bones

You can help identify specific bones (e.g., the spine or head) by drawing local axes or spheres:

```
void DrawBoneAxis(const glm::mat4& transform) {
    glm::vec3 pos = glm::vec3(transform[3]);

    DrawLine(pos, pos + glm::vec3(transform[0]) *
0.1f, glm::vec3(1, 0, 0)); // X axis
```

```
    DrawLine(pos, pos + glm::vec3(transform[1]) *
0.1f, glm::vec3(0, 1, 0)); // Y axis
    DrawLine(pos, pos + glm::vec3(transform[2]) *
0.1f, glm::vec3(0, 0, 1)); // Z axis
}
```

This helps you identify flipped axes, wrong rotation order, or unexpected scaling.

Visualizing Vertex Bone Weights

One common cause of bad deformations is broken skin weights—either missing, misnormalized, or misassigned. To debug this, write a **weight debug shader** that displays bone influence visually.

Option A: Dominant Bone Color

Use the index of the most influential bone to pick a debug color.

```
int dominant = 0;
float maxWeight = a_BoneWeights[0];

for (int i = 1; i < 4; ++i) {
    if (a_BoneWeights[i] > maxWeight) {
        maxWeight = a_BoneWeights[i];
        dominant = i;
    }
}

vec3 color = vec3(float(a_BoneIndices[dominant]) /
100.0, 0.0, 1.0 - maxWeight);
```

This shows whether a vertex is controlled by the correct bone and how strong that influence is.

Option B: Weighted RGB Blending

Use the bone weights to blend colors:

```
vec3 color =

    a_BoneWeights.x * vec3(1, 0, 0) +

    a_BoneWeights.y * vec3(0, 1, 0) +
```

```
a_BoneWeights.z * vec3(0, 0, 1) +

a_BoneWeights.w * vec3(1, 1, 0);
```

This helps you identify blending issues like abrupt seams or over-weighted vertices.

Comparing GPU and CPU Skinning

To validate that your GPU skinning shader matches your CPU's bone transforms:

Step 1: Compute CPU-Skinned Mesh

On the CPU, apply bone matrices to each vertex:

```
glm::vec3 skinnedPos = glm::vec3(0.0f);

for (int i = 0; i < 4; ++i) {

    int bone = vertex.boneIndices[i];

    float weight = vertex.boneWeights[i];

    skinnedPos += weight *
glm::vec3(boneMatrices[bone] *
glm::vec4(vertex.position, 1.0f));

}
```
Store this in a separate VBO and draw it using a different color.

Step 2: Overlay CPU and GPU Meshes

Render the GPU-skinned mesh normally, and draw the CPU-skinned mesh slightly offset or wireframed. Differences will be obvious if there's an error in the shader.

Debugging Bone Matrix Data

Incorrect bone matrices—due to wrong parenting, missing inverse bind matrices, or animation misalignment—can be hard to spot. Try:

Logging matrix rows to the console and watching for NaN, inf, or degenerate scales.

Drawing joint axes and comparing them to rest pose axes.

Highlighting bones that have `det(matrix)` < 0 (inverted scale or flipped handedness).

Also watch for this common mistake:

```
// Incorrect
finalMatrix = inverseBindMatrix * animatedMatrix;
// wrong order

// Correct
finalMatrix = animatedMatrix * inverseBindMatrix;
```

Highlight Bones with High Error

When comparing animation states (e.g., blending animation with ragdoll), measure the delta between expected and actual transforms:

```
float error = glm::length(expectedPos - actualPos);

if (error > threshold) {

    DrawSphere(actualPos, 0.05f, glm::vec3(1.0f,
0.0f, 0.0f)); // red sphere

}
```

This lets you identify bones that drift, jitter, or collapse unexpectedly.

Debugging Blending and Pose Modifiers

If you use blending systems or procedural modifiers (like leaning, IK, or recoil):

Visualize **intermediate poses**: draw lines for both the animation pose and the modified pose.

Use color-coded skeleton overlays:

White = base animation

Green = additive pose

Blue = final blended result

This makes it clear whether a bone is being overridden, skipped, or double-applied.

Exercise: Build a Bone Debug Viewer

Create a skeleton viewer that draws joints and bones over your skinned mesh.

Add toggles to switch between rest pose, animation pose, and GPU pose.

Implement a shader that colors mesh vertices based on bone weight.

Add a wireframe overlay to compare CPU and GPU results.

Create hotkeys to freeze animation or step frame-by-frame for precise analysis.

Visual debugging is an essential part of developing robust animation systems. Instead of guessing what went wrong, you expose the hidden state—skeletons, weights, matrices—and make issues visible and fixable. With these tools, you gain insight into how each part of your system works together, enabling faster development, better tools, and more reliable character behavior in the final product.

Chapter 11: Vulkan-Based Animation Rendering

When you're building a modern animation system for high-performance games or simulation software, **Vulkan** offers low-level access to the GPU and fine-grained control over memory, command submission, and rendering flow. But this control comes at the cost of complexity. Compared to OpenGL, where the driver does a lot of heavy lifting, Vulkan expects you to manage everything explicitly—including buffer memory, descriptor bindings, synchronization, and batching.

11.1 Vulkan Data Pipeline Overview

Before you can render skinned characters using Vulkan, you need a clear understanding of how animation data flows from your CPU-based animation system to the GPU's raster pipeline. Vulkan is explicit by design, meaning it won't do anything on your behalf—you must manually manage memory, buffer ownership, synchronization, and descriptor bindings. The advantage? Once your pipeline is correctly structured, it scales extremely well, giving you low-level control with high throughput.

The Core Flow of Animation Rendering in Vulkan

Each frame, animated characters follow this general flow:

Pose Calculation: You evaluate the current animation state of each character and compute bone transformation matrices.

Bone Matrix Upload: You upload those matrices to GPU-accessible memory (typically through a `VkBuffer`).

Descriptor Set Binding: You bind descriptor sets containing the bone matrix buffer.

Vertex Input Assembly: You send vertex data (positions, normals, UVs, bone indices, weights) into the pipeline.

Vertex Shader Skinning: The vertex shader fetches bone matrices using indices and applies linear blend skinning.

Rasterization and Fragment Shading: The resulting transformed geometry flows through the rest of the graphics pipeline like any other mesh.

Each of these steps must be handled explicitly, so let's expand on each part of the pipeline.

Preparing Vertex Data for Skinned Meshes

You need to define a vertex format that includes bone indices and weights.

Vertex Format in C++

```cpp
struct SkinnedVertex {

    glm::vec3 position;

    glm::vec3 normal;

    glm::vec2 uv;

    glm::uvec4 boneIndices; // up to 4 bone indices

    glm::vec4 boneWeights;  // corresponding
normalized weights

};
```

When you load a mesh (e.g., from Assimp or glTF), extract bone weights and indices per vertex and store them in this format.

Vertex Input Description in Vulkan

```cpp
VkVertexInputBindingDescription bindingDesc = {
    .binding = 0,
    .stride = sizeof(SkinnedVertex),
    .inputRate = VK_VERTEX_INPUT_RATE_VERTEX
};

std::array<VkVertexInputAttributeDescription, 5>
attrDescs = {{
    { 0, 0, VK_FORMAT_R32G32B32_SFLOAT,
offsetof(SkinnedVertex, position) },
    { 1, 0, VK_FORMAT_R32G32B32_SFLOAT,
offsetof(SkinnedVertex, normal) },
```

```
    { 2, 0, VK_FORMAT_R32G32_SFLOAT,
offsetof(SkinnedVertex, uv) },
    { 3, 0,
VK_FORMAT_R32G32B32A32_UINT,offsetof(SkinnedVertex,
boneIndices) },
    { 4, 0, VK_FORMAT_R32G32B32A32_SFLOAT,
offsetof(SkinnedVertex, boneWeights) }
}};
```

Upload vertex data to a `VkBuffer` and bind it during rendering using `vkCmdBindVertexBuffers`.

Computing Bone Transforms on the CPU

Each frame, you evaluate all animations and compute final bone transforms as:

finalTransform = animatedTransform * inverseBindPose;

For each animated character, you generate an array of 60–100 `glm::mat4` bone matrices, depending on rig complexity.

Uploading Bone Matrices to GPU Memory

Allocate a uniform buffer (or dynamic uniform buffer) and copy the matrices:

```
VkBuffer boneUBO;

VkDeviceMemory boneMemory;

VkDeviceSize size = sizeof(glm::mat4) * maxBones;


CreateUniformBuffer(device, size, &boneUBO,
&boneMemory);


// each frame:

void* mapped;
```

```
vkMapMemory(device, boneMemory, 0, size, 0,
&mapped);

memcpy(mapped, boneMatrices.data(), size);

vkUnmapMemory(device, boneMemory);
```

This `VkBuffer` will later be referenced in a **descriptor set** and bound to the shader at draw time.

Creating and Binding Descriptor Sets

Each animated character typically has its own descriptor set that contains its bone matrix buffer:

```
layout(set = 0, binding = 0) uniform BoneBlock {

    mat4 u_BoneMatrices[100];

};
```

You allocate a `VkDescriptorSet` from a descriptor pool, and write the buffer binding like this:

```
VkDescriptorBufferInfo bufferInfo = {
    .buffer = boneUBO,
    .offset = 0,
    .range = sizeof(glm::mat4) * boneCount
};

VkWriteDescriptorSet write = {
    .sType =
VK_STRUCTURE_TYPE_WRITE_DESCRIPTOR_SET,
    .dstSet = descriptorSet,
    .dstBinding = 0,
    .descriptorType =
VK_DESCRIPTOR_TYPE_UNIFORM_BUFFER,
    .descriptorCount = 1,
    .pBufferInfo = &bufferInfo
};

vkUpdateDescriptorSets(device, 1, &write, 0,
nullptr);
```

Bind it during rendering:

```
vkCmdBindDescriptorSets(commandBuffer,
VK_PIPELINE_BIND_POINT_GRAPHICS, pipelineLayout,

                           0, 1, &descriptorSet, 0,
nullptr);
```

Skinning in the Vertex Shader

The vertex shader reads vertex attributes (boneIndices, boneWeights) and uses them to blend the appropriate bone transforms:

```
mat4 skinMatrix =

    boneWeights.x * u_BoneMatrices[boneIndices.x] +

    boneWeights.y * u_BoneMatrices[boneIndices.y] +

    boneWeights.z * u_BoneMatrices[boneIndices.z] +

    boneWeights.w * u_BoneMatrices[boneIndices.w];


vec4 skinnedPos = skinMatrix * vec4(position, 1.0);
```

The resulting skinnedPos is transformed to clip space using your model-view-projection matrices.

Rendering: Submitting Commands

Everything is wrapped into a VkCommandBuffer. For each animated character:

```
vkCmdBindPipeline(commandBuffer,
VK_PIPELINE_BIND_POINT_GRAPHICS,
animationPipeline);
vkCmdBindDescriptorSets(commandBuffer,
VK_PIPELINE_BIND_POINT_GRAPHICS,
                           pipelineLayout, 0, 1,
&descriptorSet, 0, nullptr);
```

```
vkCmdBindVertexBuffers(commandBuffer, 0, 1,
&vertexBuffer, offsets);
vkCmdBindIndexBuffer(commandBuffer, indexBuffer, 0,
VK_INDEX_TYPE_UINT32);

vkCmdDrawIndexed(commandBuffer, indexCount, 1, 0,
0, 0);
```

If multiple characters share the same pipeline layout and descriptor set layout, you can batch them efficiently.

Practical Example: Single Skinned Character

At minimum, to render one animated character in Vulkan:

You upload the character's skinned mesh to a vertex buffer.

You compute the current animation pose and generate an array of bone matrices.

You update a `VkBuffer` with these matrices.

You create a descriptor set pointing to this buffer.

You bind the descriptor set and draw the mesh.

This process repeats each frame, enabling smooth real-time animation.

This section gives you a solid overview of how skeletal animation works within Vulkan's rendering architecture. Instead of relying on fixed-function abstractions, you define the entire data path—from vertex input to matrix updates to shader access. This enables you to scale animation performance, integrate with compute pipelines, and even customize skinning behavior on the GPU.

11.2 Descriptor Sets and Uniform Buffers for Bones

In Vulkan, you can't pass large arrays of data like bone matrices directly as global uniforms. Instead, Vulkan introduces a clean, scalable mechanism for binding resources to shaders: **descriptor sets**. If you want your vertex shader to access a buffer containing bone matrices, you must define a uniform buffer, allocate GPU-visible memory for it, and bind it through a descriptor set. This is a core requirement for GPU-based skinning in Vulkan.

Each animated character typically needs its own array of bone matrices—one `mat4` per joint in the skeleton. These matrices must be accessible by the vertex shader to perform skinning. Passing them via descriptor sets ensures:

Efficient binding per draw call

Safe parallelism (no global state mutation)

Scalability across many animated instances

Uniform buffers are the typical mechanism, though **storage buffers** can be used when more flexibility or larger limits are needed.

Shader-Side Declaration

In your vertex shader, declare a uniform block to receive bone matrices:

```
layout(set = 0, binding = 0) uniform BoneBlock {

    mat4 u_BoneMatrices[100];

};
```
`set = 0`: This is Descriptor Set #0.

`binding = 0`: This is the first resource in the set.

`100`: The maximum number of bones supported by your shader.

This block must match the layout and binding index used on the CPU side.

Creating the Descriptor Set Layout

A **descriptor set layout** tells Vulkan what resources will be bound to each set/binding combination. For bone matrices:

```
VkDescriptorSetLayoutBinding boneBinding{};

boneBinding.binding = 0;

boneBinding.descriptorType =
VK_DESCRIPTOR_TYPE_UNIFORM_BUFFER;
```

```cpp
boneBinding.descriptorCount = 1;

boneBinding.stageFlags =
VK_SHADER_STAGE_VERTEX_BIT;

boneBinding.pImmutableSamplers = nullptr;


VkDescriptorSetLayoutCreateInfo layoutInfo{};

layoutInfo.sType =
VK_STRUCTURE_TYPE_DESCRIPTOR_SET_LAYOUT_CREATE_INFO
;

layoutInfo.bindingCount = 1;

layoutInfo.pBindings = &boneBinding;


VkDescriptorSetLayout descriptorSetLayout;

vkCreateDescriptorSetLayout(device, &layoutInfo,
nullptr, &descriptorSetLayout);
```

You'll include this layout when creating your graphics pipeline layout.

Creating the Uniform Buffer

Each animated character should have its own buffer containing bone matrices. Here's how you can create a uniform buffer sized for 100 mat4s:

```cpp
VkDeviceSize bufferSize = sizeof(glm::mat4) * 100;


VkBufferCreateInfo bufferInfo{};

bufferInfo.sType =
VK_STRUCTURE_TYPE_BUFFER_CREATE_INFO;

bufferInfo.size = bufferSize;
```

```
bufferInfo.usage =
VK_BUFFER_USAGE_UNIFORM_BUFFER_BIT;

bufferInfo.sharingMode = VK_SHARING_MODE_EXCLUSIVE;


VkBuffer boneBuffer;

vkCreateBuffer(device, &bufferInfo, nullptr,
&boneBuffer);
```

Allocate memory for it and bind:

```
VkMemoryRequirements memRequirements;

vkGetBufferMemoryRequirements(device, boneBuffer,
&memRequirements);


VkMemoryAllocateInfo allocInfo{};

allocInfo.sType =
VK_STRUCTURE_TYPE_MEMORY_ALLOCATE_INFO;

allocInfo.allocationSize = memRequirements.size;

allocInfo.memoryTypeIndex =
FindMemoryType(memRequirements.memoryTypeBits,

    VK_MEMORY_PROPERTY_HOST_VISIBLE_BIT |
VK_MEMORY_PROPERTY_HOST_COHERENT_BIT);


VkDeviceMemory boneMemory;

vkAllocateMemory(device, &allocInfo, nullptr,
&boneMemory);

vkBindBufferMemory(device, boneBuffer, boneMemory,
0);
```

Now you can write bone matrices into this buffer each frame.

Writing to the Uniform Buffer

Assuming `finalBoneMatrices` is a `std::vector<glm::mat4>`:

```
void* data;

vkMapMemory(device, boneMemory, 0, bufferSize, 0,
&data);

memcpy(data, finalBoneMatrices.data(), bufferSize);

vkUnmapMemory(device, boneMemory);
```

You can optimize this with persistent mapping and avoid mapping/unmapping every frame, but the above is safe and reliable.

Allocating and Updating the Descriptor Set

You must allocate a descriptor set from a pool and link it to the uniform buffer.

Descriptor Pool

```
VkDescriptorPoolSize poolSize{};

poolSize.type = VK_DESCRIPTOR_TYPE_UNIFORM_BUFFER;

poolSize.descriptorCount = maxCharacters;


VkDescriptorPoolCreateInfo poolInfo{};

poolInfo.sType =
VK_STRUCTURE_TYPE_DESCRIPTOR_POOL_CREATE_INFO;

poolInfo.poolSizeCount = 1;

poolInfo.pPoolSizes = &poolSize;

poolInfo.maxSets = maxCharacters;
```

```
vkCreateDescriptorPool(device, &poolInfo, nullptr,
&descriptorPool);
```

Descriptor Set Allocation

```
VkDescriptorSetAllocateInfo allocInfo{};

allocInfo.sType =
VK_STRUCTURE_TYPE_DESCRIPTOR_SET_ALLOCATE_INFO;

allocInfo.descriptorPool = descriptorPool;

allocInfo.descriptorSetCount = 1;

allocInfo.pSetLayouts = &descriptorSetLayout;


VkDescriptorSet descriptorSet;

vkAllocateDescriptorSets(device, &allocInfo,
&descriptorSet);
```

Descriptor Write

```
VkDescriptorBufferInfo bufferInfo{};

bufferInfo.buffer = boneBuffer;

bufferInfo.offset = 0;

bufferInfo.range = bufferSize;


VkWriteDescriptorSet descriptorWrite{};

descriptorWrite.sType =
VK_STRUCTURE_TYPE_WRITE_DESCRIPTOR_SET;

descriptorWrite.dstSet = descriptorSet;

descriptorWrite.dstBinding = 0;
```

```
descriptorWrite.dstArrayElement = 0;

descriptorWrite.descriptorType =
VK_DESCRIPTOR_TYPE_UNIFORM_BUFFER;

descriptorWrite.descriptorCount = 1;

descriptorWrite.pBufferInfo = &bufferInfo;


vkUpdateDescriptorSets(device, 1, &descriptorWrite,
0, nullptr);
```

Now your descriptor set is configured to point to the bone matrix buffer.

Binding the Descriptor Set at Draw Time

In your command buffer:

```
vkCmdBindDescriptorSets(

    commandBuffer,

    VK_PIPELINE_BIND_POINT_GRAPHICS,

    pipelineLayout,

    0, // first set

    1, &descriptorSet,

    0, nullptr

);
```

You do this before each `vkCmdDrawIndexed()` or `vkCmdDraw()` call. Each animated mesh will have its own descriptor set pointing to its unique bone matrix buffer.

Performance Tips

Reuse descriptor set layouts across similar characters.

Group characters with the same pipeline to minimize pipeline binding overhead.

Use dynamic UBOs or storage buffers if you want to batch many characters with a single buffer.

Double-buffer UBOs to avoid CPU-GPU synchronization stalls on write.

Use persistent mapping for uniform buffers and write directly to GPU memory (if supported and safe).

Exercise: Set Up Descriptor Binding for Animated Character

Create a `VkBuffer` for 100 bone matrices.

Allocate memory with `HOST_VISIBLE | HOST_COHERENT`.

Upload computed animation transforms each frame.

Allocate a descriptor set and bind the buffer to `binding = 0`.

Use `vkCmdBindDescriptorSets` before drawing.

Descriptor sets and uniform buffers are the backbone of Vulkan's resource binding system. By allocating per-character descriptor sets that point to character-specific bone matrices, you can keep your GPU skinning logic flexible, parallel-friendly, and efficient. With this setup, each character gets its own animation state fully managed on the GPU, allowing you to scale your animation system far beyond what would be possible with fixed-function or global state approaches.

11.3 Efficient Memory Layout and Synchronization

When working with Vulkan for real-time skeletal animation, the way you allocate and manage memory directly affects both performance and stability. Uploading bone matrices every frame—especially for dozens or hundreds of animated characters—requires careful control over memory layout, alignment, and synchronization. If you're not careful, you'll introduce stalls, memory hazards, or undefined behavior.

Understanding the Challenge

Each animated character needs a set of bone matrices (typically 60–100 `mat4s`) uploaded to the GPU each frame. If you upload this data directly into the same buffer used for rendering without any precautions, you risk the following:

CPU-GPU synchronization conflicts (writing while the GPU is still reading)

Suboptimal cache performance due to misaligned access

Exceeding device limits on buffer usage or alignment

The solution is to follow Vulkan's alignment requirements, use proper memory barriers, and design your buffer layout with **per-frame** isolation in mind.

Aligning Uniform Buffer Offsets Properly

When using a single uniform buffer for multiple characters or frames, each block of bone data must begin at an aligned offset.

Query Device Limits

```
VkPhysicalDeviceProperties properties;

vkGetPhysicalDeviceProperties(physicalDevice,
&properties);



VkDeviceSize alignment =
properties.limits.minUniformBufferOffsetAlignment;
```

On many systems, this value is **256 bytes**. This means each bone matrix block must start on a 256-byte boundary.

Compute Aligned Stride

If each character's bone block is `sizeof(glm::mat4) * 100 = 6400` bytes:

```
VkDeviceSize stride = AlignTo(sizeof(glm::mat4) *
100, alignment);
```

Where `AlignTo(x, align)` is:

```
inline VkDeviceSize AlignTo(VkDeviceSize value,
VkDeviceSize alignment) {
    return (value + alignment - 1) & ~(alignment -
1);
}
```

Use this stride to calculate memory offsets when uploading or binding per-character data in the uniform buffer.

Avoiding CPU-GPU Write Conflicts

If you overwrite a buffer that the GPU is still reading from, you'll get undefined behavior. Vulkan does not protect you from this—it's up to you.

Option 1: Double Buffering

Use **two buffers**, one for writing and one for rendering. Swap them each frame:

```
int frameIndex = frameNumber % 2;

VkBuffer activeBoneBuffer =
boneBuffers[frameIndex];
```

This avoids hazards because the write and read operations never touch the same memory.

Option 2: Dynamic UBO with Per-Frame Offsets

You can store multiple bone matrices blocks in a single large buffer and bind per-character blocks via dynamic offsets:

```
VkDeviceSize offset = stride * characterIndex;


vkCmdBindDescriptorSets(

    commandBuffer,

    VK_PIPELINE_BIND_POINT_GRAPHICS,

    pipelineLayout,
```

```
    0, 1, &descriptorSet,

    1, &offset
);
```

This lets you bind the same descriptor set for all characters and just change the dynamic offset.

Important: You must ensure the GPU has finished reading from `offset` before overwriting it.

Using `VK_MEMORY_PROPERTY_HOST_COHERENT_BIT`

When creating your buffer memory, you have two options:

Host coherent: Automatically visible to the GPU when you `memcpy`.

Host visible (non-coherent): Requires manual flushing.

Use host-coherent memory for simplicity:

```
memoryType = VK_MEMORY_PROPERTY_HOST_VISIBLE_BIT |
VK_MEMORY_PROPERTY_HOST_COHERENT_BIT;
```

If you use non-coherent memory, you must call:

```
VkMappedMemoryRange flushRange = {

    .sType = VK_STRUCTURE_TYPE_MAPPED_MEMORY_RANGE,

    .memory = boneMemory,

    .offset = 0,

    .size = bufferSize

};


vkFlushMappedMemoryRanges(device, 1, &flushRange);
```

For performance, you can batch multiple updates before flushing.

Buffer Usage Flags and Access Hints

When creating your buffer, always set appropriate usage flags:

```
bufferInfo.usage = VK_BUFFER_USAGE_UNIFORM_BUFFER_BIT;
```

For dynamic updates and multipurpose usage, also consider:

```
VK_BUFFER_USAGE_TRANSFER_DST_BIT |
VK_BUFFER_USAGE_STORAGE_BUFFER_BIT
```

For example, you might later switch to using compute shaders or GPU-driven skinning with storage buffers.

Proper Synchronization with Fences

To ensure you don't overwrite memory in use by the GPU:

Use **per-frame fences** to wait until the previous frame is finished:

```
vkWaitForFences(device, 1,
&frameFences[currentFrame], VK_TRUE, UINT64_MAX);

vkResetFences(device, 1,
&frameFences[currentFrame]);
```

Avoid overwriting memory from frame N-1 before its fence signals.

You can tie fence state to uniform buffer use to track exactly when each region of memory is safe to reuse.

Advanced: Persistent Mapping with Ring Buffers

For high-frequency updates, map the buffer once at startup and leave it mapped:

```
void* mappedPtr;

vkMapMemory(device, boneMemory, 0, totalSize, 0,
&mappedPtr);
```

You then write directly into offsets within mappedPtr, using your computed aligned stride:

```
void* dst = (uint8_t*)mappedPtr + offset;

memcpy(dst, finalBoneMatrices.data(), stride);
```

This avoids `vkMapMemory` and `vkUnmapMemory` overhead entirely.

Exercise: Frame-Safe UBO Updates

Query device's `minUniformBufferOffsetAlignment`.

Compute stride-aligned offset for each character's bone matrices.

Allocate a single UBO large enough for all characters across multiple frames (e.g., 100 bones × 64 characters × 3 frames).

On each frame, write to a frame-specific region of the buffer.

Bind each character's data using dynamic offset.

Efficient memory layout and synchronization are critical to Vulkan's performance. You must manually align your data to meet GPU requirements, avoid writing to memory the GPU is still using, and structure your buffers to support per-frame or per-character data safely. Once these patterns are in place, your animation system becomes scalable, fast, and suitable for complex real-time applications—whether you're animating 10 characters or 1,000.

11.4 Command Buffer Optimization for Animated Characters

When rendering animated characters in Vulkan, it's not just what you draw— but how and when you record commands to draw—that determines how well your system scales. With Vulkan's explicit design, each draw call, descriptor binding, and pipeline switch adds cost to the CPU side of your frame. So, if you're animating 50 or more characters, you need to think carefully about command buffer efficiency.

Vulkan distinguishes between **primary** and **secondary** command buffers:

Primary command buffers are submitted directly to the GPU queue.

Secondary command buffers are recorded independently and executed from within a primary buffer.

This separation allows you to **record character draws independently**, potentially in parallel, and merge them before submission.

Batch Animation Draw Calls by Pipeline and Descriptor Layout

Minimizing state changes inside a command buffer improves performance. For animated characters:

Use a **shared graphics pipeline** for all characters using the same vertex layout and shaders.

Create **descriptor set layouts** that can be reused across all characters with the same bone matrix block size.

By doing this, you avoid:

Rebinding pipelines per character

Reallocating descriptor sets unnecessarily

Excessive driver validation overhead

Key Principle: Record batches of characters that share the same pipeline and descriptor set layout.

Record Per-Character Draws Using Secondary Buffers

Secondary command buffers are perfect for recording draw calls for characters independently—useful for multithreaded recording.

How to Do It

For each character:

Compute animation state and bone matrices.

Write into its uniform buffer or region in a shared buffer.

Record a secondary command buffer with its draw commands.

In the main thread:

Begin a primary command buffer.

Call `vkCmdExecuteCommands()` to append all per-character secondaries.

End and submit the primary buffer.

Sample Code

```
vkBeginCommandBuffer(primaryCmd, &beginInfo);

vkCmdBindPipeline(primaryCmd,
VK_PIPELINE_BIND_POINT_GRAPHICS, sharedPipeline);

vkCmdExecuteCommands(primaryCmd, characterCount,
secondaryBuffers);

vkEndCommandBuffer(primaryCmd);

Each secondaryBuffer contains:

vkCmdBindDescriptorSets(...); // character-specific
descriptor

vkCmdBindVertexBuffers(...);

vkCmdBindIndexBuffer(...);

vkCmdDrawIndexed(...);
```

You can record these secondaries in parallel across threads.

Use Dynamic Offsets to Minimize Descriptor Set Allocation

If all characters share a large **dynamic uniform buffer**, you can bind the same descriptor set for all of them and just change the offset.

This drastically reduces descriptor pool usage and avoids the cost of updating descriptor sets per frame.

```
VkDeviceSize dynamicOffset = characterIndex *
alignedStride;

vkCmdBindDescriptorSets(commandBuffer,
VK_PIPELINE_BIND_POINT_GRAPHICS,

                        pipelineLayout, 0, 1,
&sharedDescriptorSet, 1, &dynamicOffset);
```

This is most effective when all characters use the same shader and uniform layout.

Avoid Pipeline State Changes

Rebinding a pipeline is expensive. If you mix animated and static characters in the same buffer:

Group by **render type**

Sort characters by **pipeline layout**

For example:

```
for (const DrawGroup& group : drawGroupsByPipeline)
{
    vkCmdBindPipeline(cmd, ..., group.pipeline);
    for (const CharacterDraw& draw :
group.characters) {
        vkCmdBindDescriptorSets(...);
        vkCmdDrawIndexed(...);
    }
}
```

This reduces `vkCmdBindPipeline()` calls to once per batch.

Push Constants for Per-Draw Data

For small per-character state like a model matrix, use push constants instead of uniforms:

```
vkCmdPushConstants(cmd, pipelineLayout,
VK_SHADER_STAGE_VERTEX_BIT,

                   0, sizeof(glm::mat4),
&character.modelMatrix);
```

This avoids needing additional descriptor bindings and is very fast (<128 bytes).

In your shader:

```
layout(push_constant) uniform PushConstants {
    mat4 u_ModelMatrix;
```

```
};
```

Preallocate and Reuse Command Buffers

Avoid allocating and freeing command buffers every frame. Instead:

Create a **pool of secondary command buffers**, one per character.

Record them each frame but reuse the allocated handles.

Only reset command buffers, not destroy/allocate:

```
vkResetCommandBuffer(cmd, 0);
```

Exercise: Optimized Animated Draw Submission

Create a pool of secondary command buffers, one for each animated character.

In each frame:

Update animation pose

Write bone matrices into uniform buffer

Record character's draw call in a secondary command buffer

In the main thread:

Record a primary command buffer

Bind the shared pipeline

Execute all character draw command buffers

Submit the primary buffer once.

This structure gives you the flexibility to render 100+ characters efficiently with minimal CPU overhead.

Efficient command buffer usage is what makes Vulkan's explicit model truly shine—especially for complex systems like character animation. By batching draw calls, using secondary command buffers, avoiding redundant pipeline bindings, and leveraging dynamic offsets and push constants, you significantly reduce overhead and unlock performance that scales with hardware capability. These practices turn a naive animation renderer into a robust system suitable for professional-grade, high-load rendering scenarios.

Chapter 12: Architecting an Animation System in C++

By this point in the book, you've learned how to construct and render skeletal animations in real time—from pose evaluation to GPU skinning using OpenGL or Vulkan. But building isolated features isn't enough to scale a full game or simulation system. What you need now is **architecture**: a way to design your animation system so it's maintainable, extensible, thread-safe, and cleanly decoupled from unrelated concerns like rendering or physics.

This chapter is focused on system design. We'll look at how to structure your animation codebase in modern C++, how to integrate with an entity-component-system (ECS), how to perform parallel updates using a job system, and how to serialize animation state for saving and loading. These patterns are field-tested in real engines and are designed to help you ship stable, high-performance code in production.

12.1 Decoupling Animation from Rendering and Physics

If you want your animation system to scale cleanly, remain testable, and support advanced features like blend trees, ragdoll overrides, and procedural motion, then the most important architectural principle to follow is this: **do not couple animation with rendering or physics.**

The animation system should be concerned with **motion logic and pose generation only**. It computes bone transforms based on time, state, and animation graphs. Once the poses are calculated, the data is handed off. What happens afterward—whether the pose is used for rendering, fed into a physics solver, or manipulated procedurally—is outside animation's concern.

Animation's Responsibility: Output a Pose

Your animation system evaluates characters' states and animations, then generates a **pose**—typically a list of joint transformations in model or global space.

This output is **pure data**, and should look something like this:

```
struct LocalTransform {
    glm::vec3 translation;
    glm::quat rotation;
    glm::vec3 scale;
};

using Pose = std::vector<LocalTransform>;
```

Once this pose is computed, your animation system is done. From this point onward, rendering and physics can read it, modify it, or consume it however they need. But the animation system itself should never:

Call OpenGL, Vulkan, or DirectX APIs

Allocate or bind render resources

Directly access or resolve physics constraints

Data Flow Architecture

Here's the recommended **one-way data flow** between animation and other systems:

[Animation System] → **[Pose Buffer]** → **[Renderer]**

                                |

                                └──→ **[Physics]**

The **Pose Buffer** is a memory structure that holds the current animation results. It's typically owned by the ECS or a central animation manager and updated every frame.

Each frame:

The animation system evaluates active animations, blend nodes, and any IK solvers under its scope.

It writes the result to a Pose—one per entity or per skeleton.

The render system reads the pose to perform GPU skinning.

The physics system may also read the pose for foot placement, ragdoll blending, or hit reaction adjustments.

This separation keeps responsibilities clean and predictable.

Minimal Interface: Animation System API

Here's what the **public interface** of your animation system might look like:

```
class AnimationSystem {
public:
    void Update(float deltaTime); // Runs animation
logic
    const Pose& GetPose(EntityID entity) const; //
Read-only access to pose
};
```

This ensures external systems can read poses, but never alter internal animation state. If you allow bidirectional coupling (e.g., renderer tells animation what to do), you quickly run into ordering problems, tight dependencies, and hard-to-test logic.

Real-World Pitfall: Renderer-Modifies-Pose

A bad but common pattern:

```
// BAD: Renderer modifies animation state based on
render visibility

if (IsVisible(entity)) {

    animationSystem.AdvanceAnimation(entity,
deltaTime);

}
```

This seems harmless, but it means your animation system's output depends on renderer logic—breaking determinism. Worse, it introduces hidden bugs: if visibility culling is done later, animation becomes one frame off or fails entirely.

Instead, do this:

```
animationSystem.Update(deltaTime); // Independent
of visibility
```

```
renderer.Submit(animationSystem.GetPose(entity));
// Pure read
```

Even invisible characters should advance animations to maintain continuity and ensure future blend transitions are smooth.

Optional Pose Modification: Procedural Layers or Physics

Let's say you want physics to modify the pose before rendering—for instance, when applying ragdoll motion or spring-based head movement. This should be done **after animation completes** and before rendering begins:

```
Pose pose = animationSystem.GetPose(entity);

if (isRagdollActive(entity)) {
    ragdollSolver.ModifyPose(entity, pose); //
Modifies the pose
}

renderer.Submit(pose); // Renderer reads final
version
```

This pattern allows you to keep animation deterministic and pure, while still supporting dynamic procedural overrides in a well-defined place.

Example: Clean Integration with Rendering

Let's look at how you would use the animation system in practice, decoupled from rendering:

```
void AnimationSystem::Update(float dt) {

    for (auto& [entity, animState, poseOut,
skeleton] : entities) {

        animState.graph->Update(dt);

        animState.graph-
>Evaluate(poseOut.localPose);

        ApplySkeletonHierarchy(poseOut.localPose,
poseOut.globalPose, skeleton);
```

```
        }
    }
}
```

Later in the frame:

```
void RenderSystem::DrawCharacters() {
    for (auto& entity : visibleCharacters) {
        const Pose& pose =
animationSystem.GetPose(entity);

        UploadBoneMatricesToGPU(pose); // This is
now the renderer's job

        DrawSkinnedMesh(entity.mesh);
    }
}
```

This level of separation allows you to:

Parallelize animation updates separately from rendering

Pause rendering without affecting animation (e.g., for remote sim)

Save animation state without worrying about visual state

Reuse the animation system in a headless server environment

Exercise: Implement a One-Way Animation Pose Buffer

Create a `PoseComponent` that stores a pose for each character.

In the animation update loop, write to `PoseComponent.localPose` and `globalPose`.

In the render system, read from `PoseComponent.globalPose` and convert to bone matrices.

Never allow the renderer or physics system to write to animation state directly.

This clean break will help you debug faster and scale animation complexity over time.

By decoupling animation from rendering and physics, you create a more modular, testable, and efficient system. The animation system focuses purely on character state and pose evaluation, while rendering and physics become consumers of that output. This separation is foundational for building scalable animation pipelines—whether you're rendering 10 animated characters or 10,000.

12.2 ECS-Friendly Animation Design

When you're working within an Entity-Component-System (ECS) architecture, animation must be designed in a way that complements ECS principles. That means animation logic should operate on **stateless systems** and **data-driven components**. You should avoid OOP-style object ownership and instead rely on pure functions acting over groups of related components.

Each system must do one job, operate only on the data it needs, and never store per-entity state internally.

That means your animation update system should look like this:

```
void UpdateAnimations(World& world, float deltaTime);
```

It reads and writes components for each relevant entity, and nothing more. There's no inheritance, no virtual method tables, and no entity-specific logic embedded in the system.

Defining ECS Animation Components

Let's define the minimal set of components to support runtime skeletal animation.

1. SkeletonComponent

This is the static rig definition: joint hierarchy and bind pose.

```
struct SkeletonComponent {
    Skeleton* skeleton; // Shared pointer to joint
hierarchy and metadata
};
```

All entities that share the same rig (e.g., humanoids) can point to the same `Skeleton` instance.

2. AnimationStateComponent

This holds the runtime state machine, blend tree, or procedural motion logic.

```
struct AnimationStateComponent {

    AnimationGraphInstance stateMachine;

    float playbackTime = 0.0f;

};
```

Each entity can have its own animation state logic, which may include transitions, layer weights, current clip time, and so on.

3. PoseComponent

This stores the output of animation: one pose per frame, per entity.

```
struct PoseComponent {

    std::vector<LocalTransform> localPose;

    std::vector<glm::mat4> globalPose;

};
```

The local pose holds joint-relative transforms. The global pose holds world-space matrices for rendering or physics. These are rewritten every frame during animation evaluation.

Evaluating Animations in an ECS System

Your animation system processes all entities with the above components and evaluates their current pose.

Basic System Logic

```
void UpdateAnimations(World& world, float
deltaTime) {
    auto view = world.view<AnimationStateComponent,
SkeletonComponent, PoseComponent>();
```

```
    for (auto entity : view) {
        auto& state =
view.get<AnimationStateComponent>(entity);
        auto& skeleton =
view.get<SkeletonComponent>(entity);
        auto& pose =
view.get<PoseComponent>(entity);

        state.stateMachine.Update(deltaTime);

state.stateMachine.Evaluate(pose.localPose);

        ApplySkeletonHierarchy(pose.localPose,
pose.globalPose, *skeleton.skeleton);
    }
}
```

ApplySkeletonHierarchy

This is the function that propagates transforms down the joint hierarchy:

```
void ApplySkeletonHierarchy(const
std::vector<LocalTransform>& local,
                            std::vector<glm::mat4>&
global,
                            const Skeleton&
skeleton) {
    global[0] = local[0].ToMatrix();

    for (size_t i = 1; i < skeleton.joints.size();
++i) {
        int parent =
skeleton.joints[i].parentIndex;
        global[i] = global[parent] *
local[i].ToMatrix();
    }
}
```

You call this once per entity after local pose evaluation to produce global matrices.

Memory Efficiency and Pooling

To avoid allocating pose buffers every frame:

Allocate the `PoseComponent.localPose` and `globalPose` arrays once, based on skeleton joint count.

Do this during entity setup when the `SkeletonComponent` is first attached.

```
void InitializePoseComponent(EntityID entity,
SkeletonComponent& skeleton, PoseComponent& pose) {

    size_t jointCount = skeleton.skeleton-
>joints.size();

    pose.localPose.resize(jointCount);

    pose.globalPose.resize(jointCount);

}
```

If you use `entt`, this can be handled in a construction callback:

```
registry.on_construct<SkeletonComponent>().connect<
&InitializePoseComponent>();
```

Animation Systems as Stateless Jobs

This design allows your animation evaluation to be trivially multithreaded.

Each entity is independent, so you can batch update them using a job system:

```
for (auto& entity : view) {
    jobSystem.Submit([=]() {
        UpdateOneAnimation(entity, world,
deltaTime);
    });
}
jobSystem.WaitForAll();
```

Where `UpdateOneAnimation()` mirrors the loop body shown earlier.

Optional: Animation Output Component for GPU Skinning

If you want to pass final matrices to the GPU, include a separate component for skinning data:

```cpp
struct SkinningMatricesComponent {
    std::vector<glm::mat4> boneMatrices; // 
Computed from globalPose * inverseBind
};
```
You update this after pose evaluation:
```cpp
void ComputeSkinningMatrices(const Skeleton&
skeleton,
                                const
std::vector<glm::mat4>& globalPose,

std::vector<glm::mat4>& outSkinning) {
    size_t count = skeleton.joints.size();
    outSkinning.resize(count);
    for (size_t i = 0; i < count; ++i) {
        outSkinning[i] = globalPose[i] *
skeleton.joints[i].inverseBindMatrix;
    }
}
```

Component Relationships Summary

Component	Role
SkeletonComponent	Static joint structure and bind poses
AnimationStateComponent	Dynamic state machine / playback logic
PoseComponent	Per-frame joint transforms
SkinningMatricesComponent (optional)	Final matrices for GPU skinning

This breakdown ensures that animation systems only touch what they need, and rendering can consume the result without knowing how it was created.

Exercise: Build a Minimal ECS-Based Animation System

Create an ECS registry with the above four components.

Initialize one animated character with a test skeleton and simple walk animation.

Each frame:

Advance the animation state graph

Evaluate and apply the skeleton hierarchy

Compute final matrices for skinning

Render the result using GPU skinning (optional)

This workflow gives you a robust foundation for dozens of animated characters.

ECS-friendly animation design is all about clean data boundaries, stateless update systems, and scalable processing. By defining animation as a set of independent components—skeletons, animation graphs, and poses—you keep your system extensible and testable. You avoid tightly coupling animation logic to rendering or physics, and you prepare your system to scale cleanly across hundreds of entities and multiple threads.

12.3 Job System and Multithreaded Animation Updates

When your game or simulation scales to dozens—or hundreds—of animated characters, updating each one serially becomes a bottleneck. Animation evaluation can be CPU-intensive, especially when working with layered blend trees, pose modifiers, or inverse kinematics. To meet modern performance expectations, your animation system must leverage **multithreading**, and the most effective way to do this is by integrating a **job system**.

A job system is a lightweight task scheduler that lets you split work into small, independent jobs. These jobs are distributed across a fixed pool of worker threads and executed in parallel. Unlike raw threads, job systems are:

Efficient (no OS thread creation/destruction overhead)

Fine-grained (you can schedule thousands of tasks per frame)

Synchronizable (via counters, fences, or dependency graphs)

In animation, this allows you to evaluate each character independently and in parallel.

Animation Is Naturally Parallel

Each animated character's state update and pose evaluation is typically independent of others. If your engine uses ECS, and animation writes only to per-entity components like `PoseComponent` and `AnimationStateComponent`, there's no shared state to protect.

This makes each character a perfect candidate for its own job.

Basic Job Interface

Let's start with a minimal C++ job system API:

```cpp
class JobSystem {
public:
    using JobHandle = std::shared_ptr<Job>;

    JobHandle Submit(std::function<void()> task);
    void Wait(JobHandle handle);
    void WaitAll();
};
```

Each call to `Submit` schedules a new job to the internal thread pool.

Job Example: One Character's Animation Evaluation

```cpp
struct AnimationJob {
    Skeleton* skeleton;
    AnimationGraphInstance* graph;
    std::vector<LocalTransform>* localPose;
    std::vector<glm::mat4>* globalPose;
    float deltaTime;

    void operator()() {
        graph->Update(deltaTime);
        graph->Evaluate(*localPose);
        ApplySkeletonHierarchy(*localPose,
*globalPose, *skeleton);
    }
};
```

The operator overload allows this struct to be used like a lambda.

You submit this like so:

```
jobSystem.Submit(AnimationJob {

    skeleton,

    &stateGraph,

    &pose.localPose,

    &pose.globalPose,

    deltaTime

});
```

Scheduling All Entities

Within your ECS-based animation update system:

```
std::vector<JobSystem::JobHandle> animationJobs;

auto view = world.view<AnimationStateComponent,
SkeletonComponent, PoseComponent>();
for (auto entity : view) {
    auto& graph =
view.get<AnimationStateComponent>(entity).stateMach
ine;
    auto& skeleton =
*view.get<SkeletonComponent>(entity).skeleton;
    auto& pose = view.get<PoseComponent>(entity);


animationJobs.push_back(jobSystem.Submit(AnimationJ
ob {
        &skeleton,
        &graph,
        &pose.localPose,
        &pose.globalPose,
        deltaTime
    }));
}

jobSystem.WaitAll(); // Blocks until all animations
are evaluated
```

This code allows each character's update to run in parallel, as long as your job system is built with thread-safe scheduling.

Ensuring Thread-Safe Data Access

The key to correctness in multithreaded animation is to avoid shared writes.

Rules to follow:

Never share `std::vector` instances across jobs unless properly locked.

Avoid modifying `Skeleton` or animation graph definitions inside jobs.

Allocate each character's `PoseComponent` and `AnimationStateComponent` separately.

You can share read-only assets (like animation clips or rig definitions), but any runtime state must be per-entity.

Avoiding False Sharing

False sharing happens when multiple threads write to variables that are close in memory but technically independent. It causes unnecessary cache line contention and kills performance.

To avoid this:

```
struct PoseComponent {
    alignas(64) std::vector<LocalTransform>
localPose;
    alignas(64) std::vector<glm::mat4> globalPose;
};
```

This keeps each `PoseComponent` on its own cache line, so two threads updating adjacent characters don't slow each other down.

Advanced Job Graphs and Dependencies

Some animations might depend on others (e.g., child bones following parents, ragdoll blending, or pose constraints). In such cases, your job system should support **job dependencies**:

```
JobHandle parentJob = jobSystem.Submit(...);
```

```
JobHandle childJob =
jobSystem.SubmitAfter(parentJob, ...);
```

You might also batch jobs into groups using a counter:

```
JobCounter counter;
for (auto& entity : animatedEntities) {
    jobSystem.SubmitWithCounter(AnimationJob{...},
counter);
}
jobSystem.Wait(counter);
```

This enables non-blocking parallelism and allows your engine to perform other tasks while animation finishes.

Exercise: Implement Parallel Animation Updates

Create a job system with a worker thread pool.

For each animated character:

Build an `AnimationJob` that updates the animation graph and pose.

Submit it to the job system.

Use `WaitAll()` to synchronize before rendering.

Benchmark CPU usage before and after—expect significant frame time reduction on multicore CPUs.

A job system transforms animation updates from a linear loop into a massively parallel workload. Because each character is typically independent, animation is one of the easiest systems to thread—and also one of the most rewarding. With a proper job system in place, your game or engine will run smoother, scale better, and stay responsive under heavy animation loads.

12.4 Saving and Loading Animation States

In real-time systems like games, simulators, or interactive experiences, animation is not just visual polish—it's an active part of your system's state. Whether your character is in the middle of a walking cycle, performing a combo chain, or transitioning between layers in a blend tree, preserving this runtime state is essential for features like **save/load, pausing, rewinding,** or **network synchronization**.

When we say "animation state," we're referring to all runtime data needed to:

Resume playback of animations at the exact point they left off

Maintain transitions, blend weights, and additive layers

Support dynamic state graphs (e.g. walk → run → jump)

That means **just saving the current clip name and time is not enough**. You also need the state machine's active node(s), interpolation progress, and any non-default parameters affecting motion.

Identify What Needs to Be Serialized

Basic Fields for Each Animated Entity

The current animation clip or graph node ID

The current playback time in seconds

Blend weights (if in a blend tree or layer system)

Transition progress (if in the middle of a crossfade)

Flags like looping, paused, reversed

If you're using an animation state graph or FSM, also include:

Active state name or hash

State transition info (target node, blend curve)

Any parameter values (e.g. speed = 1.2, isJumping = true)

Defining a Serializable Animation State Structure

Create a plain struct that mirrors your runtime animation logic but is designed for clean I/O:

```
struct SerializedAnimationState {
    std::string currentNodeName;
    float playbackTime = 0.0f;
```

```
    bool isTransitioning = false;
    std::string targetNodeName;
    float transitionProgress = 0.0f;
    float transitionDuration = 0.0f;

    std::unordered_map<std::string, float>
floatParameters;
    std::unordered_map<std::string, bool>
boolParameters;
};
```

This data structure should **not** contain pointers or references. It must be self-contained and portable.

Saving State from a Runtime Animation Graph

To extract a serializable state from your animation system:

```
SerializedAnimationState SaveState(const
AnimationGraphInstance& graph) {
    SerializedAnimationState state;

    state.currentNodeName =
graph.GetActiveNodeName();
    state.playbackTime = graph.GetCurrentTime();

    if (graph.IsInTransition()) {
        state.isTransitioning = true;
        state.targetNodeName =
graph.GetTargetNodeName();
        state.transitionProgress =
graph.GetTransitionProgress();
        state.transitionDuration =
graph.GetTransitionDuration();
    }

    for (const auto& param :
graph.GetFloatParameters()) {
        state.floatParameters[param.first] =
param.second;
    }
```

```
    for (const auto& param :
graph.GetBoolParameters()) {
        state.boolParameters[param.first] =
param.second;
    }

    return state;
}
```

This allows you to save the entire animation logic without knowing anything about the rendering or pose evaluation.

Restoring State into a Running Graph

To reload the animation state and apply it to a live character:

```
void LoadState(AnimationGraphInstance& graph, const
SerializedAnimationState& state) {

graph.SetActiveNodeByName(state.currentNodeName);
    graph.SetCurrentTime(state.playbackTime);

    if (state.isTransitioning) {

graph.StartTransitionTo(state.targetNodeName,
state.transitionDuration,
state.transitionProgress);
    }

    for (const auto& [key, val] :
state.floatParameters) {
        graph.SetFloatParameter(key, val);
    }

    for (const auto& [key, val] :
state.boolParameters) {
        graph.SetBoolParameter(key, val);
    }
}
```

Important: This assumes your animation graph supports runtime state manipulation (i.e., can start mid-transition or jump to a specific time in a clip).

Storing as JSON or Binary

To JSON (for easy debugging and inspection)

```cpp
nlohmann::json SerializeToJson(const
SerializedAnimationState& state) {

    json j;

    j["currentNodeName"] = state.currentNodeName;

    j["playbackTime"] = state.playbackTime;

    j["isTransitioning"] = state.isTransitioning;

    j["targetNodeName"] = state.targetNodeName;

    j["transitionProgress"] =
state.transitionProgress;

    j["transitionDuration"] =
state.transitionDuration;

    j["floatParameters"] = state.floatParameters;

    j["boolParameters"] = state.boolParameters;

    return j;

}
```

From JSON

```cpp
SerializedAnimationState DeserializeFromJson(const
json& j) {
    SerializedAnimationState state;
    state.currentNodeName =
j.at("currentNodeName").get<std::string>();
    state.playbackTime =
j.at("playbackTime").get<float>();
    state.isTransitioning =
j.at("isTransitioning").get<bool>();
    state.targetNodeName =
j.at("targetNodeName").get<std::string>();
```

```cpp
    state.transitionProgress =
j.at("transitionProgress").get<float>();
    state.transitionDuration =
j.at("transitionDuration").get<float>();
    state.floatParameters =
j.at("floatParameters").get<std::unordered_map<std:
:string, float>>();
    state.boolParameters =
j.at("boolParameters").get<std::unordered_map<std::
string, bool>>();
    return state;
}
```

Use libraries like `nlohmann/json` or `cereal` to keep your serialization code clean and maintainable.

Handling Legacy and Versioned Data

Your animation system will evolve. So always add a `version` field when storing:

```json
{

  "version": 2,

  "currentNodeName": "Run",

  "playbackTime": 1.53,

  . . .

}
```

In your loading code, use the version field to ensure compatibility:

```cpp
if (j["version"].get<int>() < 2) {

    // Apply fallback logic or defaults

}
```

This helps when loading old save games or transitioning between engine versions.

Network Use Case: State Snapshots for Multiplayer

When replicating animation across networked entities:

Serialize a lightweight subset of the state (e.g., clip name and time).

Stream this every few frames (not every tick).

Use interpolation and prediction on the receiving side.

You can reuse the same serialization logic, just omit heavy or unnecessary fields like blend weights.

Exercise: Implement Runtime Animation Save/Load

Add `SerializedAnimationState` support to your animation graph instance.

Implement `SaveState()` and `LoadState()` functions.

Hook them up to your game's save/load logic.

Test by pausing mid-animation, saving to file, restarting the app, and restoring from file.

Confirm that characters resume animations without jumps or glitches.

Saving and restoring animation state is not just about pausing and resuming animations—it's about enabling full system reliability. Whether you're building save games, loading screens, rollback support, or multiplayer synchronization, consistent animation state serialization ensures smooth continuity and immersive experiences. With a clean data structure, versioned format, and explicit separation from rendering logic, your system stays robust as it grows.

Chapter 13: Optimization, Debugging, and Profiling

Even the most elegant animation system can suffer from performance issues if you're not careful. Real-time animation pipelines involve multiple stages—CPU evaluation, GPU skinning, memory access, buffer updates—and they all cost something. When you scale up to dozens or hundreds of animated characters, the impact can grow exponentially.

13.1 Visualizing Skeletons and Motion Paths

Debugging animation problems without visualization is like debugging physics without collision shapes—you're working blind. When your character isn't animating correctly, when bones appear flipped, or when an animation graph isn't behaving as expected, visualizing the skeleton and motion path becomes your best diagnostic tool. It's the fastest way to see if joint transforms are correct, if hierarchy propagation is working, and if root motion is stable across frames.

Visualizing the Skeleton

The first step is to render the bones and joints of your animated character. This is done in a debug overlay pass and does **not** require a skinned mesh or full GPU animation to be working. You're simply visualizing joint positions and parent-child connections derived from the current pose.

Skeleton Debug Function

Assume you have this basic `Pose` structure populated each frame:

```
struct Pose {

    std::vector<glm::mat4> globalPose; // One
matrix per joint

};
```

And your skeleton defines the hierarchy:

```
struct Joint {
    int parentIndex;
```

```cpp
    std::string name;
};

struct Skeleton {
    std::vector<Joint> joints;
};
```

You can draw the skeleton with a simple debug function:

```cpp
void DebugDrawSkeleton(const Pose& pose, const
Skeleton& skeleton) {
    const size_t jointCount =
skeleton.joints.size();
    for (size_t i = 0; i < jointCount; ++i) {
        int parent =
skeleton.joints[i].parentIndex;
        if (parent < 0) continue;

        glm::vec3 childPos =
glm::vec3(pose.globalPose[i][3]);
        glm::vec3 parentPos =
glm::vec3(pose.globalPose[parent][3]);

        DebugDrawLine(parentPos, childPos,
glm::vec3(1.0f, 0.0f, 0.0f)); // red line
        DebugDrawSphere(childPos, 0.01f,
glm::vec3(1.0f, 1.0f, 0.0f));    // yellow joint
    }
}
```

Why It Matters

This lets you:

Confirm that the bone hierarchy is applied correctly

Verify joint transforms during animation

Catch flipped axes, scale issues, or zero-length bones

Validate skeleton loading from DCC tools (e.g., Blender, Maya)

You can also draw joint names next to each sphere for easier debugging of rig mismatches.

Motion Path Trails

Next, you'll want to verify motion over time. This helps with problems like:

Incorrect root motion extraction

Inconsistent walk/run transitions

Blend tree artifacts (e.g., foot slipping)

IK issues when moving targets

The simplest form of motion tracking is a **position trail** for a particular joint, usually the root.

Tracking Motion

```cpp
std::deque<glm::vec3> motionTrail;

const size_t maxTrailLength = 120; // 2 seconds at
60 FPS


void TrackRootMotion(const glm::mat4&
rootGlobalMatrix) {

    glm::vec3 position =
glm::vec3(rootGlobalMatrix[3]);

    motionTrail.push_back(position);


    if (motionTrail.size() > maxTrailLength) {

        motionTrail.pop_front();

    }

}
```

Call this every frame during animation update. Then draw the path:

```cpp
void DebugDrawMotionPath() {
```

```
    for (size_t i = 1; i < motionTrail.size(); ++i)
{
        DebugDrawLine(motionTrail[i - 1],
motionTrail[i], glm::vec3(0.0f, 1.0f, 1.0f)); //
cyan
    }
}
```

Multiple Trails

You can extend this to track other joints—like feet, hands, or the head—to validate IK and look-at systems:

```
std::unordered_map<std::string,
std::deque<glm::vec3>> jointTrails;
```
Then store and render per-joint trails over time.

Animating Skeletons Without Meshes

When debugging blend trees, you don't always want to run skinning or even load the mesh. You can evaluate animation and pose without rendering the mesh at all, and just draw the skeleton. This helps isolate whether the problem is in:

Animation playback logic

Skinning calculations

Mesh attachment or binding

Doing this early saves time and avoids being misled by mesh artifacts.

Visual Debug Controls

To avoid clutter and improve usability, hook up controls:

Toggle debug skeletons with a key (e.g., F1)

Select which joints to track with motion trails

Toggle display of joint names or hierarchy depth

Allow scrubbing back and forth through stored poses

These can be integrated into your in-game debug UI using a system like **Dear ImGui** or a custom overlay.

Practical Debug Workflow Example

Character's foot appears to be slipping in walk → run blend.

You activate debug skeletons and motion trails.

You notice the root joint moves forward linearly, but the pelvis follows a curved path.

You realize the blend tree isn't using root motion blending correctly.

You adjust the blend weights or add a curve editor to fix the transition.

This sort of problem is difficult to solve without direct skeleton visualization.

Exercise: Build a Minimal Debug Skeleton Viewer

Use a test character and rig loaded from your preferred format (e.g., glTF).

Evaluate its animation pose every frame.

Draw a debug skeleton using lines and spheres for each bone.

Record root joint position over time and draw its motion trail.

Add a toggle key to enable/disable debug overlays.

Once this is in place, leave it on by default during animation development. It'll save you hours every week.

Visualization tools are not luxuries—they are critical development tools. Seeing your skeleton and motion paths directly exposes structural problems, animation bugs, blend errors, and graph mistakes that would otherwise go unnoticed. It gives you the confidence that your runtime animation system is behaving exactly as intended, from joint hierarchy to motion deltas. And once you can see the problem, fixing it becomes a straightforward technical task instead of guesswork.

13.2 Performance Profiling

A slow animation system can cripple your game's frame rate long before you hit GPU fill limits or draw call ceilings. Profiling isn't guesswork—it's measurement. In this section, you'll learn how to profile your animation system effectively on both the CPU and GPU. You'll identify bottlenecks in animation evaluation, pose propagation, GPU skinning, and data upload, then optimize based on concrete evidence.

The Anatomy of an Animation Frame

Here's a breakdown of where your frame budget can be spent:

CPU Animation Evaluation:

State machine traversal

Keyframe interpolation

Pose blending

Skeleton hierarchy propagation

Skinning matrix generation

GPU Animation Processing:

Bone matrix upload

Vertex skinning in the vertex shader

Memory bandwidth for skinning inputs

If your system is lagging, the question is: *where?*

Profiling CPU Bottlenecks

Use Per-Frame Timers

Start by instrumenting your animation system using a high-resolution timer or a profiling library like Tracy, Remotery, or platform-specific tools like Intel VTune, Windows Performance Analyzer, or Linux `perf`.

Minimal example using `std::chrono`:

```
auto start =
std::chrono::high_resolution_clock::now();

UpdateAnimations(world, deltaTime);

auto end =
std::chrono::high_resolution_clock::now();


double ms = std::chrono::duration<double,
std::milli>(end - start).count();

std::cout << "[Profiler] Animation Update took " <<
ms << " ms" << std::endl;
```

This gives you coarse-grained timing. Break it down into finer sections for meaningful diagnostics.

Profiling Breakdown

Instrument sub-stages:

```
ZoneScopedN("Animation.StateUpdate");


for (auto entity : view) {

    auto& state = ...;

    state.Update(deltaTime);

}

ZoneScopedN("Animation.PoseBlend");

stateGraph.Evaluate(localPose);

ZoneScopedN("Animation.Hierarchy");

ApplySkeletonHierarchy(localPose, globalPose,
skeleton);
```

Look for:

High-cost blend trees (especially nested ones)

Expensive pose blending with many layers

Per-frame allocations (e.g., re-allocating vectors or copying data)

Cache misses from non-contiguous memory access

If a 60-FPS budget gives you **16.67ms** per frame, you should target <1ms total for animation on the CPU. Anything more needs attention.

Key Optimization Targets (CPU)

Avoid memory allocations during evaluation:

Use pre-allocated `std::vector` or custom pools for pose data.

Avoid creating new objects in the hot path.

Avoid evaluating inactive branches of blend trees:

Skip branches with 0 blend weight.

Use caching to short-circuit evaluation where applicable.

Batch operations where possible:

Use SoA (Structure of Arrays) layouts for joint data if needed.

Move per-character evaluation into job system for parallelism (as shown in 12.3).

Use flat arrays over pointer-heavy trees:

Store blend tree nodes in contiguous memory and interpret as a DAG.

Avoid pointer chasing inside graph traversal logic.

Profiling GPU Bottlenecks

Use tools like:

RenderDoc (cross-platform, powerful frame debugger)

NVIDIA Nsight Graphics / Nsight Systems

Radeon GPU Profiler (RGP)

Intel Graphics Performance Analyzers

These tools show:

Draw call timing

Shader execution cost

UBO/SSBO memory bandwidth

Cache hit/miss ratios

Key GPU Hotspots in Animation

Vertex Skinning Shader

For each vertex:

Load 4 bone indices and weights

Fetch 4 matrices from the bone matrix buffer

Perform matrix * position blend

GLSL skinning vertex snippet:

```
mat4 skinMatrix =

    boneWeights.x * boneMatrices[boneIndices.x] +

    boneWeights.y * boneMatrices[boneIndices.y] +

    boneWeights.z * boneMatrices[boneIndices.z] +

    boneWeights.w * boneMatrices[boneIndices.w];


vec4 skinnedPosition = skinMatrix *
vec4(vertexPosition, 1.0);
```

Optimization Tips:

Prefer `mat3` if you don't use non-uniform scaling.

Use `half` or 16-bit floats if your platform supports it.

Minimize branches or conditionals in shader logic.

Bone Matrix Upload

This usually comes from a UBO or SSBO updated every frame. Make sure:

UBO is properly aligned to `std140` or `std430`

You're not mapping/unmapping memory every frame (use persistent mapping)

You avoid buffer orphaning (either map persistently or triple-buffer)

Draw Call Overhead

Each animated character may require:

Binding a unique descriptor set (for bone data)

Uploading dynamic offsets

Separate draw call

Batching helps:

Use dynamic uniform buffers with per-character offsets

Reuse descriptor sets across characters with shared layouts

Instancing only helps if animations are shared or driven procedurally

Exercise: Profile and Optimize Skinning Performance

Run a test scene with 50+ characters using real animation data.

Use RenderDoc or Nsight to measure vertex shader cost.

Look at bone matrix fetch bandwidth per frame.

Try replacing the matrix fetch with a simplified transform and re-measure.

Try batching characters with shared skinning data and observe frame time impact.

Summary of Symptoms and Likely Causes

Symptom	Likely Cause
CPU animation time > 2ms	Deep blend trees, non-threaded update
Frequent memory reallocations	Per-frame `std::vector::resize()`
Vertex shader > 5ms	Complex skinning, unoptimized matrix fetch
UBO update stalls	Improper buffer sync or mapping strategy
Jittering or inconsistent FPS	Frame spikes due to large character batches

Profiling is not about intuition—it's about measurement and iteration. With the right tools and instrumentation, you can isolate CPU bottlenecks in animation graphs, identify slow shader paths in skinning, and optimize both data structures and execution flow. Once you have this level of visibility, you're no longer guessing where the time goes. You're tuning with precision.

13.3 Animation Culling and LOD Strategies

As your scene complexity grows—whether it's a battlefield with hundreds of soldiers or a city full of NPCs—running full animation graphs on every character becomes unsustainable. The majority of those characters aren't close to the camera. Many are not even visible. So why would you spend CPU and GPU cycles evaluating, blending, and skinning them? You shouldn't.

Animation culling and level-of-detail (LOD) strategies are performance multipliers. They reduce CPU cost by avoiding unnecessary pose evaluation, and they ease GPU load by skipping or simplifying skinning. These systems are invisible to the player but essential to keeping your framerate stable and your simulation scalable.

Frustum-Based Animation Culling

Before you run animation on a character, ask: *is it currently visible to the camera?*

You should already be doing view frustum culling for rendering. Extend that logic to gate animation updates:

```
if (!CameraFrustum.Intersects(entity.worldBounds))
{
    // Skip animation update for this character
    continue;
}
```

This means you only evaluate the animation state graph and pose if the character could be drawn.

Important note: Be careful not to skip animation if the entity still affects gameplay (e.g. for AI or physics interactions). In those cases, you can evaluate in a minimal, headless mode without producing a renderable pose.

Distance-Based Animation LOD

Not all visible characters need the same animation fidelity. The further a character is from the camera, the less precision the viewer perceives. Animation LOD allows you to reduce CPU and GPU cost proportionally to screen impact.

Define Discrete LOD Tiers

Let's define four levels:

LOD 0 – Full animation: layered blends, additive poses, GPU skinning, IK.

LOD 1 – Simplified blend graph: no additive layers, cheaper transitions.

LOD 2 – Single baked animation or looping clip, minimal evaluation.

LOD 3 – Completely culled: no animation update or render.

Assign LOD Based on Distance

Each frame, compute the distance from the camera to the character:

```
float distance = glm::length(cameraPosition -
entityPosition);
```

Then assign an LOD tier:

```
if (distance > 100.0f)

    entity.lod = 3;
```

```
else if (distance > 60.0f)

    entity.lod = 2;

else if (distance > 30.0f)

    entity.lod = 1;

else

    entity.lod = 0;
```

You can use screen-space size or dot-product angle from the camera as well for more precise control.

Integrating LOD into Animation Evaluation

Once you know which LOD level each character is in, update their animation accordingly.

Example:

```
switch (entity.lod) {

    case 0:

        EvaluateFullBlendGraph(entity);

        break;

    case 1:

        EvaluateSimplifiedGraph(entity);

        break;

    case 2:

        EvaluateLoopingClipOnly(entity);

        break;

    case 3:

        // Skip animation entirely
```

```
        break;
}
```

Make sure each version of the evaluation code writes a consistent pose format (`PoseComponent`) so the render system can still function without branching.

GPU Skinning LOD

Even if the CPU sends you a pose, you don't always need to skin every character the same way. GPU cost can be reduced by:

Skinning fewer bones (e.g. skip fingers or facial joints)

Using simpler shaders with fewer blend weights

Caching previous bone matrices for use across several frames (temporal reuse)

Shader example with LOD:

```
#ifdef LOD_HIGH
    // Full bone matrix blend (4 weights)
#else
    // Simple blend (2 weights)
#endif
```

At draw time, choose a simpler shader variant or precompiled material based on `entity.lod`.

Pose Freezing and Frame Skipping

For characters in the far background, you don't need to animate them every frame. You can update their pose every N frames or even freeze it for several seconds at a time.

Example:

```
if (frameCount % 5 != 0 && entity.lod == 2) {

    // Skip update, use previously cached pose

    continue;
```

```
}
```

This is great for crowd characters, audience members, or large-scale background armies. They're still moving, but slowly and at very low cost.

Culling Overhead and Safety

Even culling logic adds CPU cost if done poorly. Profile your culling code. Use bounding spheres instead of AABBs when possible—they're faster to test against the frustum.

Make sure to **never** cull or LOD a character if:

The camera is attached to them

They affect gameplay (e.g. local player, active enemy)

They are interacting with physics or another actor

Always include overrides or flags to mark characters as "always update" or "never skip."

Debugging Tools for LOD and Culling

To validate your system:

Draw bounding boxes or spheres for characters, color-coded by LOD level

Overlay text tags showing LOD tier and update frequency

Log or count characters culled per frame to catch anomalies

Example:

```
DebugDrawText(entityPosition, "LOD: 2",
glm::vec3(1, 1, 0));
```

This lets you instantly spot if a foreground character is being downgraded or a background one is wasting resources.

Exercise: Implement Animation LOD in Your Engine

Add a `lod` field to your animation or render component.

Assign LOD based on camera distance every frame.

Create a simplified animation graph for LOD 1.

Add a loop-only pose playback for LOD 2.

Skip evaluation entirely for LOD 3.

Validate visually using color overlays or text.

You should see your CPU and GPU cost decrease dramatically with hundreds of characters, while maintaining visual fidelity in the player's focus area.

Animation LOD and culling are not luxuries—they are essential parts of a real-time animation system. They allow you to scale up character counts, support large environments, and maintain frame rate without sacrificing quality where it matters. With proper culling logic, frame skipping, and hierarchical LOD graphs, you can control every part of the animation pipeline dynamically based on importance and visibility.

13.4 Reducing Memory Usage and Runtime Cost

A high-fidelity animation system doesn't just put pressure on the CPU and GPU—it can also consume substantial memory. Keyframes, blend graphs, inverse bind poses, pose buffers, and per-entity runtime state all add up fast. This becomes a problem when you scale to hundreds of characters or support large animation libraries.

Reducing memory usage isn't just about compression—it's about smart structuring of your data, minimizing duplication, avoiding waste, and delaying or skipping allocation where possible. Every pointer you eliminate, every redundant buffer you remove, and every structure you flatten contributes to a faster, lighter, and more scalable animation runtime.

Use Shared, Read-Only Animation Data

Most characters using the same rig and animations can share all static data:

Skeleton structure

Animation clips

Inverse bind matrices

Joint names or metadata

This data should never be duplicated per entity.

```cpp
struct Skeleton {
    std::vector<Joint> joints; // read-only
    std::vector<glm::mat4> inverseBindMatrices;
};

struct AnimationClip {
    std::vector<KeyframeTrack> tracks;
    float duration;
};
```

Use `std::shared_ptr` or a global asset registry to reference these from each character:

```cpp
struct SkeletonComponent {

    std::shared_ptr<Skeleton> skeleton;

};



struct AnimationComponent {

    std::shared_ptr<AnimationClip> currentClip;

};
```

If you're duplicating these per character, you're wasting megabytes for no benefit.

Pre-allocate Pose Buffers and Avoid Reallocation

Each animated character requires at least two pose buffers:

`localPose`: joint-local transforms

`globalPose`: world-space joint transforms

Instead of allocating these vectors on each update, allocate them once when the entity is initialized:

```
void InitPose(PoseComponent& pose, size_t
jointCount) {

    pose.localPose.resize(jointCount);

    pose.globalPose.resize(jointCount);

}
```

Never do this:

```
// BAD: causes reallocations every frame

std::vector<Transform> localPose =
EvaluatePose(...);
```

Also, ensure they use proper memory alignment and pooling when needed. If hundreds of characters share the same joint count, consider pooling buffers to reduce allocation churn.

Minimize Per-Frame Animation State

Only store what must be updated per character per frame.

Good examples:

Current node in the blend graph

Playback time

Transition weights (if blending)

Per-layer or per-channel blend factors (optional)

Avoid per-frame dynamic memory. Avoid storing past poses unless you need them for delta motion or blend-back. Never keep keyframe arrays or clip data inside runtime state—use references instead.

Compress Keyframes on Load

Uncompressed animation keyframe data is one of the largest contributors to runtime memory use. Even a single character with full-body motion can require thousands of floats per clip.

Techniques to reduce this:

Quaternion Compression

Instead of storing full 4-float quaternions, store 3 and reconstruct the fourth:

```
// Store x, y, z — infer w
float w = sqrt(1.0f - x*x - y*y - z*z);
```

You can quantize the 3 floats to 16-bit integers for additional savings.

Keyframe Reduction

Use error-tolerant curve simplification. For each joint:

Compare the linear interpolation error to an epsilon threshold.

Remove intermediate keys if the error is below the threshold.

This reduces file size and memory while preserving perceptual fidelity.

Delta Encoding and Run-Length Storage

Store transforms as deltas from a base pose or previous key:

```
deltaPosition = currentPosition - previousPosition;
```

If a joint doesn't move, store a flag and skip storing keyframes entirely.

Use Runtime Masks and Bone Filters

If you're only animating the upper body for a particular layer or character, you can avoid updating and storing the full pose.

Use a **bone mask** to restrict which joints are included in evaluation:

```
std::vector<bool> boneMask; // true = animate,
false = skip
```

When evaluating pose data:

```
for (size_t i = 0; i < jointCount; ++i) {
    if (!boneMask[i]) continue;
    // Apply pose update
}
```

This helps for upper-body-only overlays (e.g., shooting while running), facial animation, or layered control rigs.

Use Animation Clips with Shared Sampling Tables

Many animation systems resample every joint at every time point. Instead, decouple **time steps** from **per-joint samples** by using a shared keyframe time table.

```
struct KeyframeTrack {

    std::vector<float> keyTimes; // shared across
all joints

    std::vector<glm::vec3> translations;

    std::vector<glm::quat> rotations;

};
```

All joints can use the same keyTimes if sampled at the same rate. This reduces storage cost significantly.

Use Bone Index Ranges to Prune Skinned Meshes

Most mesh rigs include more bones than are used in a specific mesh. When loading skinning data:

Analyze the vertex influences.

Store only the subset of joints actually referenced.

```
std::unordered_set<int> usedJointIndices =
ExtractInfluencedJoints(mesh.vertices);
```

This reduces skinning matrix upload size and avoids sending irrelevant data to the GPU.

Pool Bone Matrices in a Shared Buffer

Instead of giving each character its own GPU buffer for bone matrices, allocate a single large dynamic buffer and pack each character's matrices into separate aligned regions:

```
const size_t maxCharacters = 100;

const size_t maxBones = 64;

const size_t matrixSize = sizeof(glm::mat4);

const size_t stride = AlignTo(matrixSize *
maxBones, 256); // GPU UBO alignment


GpuBuffer boneBuffer =
CreateDynamicBuffer(maxCharacters * stride);
```

Each frame:

```
void* dst = mappedPtr + characterIndex * stride;

memcpy(dst, characterBoneMatrices.data(),
matrixSize * numBones);
```

This avoids hundreds of small allocations and allows efficient dynamic offset binding per character.

Exercise: Compress and Evaluate a Real Animation Clip

Load a sample keyframe animation in uncompressed format (e.g. 30fps, 50 joints, 300 frames).

Quantize each joint's translation to 16-bit per axis.

Convert quaternions to 3-float compressed form.

Remove intermediate keyframes within a small error threshold.

Compare the memory size before and after compression.

Replay the animation and visually verify it still looks correct.

You'll see how much redundant data exists even in professionally authored clips—and how little perceptual loss occurs when removed.

Reducing memory usage in animation systems is not just about shrinking your binary size—it directly impacts load times, runtime performance, and how many characters you can animate per frame. With careful data design, shared references, keyframe compression, pose memory pooling, and smart LOD aware evaluation, you can build an animation system that scales gracefully from indie games to large-scale open-world simulations.

Chapter 14: Case Study – Third-Person Character Animation

Up to this point, we've covered the architecture, math, data structures, GPU integration, debugging strategies, and performance optimizations required to build a scalable animation system. But theory isn't enough. This chapter applies everything you've learned to build a real, playable third-person character animation system—one that includes a full state machine, proper motion blending, procedural foot IK, and runtime integration.

We'll start from a clean base and build up to a live, testable character controller that blends idle, walk, run, and jump animations, aligns feet to the ground using IK, and integrates weapon aiming using joint overrides. Then we'll test and validate it in a working environment.

14.1 Designing a Complete State Machine

A third-person character in a real-time application—whether it's a game or a simulation—relies on more than just linear animation playback. You need a robust **animation state machine** that interprets inputs, transitions smoothly between states, and ensures continuity between motion clips. A well-structured state machine doesn't just make characters feel responsive—it prevents visual artifacts, sync issues, and janky transitions.

An animation state machine organizes your character's motion logic into well-defined **states** and **transitions**. Each state plays an animation clip or blend and defines conditions for moving to another state. This keeps your animation logic predictable and modular.

Without a state machine, you'll end up with dozens of `if-else` blocks scattered throughout your update code—hard to read, harder to debug, and nearly impossible to scale.

Define Your States Clearly

Start with a minimal, extensible enum to represent states. Each state should map to one or more animation clips or blend nodes.

```
enum class AnimState {
    Idle,
```

```
    Walk,
    Run,
    Jump,
    Fall,
    Land
};
```

Store your state machine per character. This allows each instance to track its own animation playback independently.

```
struct AnimationStateMachine {

    AnimState currentState = AnimState::Idle;

    AnimState nextState = AnimState::Idle;

    float playbackTime = 0.0f;

    float transitionDuration = 0.2f;

    float transitionTimer = 0.0f;

    bool inTransition = false;

};
```

This struct will evolve as we add blend logic and control timing, but keep it minimal to begin.

3. Input-Driven State Transitions

The state machine doesn't work on its own—it responds to inputs. In a third-person setup, you typically have:

A movement vector from the left stick or WASD keys

A jump trigger

Grounded state from physics

Let's define a control struct:

```
struct CharacterControl {
    glm::vec3 velocity;
```

```
    bool isGrounded;
    bool wantsToJump;
};
```

From this, derive movement speed:

float speed = glm::length(control.velocity);

And then determine target state:

```
AnimState DetermineTargetState(const
CharacterControl& control) {
    if (!control.isGrounded) {
        return control.velocity.y > 0.0f ?
AnimState::Jump : AnimState::Fall;
    }

    if (control.wantsToJump) {
        return AnimState::Jump;
    }

    if (speed < 0.1f) return AnimState::Idle;
    if (speed < 3.0f) return AnimState::Walk;
    return AnimState::Run;
}
```

This logic isolates the decision-making from the transition mechanics, making it easier to change later without touching playback logic.

Managing State Transitions and Blending

When a transition occurs, you typically blend from one pose to another over time. First, compare the current and target state:

```
AnimState target = DetermineTargetState(control);



if (target != sm.currentState && !sm.inTransition)
{

    sm.nextState = target;

    sm.inTransition = true;
```

```
    sm.transitionTimer = 0.0f;

}
```

During each update tick, update playback time and transition:

```
float dt = GetDeltaTime();

if (sm.inTransition) {
    sm.transitionTimer += dt;
    float t = sm.transitionTimer /
sm.transitionDuration;

    if (t >= 1.0f) {
        sm.currentState = sm.nextState;
        sm.inTransition = false;
        sm.playbackTime = 0.0f;
    }
} else {
    sm.playbackTime += dt;
}
```

This gives you deterministic state transitions and proper clip restart logic.

Pose Evaluation Per State

Each state corresponds to a clip or a blend tree. During evaluation, blend the two active poses (from current and next states) if in transition, otherwise just evaluate one.

```
Pose EvaluateCharacterPose(const
AnimationStateMachine& sm, float deltaTime) {
    Pose currentPose =
EvaluateClip(sm.currentState, sm.playbackTime);

    if (!sm.inTransition) {
        return currentPose;
    }

    float t = sm.transitionTimer /
sm.transitionDuration;
    Pose nextPose = EvaluateClip(sm.nextState,
sm.playbackTime);
```

```
    return LerpPose(currentPose, nextPose,
glm::smoothstep(0.0f, 1.0f, t));
}
```

`EvaluateClip` samples a pose from the animation clip based on time, and `LerpPose` blends the two poses bone by bone.

State-Specific Timing and Logic

Some states need special treatment. For example, jumping may have a specific clip length, and you may want to transition out only after the clip ends.

Extend your state handler like this:

```
if (sm.currentState == AnimState::Jump &&
sm.playbackTime > jumpClip.duration) {

    sm.currentState = AnimState::Fall;

    sm.playbackTime = 0.0f;

}
```

Likewise, use landing detection to switch from `Fall` to `Land`, then back to locomotion.

Visual Debugging Support

Add tools to print or render the current state for live debugging:

```
DebugDrawText(character.position + glm::vec3(0,
2.0f, 0), StateToString(sm.currentState),
glm::vec3(1, 1, 0));
```

This helps you verify state transitions in real time.

Exercise: Build a Runtime State Machine Test

Set up a simple third-person controller with velocity input.

Implement a state machine using the structure above.

Assign mock animation clips (use distinct poses per state for testing).

Evaluate and blend poses in real-time.

Render the result using debug skeleton visualization.

Trigger jump manually using keyboard input or controller.

Observe how transitions respond to real input and physics. Ensure transitions are smooth, clips don't reset too early, and states return correctly after landings.

Your animation state machine is the backbone of responsive character motion. It governs when animations start, stop, blend, or shift between modes—and makes the difference between a character that feels janky and one that feels alive. With a clean structure, modular logic, and responsive input integration, your state machine will scale with your game while remaining easy to maintain and debug.

14.2 Blending Idle, Walk, Run, and Jump

In a third-person character system, one of the most important factors for immersion and control fidelity is how smoothly the animation responds to movement input. Characters that snap between idle and running, or glitch during jumps, immediately break believability. This is where motion blending becomes essential.

Drive Blending from Player Input and Movement

Start by extracting the **speed** from your movement input. This will be the primary scalar used to blend between idle, walk, and run.

```
float speed = glm::length(control.velocity);
```

Clamp and normalize this value for blending:

```
float walkSpeed = 2.0f;

float runSpeed  = 6.0f;

float blendFactor = glm::clamp((speed - walkSpeed)
/ (runSpeed - walkSpeed), 0.0f, 1.0f);
```

If `speed` is 0, you're fully in idle. If it's greater than or equal to `runSpeed`, you're fully in run. Between those, blend gradually.

Sample Poses from Base Movement Clips

You need three base clips:

Idle: looping idle pose

Walk: looping walk forward

Run: looping run forward

At a given `playbackTime`, sample each pose:

```
Pose idlePose = SampleAnimation(idleClip, playbackTime);

Pose walkPose = SampleAnimation(walkClip, playbackTime);

Pose runPose  = SampleAnimation(runClip, playbackTime);
```

Now blend in two stages:

First blend between idle and walk

Then blend between that and run

```
Pose blendA = LerpPose(idlePose, walkPose,
glm::smoothstep(0.0f, 0.5f, blendFactor));

Pose finalPose = LerpPose(blendA, runPose,
glm::smoothstep(0.5f, 1.0f, blendFactor));
```

Use `smoothstep` to ensure the motion transitions feel natural and non-linear.

Match Playback Speed to Movement Speed

To keep the feet from sliding or stuttering, adjust the animation playback rate based on movement speed:

```
float walkClipSpeed = 2.0f; // m/s
float runClipSpeed  = 6.0f;

float desiredSpeed = glm::length(control.velocity);

float walkWeight = 1.0f - blendFactor;
float runWeight  = blendFactor;
```

```
float blendClipSpeed = walkWeight * walkClipSpeed +
runWeight * runClipSpeed;

float playbackSpeed = desiredSpeed /
blendClipSpeed;
```

This synchronizes the character's velocity with the looped walk/run animations.

Apply this when updating `playbackTime`:

playbackTime += deltaTime * playbackSpeed;

Handling Direction and Strafe Blends (Optional)

For more advanced control, use a 2D blend space with both **speed** and **direction**:

X-axis = movement direction angle (e.g., forward, left, right)

Y-axis = speed

Use multiple clips: walk forward, walk left, walk right, run forward, etc.

Sample and blend with bilinear or barycentric weights. While outside this chapter's scope, it becomes critical for strafe systems or root motion locomotion.

Jumping and Vertical Transitions

Jumping introduces vertical dynamics that aren't easily covered by speed alone. The character is no longer grounded, and vertical velocity becomes meaningful.

When jumping:

Start with a **JumpStart** clip that plays once

Transition to **Fall** with a looping **Airborne** or **FallLoop** animation

Blend into **Land** once the character hits the ground

Jump Pose Evaluation

```
if (state == AnimState::Jump) {
```

```
    Pose jumpPose = SampleAnimation(jumpClip,
jumpTime);
    Pose airPose  = SampleAnimation(fallLoopClip,
fallTime);

    float t = glm::clamp(jumpTime /
jumpClip.duration, 0.0f, 1.0f);
    finalPose = LerpPose(jumpPose, airPose, t);
}
```

When grounded again, play **Land** clip:

```
if (wasAirborne && isGrounded) {

    state = AnimState::Land;

    landTime = 0.0f;

}
```

After the `landClip.duration`, resume from movement logic.

Pose Blending Function

Ensure your `LerpPose()` function blends both translation and rotation of joints:

```
Pose LerpPose(const Pose& a, const Pose& b, float
t) {
    Pose out;
    size_t jointCount = a.jointTransforms.size();
    out.jointTransforms.resize(jointCount);

    for (size_t i = 0; i < jointCount; ++i) {
        out.jointTransforms[i].position = glm::mix(
            a.jointTransforms[i].position,
            b.jointTransforms[i].position,
            t
        );

        out.jointTransforms[i].rotation =
glm::slerp(
            a.jointTransforms[i].rotation,
```

```
                b.jointTransforms[i].rotation,
            t.
        );
    }

    return out;
}
```

This guarantees bone transforms blend smoothly—no harsh snapping, no flipped orientations.

Testing Blends with Visual Feedback

To verify blending correctness:

Toggle between speeds using keyboard input (0 for idle, 1 for walk, 2 for run)

Overlay joint names or draw foot paths to inspect smoothness

Debug log blend weights and final animation state

You can also draw a real-time blend factor indicator on-screen to watch the interpolation visually:

```
DrawBar(blendFactor, glm::vec3(1.0f, 1.0f, 0.0f));
```

This helps catch unexpected jumps or bad transitions in tuning.

Exercise: Implement Blended Movement Locomotion

Load three clips: Idle, Walk, and Run.

Compute blendFactor from movement speed.

Adjust playback speed dynamically based on actual movement.

Sample and blend poses every frame using LerpPose().

Test by moving the character with a gamepad or keyboard.

Add Jump/Fall logic using a separate vertical state transition.

The goal is a fully functional third-person locomotion controller that looks visually seamless and reacts immediately to input.

Blending is not just about interpolating frames—it's about aligning visuals with player expectations. Done right, it hides the complexity of state transitions, keeps feet from sliding, and turns abrupt motion changes into believable animation. By blending idle, walk, run, and jump with timing-aware pose evaluation and speed-based control, you deliver fluid, polished character movement that feels responsive and grounded.

14.3 IK-Based Foot Placement and Weapon Aiming

When you're building a character system that needs to feel grounded, physically consistent, and immersive, it's not enough to simply play a nice walk or run animation. The environment changes. Characters stand on slopes, aim at different elevations, or shift weight during combat. That's where **Inverse Kinematics (IK)** becomes a critical tool. IK enables you to dynamically adjust joint chains in response to context—placing feet accurately on uneven ground and aiming weapons precisely at targets without needing dozens of baked animations.

IK-Based Foot Placement

Foot IK ensures that each foot aligns to the surface under it—accounting for terrain height, slope, and even subtle inclines like stairs or ramps. Without it, characters will float, clip into geometry, or walk in a visually disconnected way.

How It Works

At runtime:

Detect where the foot should go (target position).

Use a two-bone IK solver to adjust hip and knee joints.

Optionally rotate the foot to match surface normal.

Blend the IK result with the original pose for stability.

Step 1: Raycast From the Foot

Cast a ray down from the current foot position to find the ground.

```
glm::vec3 footWorldPos =
glm::vec3(globalPose[foot.JointIndex][3]);

glm::vec3 down = glm::vec3(0.0f, -1.0f, 0.0f);



RaycastHit hit;

if (PhysicsRaycast(footWorldPos + glm::vec3(0.0f,
0.1f, 0.0f), down, 0.3f, &hit)) {

    glm::vec3 ikTarget = hit.point;

    glm::vec3 surfaceNormal = hit.normal;

    ...

}
```

Make sure you cast from just above the foot to avoid missing the ground due to pose compression.

Step 2: Solve Two-Bone IK

We'll use a common analytic solution for two-bone chains—hip, knee, and foot. Your inputs are:

Hip position (start of the chain)

Knee and foot joints from your skeleton

IK target (where you want the foot to end up)

Use cosine law to solve joint angles.

Example solver:

```
bool SolveTwoBoneIK(
    const glm::vec3& hip,
    const glm::vec3& knee,
    const glm::vec3& foot,
    const glm::vec3& target,
    float upperLen,
    float lowerLen,
```

```
    glm::vec3& outNewKnee,
    glm::vec3& outNewFoot)
{
    glm::vec3 dir = glm::normalize(target - hip);
    float dist = glm::clamp(glm::length(target -
hip), 0.001f, upperLen + lowerLen - 0.001f);

    float a = upperLen;
    float b = lowerLen;
    float c = dist;

    float angleA = acosf(glm::clamp((b*b + c*c -
a*a) / (2 * b * c), -1.0f, 1.0f));
    float bendDir = 1.0f; // Or use a bend hint
vector

    glm::vec3 mid = hip + dir * (a * sin(angleA));

    outNewKnee = mid;
    outNewFoot = target;
    return true;
}
```

Update your local transforms or overwrite the global pose directly depending on your engine's structure.

Step 3: Apply Foot Rotation (Optional)

Align the foot joint to the surface normal using a rotation that matches local Y-up to surface normal.

```
glm::vec3 forward = ExtractForwardFromJoint(); //
Based on character direction

glm::vec3 right =
glm::normalize(glm::cross(forward, surfaceNormal));

glm::vec3 adjustedForward =
glm::normalize(glm::cross(surfaceNormal, right));

glm::mat3 rotationMatrix = glm::mat3(right,
surfaceNormal, adjustedForward);
```

```
glm::quat finalRotation =
glm::quat_cast(rotationMatrix);
```

Use this rotation to override the foot joint orientation.

Step 4: Blend Smoothly Into IK Result

Avoid hard snapping by interpolating between the original and adjusted pose.

```
float ikWeight = ComputeFootContactWeight(...); //
Based on grounded status or phase

pose[footJoint].position =
glm::mix(original.position, ikPosition, ikWeight);

pose[footJoint].rotation =
glm::slerp(original.rotation, ikRotation,
ikWeight);
```

Apply similar blending to hip and knee if you're modifying those joints too.

IK-Based Weapon Aiming

In aiming systems, you often want the upper body (or at least the arms) to rotate to face a target, even if the base animation doesn't. IK is great for this.

Step 1: Choose Joint Chain

You need a chain of joints from the spine through the shoulder and upper arm, possibly including the hand.

For example:

```
std::vector<int> spineChain = {

    jointMap["spine1"],

    jointMap["spine2"],

    jointMap["neck"],

    jointMap["right_shoulder"],

    jointMap["right_elbow"],
```

```
    jointMap["right_hand"]

};
```

Step 2: Compute Look-At Rotation

Calculate a rotation from current aim direction to target direction.

```
glm::vec3 jointWorldPos =
glm::vec3(globalPose[spineChain.front()][3]);

glm::vec3 currentForward =
ExtractForward(globalPose[spineChain.front()]);

glm::vec3 targetDir = glm::normalize(target -
jointWorldPos);



glm::quat lookRotation =
glm::rotation(currentForward, targetDir);
```

You can clamp or damp this rotation to keep it subtle.

Step 3: Distribute Rotation Down the Chain

Apply portions of the rotation down the joint chain so that the movement is smooth and believable.

```
float weightPerJoint = 1.0f / spineChain.size();

for (size_t i = 0; i < spineChain.size(); ++i) {

    float t = (i + 1) * weightPerJoint;

    glm::quat blended = glm::slerp(glm::quat(1, 0,
0, 0), lookRotation, t);

    pose[spineChain[i]].rotation = blended *
pose[spineChain[i]].rotation;

}
```

Apply this **after pose evaluation and before GPU upload.**

Real-World Example: Character Aiming with Upper Body Override

Player rotates camera to aim.

Base animation (walk, run) plays as normal.

After pose evaluation, override upper spine/shoulder joints with IK aim.

GPU receives updated pose, and the gun tracks precisely to the target.

This avoids requiring hundreds of baked aim offsets and works for any aim direction.

Debug Visualization

For development:

Draw lines from hip to foot target

Draw aim vectors and look-at axes

Color joints affected by IK

```
DebugDrawLine(hip, footTarget, glm::vec3(1, 0, 0));

DebugDrawArrow(spineJoint, spineJoint + aimDir *
0.5f, glm::vec3(0, 1, 0));
```

This confirms that your inputs and outputs are aligned properly.

IK isn't a silver bullet—but used correctly, it's a powerful complement to baked animation. It gives you physical plausibility and runtime reactivity without multiplying asset cost. Foot placement ensures characters don't look disconnected from the terrain, and upper-body IK makes weapon aiming crisp and believable. When integrated as a post-process step after pose evaluation but before rendering, IK gives your third-person character the final polish it needs to feel like part of the world.

14.4 Exporting and Testing in a Real-Time Demo

By this point, you've built a complete character animation system: a working state machine, smooth motion blending, procedural IK enhancements, and pose evaluation logic. But all of that is theory until you see it in action. This section focuses on how to **export animation assets**, **load and use them in a real-time engine**, and **interactively test your full third-person character controller** in a game-like environment.

Exporting Assets from a DCC Tool

Rig and Animation Preparation

Before exporting, ensure your character meets the following criteria in Blender (or another tool):

One armature (skeleton) with consistent naming

No constraints or modifiers applied to animation bones (bake transforms)

Consistent scale and orientation (typically +Y forward, +Z up)

Animation clips clearly named and separated into **actions** or **takes**

If you use Blender:

Use one `.blend` file with separate actions for Idle, Walk, Run, Jump, Land, etc.

Export using the **glTF 2.0** exporter:

Include **Animations**

Export in **Y-up**

Apply transform (scale and rotation baked)

Use `+z up` or reorient post-import depending on your engine

`export/character.glb`

    ↳ `Contains: mesh, skeleton, all animation clips`

Alternatively, you can export `.fbx` and process it with a pipeline like **Assimp**.

Loading Assets in Code

Assuming you're using Assimp to load the glTF or FBX file, extract:

The **mesh** (for rendering and skinning)

The **skeleton hierarchy** (joint names, parent indices)

The **inverse bind pose matrices**

The **animation clips**, each with keyframes per joint

Sample loader:

```
Assimp::Importer importer;

const aiScene* scene =
importer.ReadFile("character.glb",
aiProcessPreset_TargetRealtime_MaxQuality);



Skeleton skeleton = LoadSkeleton(scene);

std::unordered_map<std::string, AnimationClip>
clips = LoadAnimations(scene, skeleton);

SkinnedMesh mesh = LoadMesh(scene, skeleton);
```

Structure each `AnimationClip` as:

```
struct AnimationClip {
    float duration;
    float frameRate;
    std::vector<Track> tracks; // One per joint
};

struct Track {
    std::vector<float> times;
    std::vector<glm::vec3> positions;
    std::vector<glm::quat> rotations;
};
```

This format gives you per-joint interpolation capability and clean time-based sampling.

Real-Time Character Controller Integration

Hook the animation system to a third-person controller:

Map WASD or gamepad input to movement direction

Use a physics or character controller to produce a velocity vector

Feed velocity and grounded status into the animation state machine

Each frame, evaluate the pose using the current animation state

Apply procedural IK (e.g., foot placement)

Upload bone matrices to the GPU and render the skinned mesh

Main Loop Snippet

```
CharacterControl input = ReadPlayerInput();

UpdateCharacterPhysics(input);


AnimationStateMachine& sm = character.animState;

sm.Update(input, deltaTime);


Pose pose = EvaluateCharacterPose(sm, deltaTime);

ApplyFootIK(pose, character.groundContacts);


UploadPoseToGPU(pose, character.skeleton);

RenderCharacter(character.mesh,
character.material);
```

You should be able to move, jump, and land while seeing correct animation transitions, foot alignment, and aiming behavior.

Visual Debugging and Validation

During testing, build in as much debug visualization as possible:

Draw Skeletons: visualize joint transforms

Joint Labels: print joint names at world positions

Animation State: overlay current animation state as on-screen text

Motion Trails: show root joint motion over time

```
DebugDrawSkeleton(pose.globalTransforms,
character.skeleton);

DebugDrawText(character.position + glm::vec3(0,
2.0f, 0), StateToString(sm.currentState));
```

Use ImGui or a debug HUD to toggle overlays and inspect real-time data.

Test Cases for Real-Time Demo

Case 1: Grounded Movement

Walk and run using analog input or key pressure

Watch for correct idle-walk-run transitions

Verify animation speed scales with velocity (no foot slipping)

Case 2: Jump and Fall

Press jump and validate jump pose transitions into airborne

Observe fall looping until ground contact

On landing, play land animation and return to movement state

Case 3: Slope Walking with Foot IK

Walk on a ramp or uneven terrain

Confirm each foot aligns with the surface

Look for smooth transition between FK and IK-adjusted joints

Case 4: Weapon Aiming

Enable aiming mode and lock onto a target

Verify spine and shoulder rotate to match target direction

Ensure aiming blends over the base pose (walk/run/idle)

Example: Animation Graph Summary

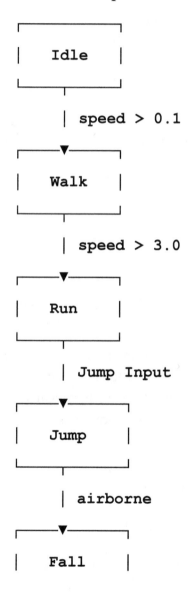

```
    ┌──────────────┐
    |    Idle      |
    └──────┬───────┘
           | speed > 0.1
    ┌──────▼───────┐
    |    Walk      |
    └──────┬───────┘
           | speed > 3.0
    ┌──────▼───────┐
    |    Run       |
    └──────┬───────┘
           | Jump Input
    ┌──────▼───────┐
    |    Jump      |
    └──────┬───────┘
           | airborne
    ┌──────▼───────┐
    |    Fall      |
```

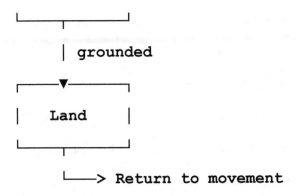

```
    └───────┬───────┘
           │ grounded
    ┌───────▼───────┐
    │     Land      │
    └───────┬───────┘
           └────> Return to movement
```

This simple flow is fully driven by input and state, with each state triggering and blending its respective animation.

Exercise: Build and Playtest Your Demo

Export a rigged character from Blender with all clips.

Load mesh, skeleton, and clips into your engine.

Implement the animation state machine and blending logic.

Integrate basic input, physics, and control flow.

Visualize animation state and motion paths.

Walk, run, jump, land, aim, and observe transitions.

Optimize and debug using the profiler and debug overlay tools.

Animation systems don't live in isolation—they operate inside engines, alongside physics, rendering, and input. Exporting, loading, and testing your character in a real-time loop is the final proof that your system is working. This chapter has shown how to connect every technical layer—from asset creation to GPU skinning—into a responsive, interactive demo.

Appendices

Appendix A: Math Reference for Game Animators

This appendix is a concise yet complete reference of the math concepts and operations every game animator should understand. Whether you're blending poses, solving IK, interpolating transforms, or skinning vertices on the GPU, animation systems rely heavily on vector and matrix math. The goal here is not to teach math from scratch but to provide clear, practical definitions and formulas you'll use daily.

All examples assume you're using a right-handed coordinate system and `glm`-style conventions (`vec3`, `quat`, `mat4`), which apply to most modern C++ game engines.

Vectors (`glm::vec3`)

Definition: A vector represents a direction and magnitude in 3D space.

`glm::vec3 a(1.0f, 0.0f, 0.0f);`

`glm::vec3 b(0.0f, 1.0f, 0.0f);`

Operations:

Addition: `a + b`

Subtraction: `a - b`

Scalar multiplication: `a * 2.0f`

Normalize: `glm::normalize(a)`

Length: `glm::length(a)`

Dot product: `glm::dot(a, b)`

Cross product: `glm::cross(a, b)`

Use Cases:

Velocity vectors

Bone directions

Surface normals

Motion deltas

Quaternions (`glm::quat`)

Definition: A quaternion represents rotation in 3D without suffering from gimbal lock.

```
glm::quat q1 = glm::angleAxis(glm::radians(90.0f),
glm::vec3(0, 1, 0));
```

Operations:

Identity: `glm::quat(1, 0, 0, 0)`

Normalize: `glm::normalize(q1)`

Inverse: `glm::inverse(q1)`

Multiply (compose rotations): `q1 * q2`

Apply to vector: `q1 * vector`

Slerp (smooth interpolation): `glm::slerp(q1, q2, t)`

Use Cases:

Joint orientation

Rotating bones

Blending animations

Smooth camera and character rotation

Transforms

Definition: A transform represents a position, orientation, and scale—usually stored as a matrix.

```
glm::mat4 transform =
glm::translate(glm::mat4(1.0f), position) *
                     glm::mat4_cast(rotation) *
```

```
                              glm::scale(glm::mat4(1.0f),
scale);
```

Decompose matrix:

```
glm::vec3 scale;

glm::quat rotation;

glm::vec3 position;

glm::vec3 skew;

glm::vec4 perspective;

glm::decompose(transform, scale, rotation,
position, skew, perspective);
```

Use Cases:

Converting local to global joint transforms

Skinning

Camera/view/projection matrices

Pose Interpolation

Linear interpolation (LERP) for positions:

```
glm::vec3 blended = glm::mix(a, b, t);
```

Spherical interpolation (SLERP) for rotations:

```
glm::quat blendedRot = glm::slerp(rotA, rotB, t);
```

Full transform blend:

```
Transform BlendTransform(const Transform& a, const
Transform& b, float t) {
    Transform result;
    result.position = glm::mix(a.position,
b.position, t);
    result.rotation = glm::slerp(a.rotation,
b.rotation, t);
```

```
    result.scale     = glm::mix(a.scale, b.scale,
t);
    return result;
}
```

Matrix Multiplication and Hierarchies

To propagate transforms through a skeleton hierarchy:

```
glm::mat4 globalPose[i] = parentMatrix *
localPose[i];
```

For skinning:

```
glm::mat4 skinMatrix = globalPose[i] *
inverseBindPose[i];
```

Inverse Kinematics (Two-Bone)

Cosine law to compute angle:

```
float angle = acos((a*a + b*b - c*c) / (2*a*b));
```

Use this in solving two-bone IK where:

a is upper leg length

b is lower leg length

c is the distance to target

Final joint positions can be solved geometrically or analytically using vector math.

Axis-Angle and LookAt

Convert direction to quaternion:

```
glm::quat q = glm::rotation(fromVector, toVector);
```

Build LookAt rotation:

```
glm::vec3 forward = glm::normalize(target -
origin);
glm::vec3 right = glm::normalize(glm::cross(up,
forward));
```

```
glm::vec3 newUp = glm::cross(forward, right);

glm::mat3 rot = glm::mat3(right, newUp, forward);
glm::quat lookAtQuat = glm::quat_cast(rot);
```

Bounding Volumes

Axis-Aligned Bounding Box (AABB):

```
struct AABB {

    glm::vec3 min;

    glm::vec3 max;

};
```

Transforming an AABB requires recomputing min/max from transformed corners. For animation culling, test bone AABBs against the camera frustum to skip pose evaluation.

The math behind animation is not abstract—it's mechanical, practical, and repeatable. With this reference, you now have all the vector, matrix, and quaternion tools needed to build robust animation features from procedural motion to GPU skinning.

You'll revisit these fundamentals constantly when debugging IK solvers, visualizing skeletons, optimizing pose blending, or adjusting real-time foot placement. Keep this appendix handy—it's your toolkit for technical animation.

Appendix B: Shader Snippets – GLSL and Vulkan

This appendix contains practical, ready-to-use shader code snippets for real-time character animation with a focus on skeletal skinning, animation blending, and GPU-friendly memory handling. All snippets are written in GLSL and suitable for use with OpenGL 4.6 or Vulkan 1.3 shader modules. The goal is to provide well-documented building blocks you can copy, adapt, and integrate directly into your graphics pipeline.

Vertex Skinning Shader (Linear Blend Skinning)

This shader deforms a character mesh by blending up to 4 bone matrices per vertex.

GLSL Vertex Shader:

```
#version 450

layout(location = 0) in vec3 inPosition;
layout(location = 1) in vec3 inNormal;
layout(location = 2) in vec2 inTexCoord;
layout(location = 3) in ivec4 inBoneIndices;
layout(location = 4) in vec4 inBoneWeights;

layout(set = 0, binding = 0) uniform BoneMatrices {
    mat4 bones[128]; // Adjust max bones as needed
} uBones;

layout(set = 1, binding = 0) uniform MVP {
    mat4 model;
    mat4 view;
    mat4 projection;
} uMVP;

layout(location = 0) out vec2 fragTexCoord;
layout(location = 1) out vec3 fragNormal;

void main() {
    mat4 skinMatrix =
        inBoneWeights.x *
uBones.bones[inBoneIndices.x] +
        inBoneWeights.y *
uBones.bones[inBoneIndices.y] +
        inBoneWeights.z *
uBones.bones[inBoneIndices.z] +
        inBoneWeights.w *
uBones.bones[inBoneIndices.w];

    vec4 worldPosition = skinMatrix *
vec4(inPosition, 1.0);
    vec4 worldNormal   = skinMatrix *
vec4(inNormal, 0.0);
```

```
    gl_Position = uMVP.projection * uMVP.view *
worldPosition;
    fragTexCoord = inTexCoord;
    fragNormal   = normalize(worldNormal.xyz);
}
```

Uniform Buffer Definition for Vulkan

Define your UBO in C++ and match the layout in GLSL.

C++ Uniform Buffer Struct (std140 layout):

```
struct alignas(16) BoneMatricesUBO {

    glm::mat4 bones[128]; // Each mat4 is aligned
to 16 bytes

};
```

GLSL Match:

```
layout(std140, set = 0, binding = 0) uniform
BoneMatrices {
    mat4 bones[128];
};
```

Make sure to use VK_DESCRIPTOR_TYPE_UNIFORM_BUFFER with proper alignment for Vulkan.

GPU-Friendly Quaternion Skinning (Optional)

For lower bandwidth, send quaternions and positions instead of full matrices. In the shader, reconstruct the matrix:

```
mat4 quatToMatrix(vec4 q, vec3 t) {
    float x2 = q.x + q.x, y2 = q.y + q.y, z2 = q.z
+ q.z;
    float xx = q.x * x2, yy = q.y * y2, zz = q.z *
z2;
    float xy = q.x * y2, xz = q.x * z2, yz = q.y *
z2;
    float wx = q.w * x2, wy = q.w * y2, wz = q.w *
z2;
```

```
    mat4 m = mat4(1.0);
    m[0][0] = 1.0 - (yy + zz);
    m[0][1] = xy + wz;
    m[0][2] = xz - wy;

    m[1][0] = xy - wz;
    m[1][1] = 1.0 - (xx + zz);
    m[1][2] = yz + wx;

    m[2][0] = xz + wy;
    m[2][1] = yz - wx;
    m[2][2] = 1.0 - (xx + yy);

    m[3].xyz = t;
    return m;
}
```

Send `vec4 rotation + vec3 translation` as SSBOs or UBOs.

Visualizing Bone Weights

For debugging skinning, visualize bone weights directly in the fragment shader:

```
layout(location = 0) in vec2 fragTexCoord;

layout(location = 1) in vec3 fragNormal;


layout(location = 0) out vec4 outColor;


void main() {

    // Show weight of first 3 bones as RGB

    outColor = vec4(fragTexCoord.x, fragTexCoord.y,
1.0 - fragTexCoord.x, 1.0);

}
```

Replace with weight-based coloring to see influence per bone.

Vertex Skinning with Skinning Index Offset (Vulkan)

When batching characters into a single draw call, use an offset into the global bone buffer.

In C++:

```cpp
uint32_t boneOffsetPerCharacter[characterCount]; //
Packed UBO
```

In GLSL:

```glsl
layout(location = 5) in uint inBoneOffset;


mat4 skinMatrix =

    inBoneWeights.x * uBones.bones[inBoneOffset +
inBoneIndices.x] +

    inBoneWeights.y * uBones.bones[inBoneOffset +
inBoneIndices.y] +

    . . .
```

Set `inBoneOffset` via a per-instance attribute or push constant.

Smoothing Animation Transitions with Blend Factors

For blending two animations in a compute shader or vertex stage, use LERP for translation and SLERP for rotation.

GLSL Pose Blend:

```glsl
vec3 blendedPos = mix(posA, posB, blendFactor);
```

```glsl
quat blendedRot = slerp(rotA, rotB, blendFactor);
```

Pre-blend CPU-side or in a compute shader if you're batching multiple animated characters with different blend weights.

Debugging Skinning Output

Send position or bone index to the fragment shader to visually confirm correct deformation.

Shader Color Based on Joint Index:

```
layout(location = 5) in ivec4 inBoneIndices;


void main() {

    float boneId = float(inBoneIndices[0]);

    vec3 color = vec3(mod(boneId, 10.0) / 10.0,
0.5, 1.0 - mod(boneId, 5.0) / 5.0);

    outColor = vec4(color, 1.0);

}
```

This helps detect if incorrect bone indices are being used or if skinning matrices are misaligned.

These shader snippets serve as a solid foundation for implementing GPU-based character animation in OpenGL or Vulkan. Whether you're skinning in the vertex stage, blending animations on the CPU or GPU, or batching character instances efficiently, these examples provide the essentials you need. Adapt them to match your bone count, joint hierarchy layout, and animation system design.

Appendix C: Recommended Tools and Libraries (Assimp, ImGui, Bullet, etc.)

Real-time animation systems require much more than raw math and shaders—they also rely on solid tools for asset import, runtime visualization, physics integration, debugging, and development productivity. This appendix covers widely used, battle-tested libraries that can help you build and debug your character animation systems faster and more reliably.

Each tool listed here is open-source or freely available, and can be used in both prototyping and production environments.

Assimp (Asset Import Library)

Use Case: Load rigged models, skeletons, and animation clips from FBX, glTF, COLLADA, and other formats.

Key Features:

Parses over 30 formats.

Extracts meshes, node hierarchies, animation keyframes, bone weights, and more.

C-compatible API with C++ wrappers.

Website: https://www.assimp.org

Example Usage:

```
Assimp::Importer importer;

const aiScene* scene =
importer.ReadFile("character.fbx",
aiProcess_Triangulate |
aiProcess_LimitBoneWeights);
```

Why Use It: Assimp makes it easy to bring data from Blender, Maya, or Mixamo into your C++ engine, including joint names, inverse bind poses, and clip data.

ImGui (Immediate Mode GUI)

Use Case: Build developer-friendly UI for debugging animation graphs, inspecting pose data, or adjusting blend weights.

Key Features:

Simple C++ API.

Immediate-mode drawing.

Works with OpenGL, Vulkan, DirectX, and Metal.

Supports real-time sliders, graphs, and hierarchical trees.

Website: https://github.com/ocornut/imgui

Example:

```
ImGui::Begin("Animation Debug");

ImGui::Text("Current State: %s",
stateMachine.GetCurrentStateName());

ImGui::SliderFloat("Blend Factor", &blendFactor,
0.0f, 1.0f);

ImGui::End();
```

Why Use It: ImGui is perfect for developing internal tools, visualizing animation transitions, or adjusting parameters without recompiling.

Bullet Physics

Use Case: Physics-based animation effects, ragdolls, hit reactions, and collision detection.

Key Features:

Rigid body dynamics and constraints.

Soft body and cloth physics.

Raycasting and overlap tests.

Compatible with custom mesh and skeleton setups.

Website: https://pybullet.org/

Integration Tip: Map skeleton joints to Bullet rigid bodies for ragdoll transitions or physics-driven animation blending.

```
btRigidBody* thigh = CreateBoneBody("thigh", position, mass);
```

Why Use It: Bullet is lightweight, cross-platform, and integrates well with game engines and animation systems.

GLM (OpenGL Mathematics)

Use Case: All core animation math—vectors, matrices, quaternions, interpolation, and transforms.

Key Features:

Header-only library modeled after GLSL syntax.

Compatible with OpenGL and Vulkan.

Includes functions for pose blending, matrix decomposition, and rotation conversions.

Website: https://github.com/g-truc/glm

Why Use It: GLM gives you everything needed for animation math without external dependencies or runtime overhead.

RenderDoc

Use Case: GPU skinning inspection, vertex debug visualization, and shader validation.

Key Features:

Frame capture and replay.

View bone matrix uploads and vertex buffer contents.

Inspect shader inputs and outputs at any stage.

Website: https://renderdoc.org

Why Use It: When something goes wrong in GPU-based animation, RenderDoc helps you inspect the exact values being fed into the shader.

Blender

Use Case: Author animation clips, edit skeletons, rig characters, and preview motion in a DCC tool.

Key Features:

Open-source 3D modeling, rigging, and animation.

Export to FBX or glTF.

Python scripting for automation.

Website: https://www.blender.org

Why Use It: It's free, capable, and flexible. Ideal for creating test data and verifying animation behavior before import.

Mixamo

Use Case: Rapid prototyping with free humanoid animations.

Key Features:

Web-based animation library.

Hundreds of pre-made motion capture clips.

Auto-rigging support for humanoid characters.

Downloads in FBX, glTF formats.

Website: https://www.mixamo.com

Why Use It: Great for testing and prototyping without needing to author your own animation data.

Tracy / Remotery / Optick (Profilers)

Use Case: Animation CPU cost tracking, pose blending performance, IK solver profiling.

Key Features:

Visual timeline views.

Real-time or post-frame profiling.

Flame graphs, FPS graphs, per-thread breakdowns.

Why Use It: Performance insight is critical for scaling up character animation. Use profilers to spot bottlenecks in clip sampling, hierarchy evaluation, and pose transforms.

stb_image and tinygltf

Use Case: Load images and glTF files directly without large dependencies.

`stb_image.h` — for PNG/JPG/EXR/8-bit and 16-bit image loading.

`tinygltf` — header-only glTF loader with animation support.

Why Use It: Minimal dependencies, good for custom pipelines or when integrating with your own data loaders.

Vulkan SDK / glslang / SPIR-V Tools

Use Case: Compile and debug shaders for Vulkan animation pipelines.

Tools:

`glslangValidator` — compile GLSL to SPIR-V.

`spirv-dis`, `spirv-opt` — inspect and optimize compiled shaders.

Vulkan SDK — reference loader, validation layers, and headers.

Website: https://vulkan.lunarg.com

These tools provide a reliable foundation for every stage of real-time animation—authoring, importing, debugging, visualizing, simulating, and profiling. Whether you're building an in-house engine or extending an existing game framework, integrating these libraries into your workflow will save time, reduce bugs, and make your animation systems more flexible and performant.

Appendix D: Further Reading and Animation Resources

No animation system is ever truly finished. As techniques evolve and tools improve, staying current with best practices, advanced methods, and engine-specific guidance is crucial. This appendix compiles essential references, books, articles, communities, and repositories that will deepen your knowledge and help you explore real-time animation from every angle—technical, artistic, and architectural.

Books and Academic References

Game Programming Gems (volumes 1–8)
Contains dozens of technical articles on animation, state machines, inverse kinematics, procedural motion, and blend trees.

Real-Time Rendering (Tomas Akenine-Möller et al.)
A foundational graphics text that explains transform hierarchies, skinning, matrix math, and GPU-friendly design.

Mathematics for 3D Game Programming and Computer Graphics (Eric Lengyel)

Excellent deep dive into the math behind animation, including quaternions, matrix interpolation, and curve evaluation.

Computer Animation: Algorithms and Techniques (Rick Parent)
Covers animation from a film and simulation perspective, including rigging, motion capture, and constraints.

Advanced Animation with DirectX (Jim Adams)
Outdated API-wise but useful for understanding animation controller logic, transition graphs, and compression.

Online Articles and Guides

"Skinning Techniques for Real-Time Characters" – NVIDIA Developer
Comprehensive overview of skinning algorithms, GPU optimizations, and memory layout:
developer.nvidia.com

"A Hierarchical Approach to Real-Time Character Animation" – GDC Vault
An excellent breakdown of state-driven animation systems from industry production.

"Understanding Matrix Skinning" – Catlike Coding
A simple, clear explanation of bone skinning for GPU and CPU pipelines.

"Real-Time Character Animation With Blend Trees" – Unity Docs
While Unity-specific, the concepts generalize to any custom animation engine.

Open-Source Engines and Frameworks

Godot Engine
Contains a fully open-source animation system including state machines, blend trees, and bone manipulation.

Ogre3D
Mature C++ rendering engine with full skeletal animation support, GPU skinning, and animation controllers.

Bevy (Rust)
An ECS-based game engine with growing support for animation graphs and pose evaluation.

Filament (Google)
High-performance rendering engine with Vulkan and OpenGL backends; animation system includes glTF2 skeletal support.

GitHub Repositories and Sample Projects

`assimp/assimp` – Asset importer with examples of extracting skeletons and clips.

`ocornut/imgui` – Immediate-mode GUI used for animation debugging.

`mixamo2gltf` – Tools to convert Mixamo FBX files to glTF with skeleton remapping.

`tgjones/gltf-transform` – A CLI toolset for inspecting and optimizing glTF skeleton and animation data.

Animation Systems in Commercial Engines

While you may be building your own engine or framework, studying how commercial engines structure animation logic is invaluable.

Unity Animator Controller
Focuses on visual state machines and blend trees. Strong documentation and Playables API for custom rigs.

Unreal Engine Animation Blueprint
Highly modular. Includes IK solvers, bone drivers, and complex blend layers. Look into Unreal's Pose Caching and Motion Matching systems.

Communities and Learning Platforms

Polycount Forums
Great for rigging and animation art pipeline discussions.

GameDev Stack Exchange
Many practical programming and math answers related to animation blending and transforms.

r/gamedev and r/animation

Reddit communities for implementation questions, career advice, and demo feedback.

Shadertoy

While focused on shaders, it's helpful for learning GLSL and animating math expressions visually.

YouTube Channels and Video Series

GDC Talks on Character Animation

Many professional studios share their animation system breakdowns.

Brackeys / Game Endeavor / Mix and Jam

Indie-focused but often show clean and understandable third-person controller setups.

Sebastian Lague (Coding Adventure)

Particularly relevant for procedural IK, vector math, and custom rendering systems.

Technical animation sits at the intersection of math, motion, and engineering. These resources can expand your knowledge beyond this book, introduce new techniques, and expose you to production-quality implementations used across the industry. Whether you're refining a custom engine or learning to plug procedural IK into an off-the-shelf framework, these tools and communities will keep you sharp and inspired.

Glossary

Additive Animation
A method that allows overlaying secondary animation—such as breathing, recoil, or head movement—on top of a base animation. Instead of replacing the base pose, it adds or offsets joint transforms based on differences.

Assimp (Open Asset Import Library)
An open-source library used to import 3D models and animations from various file formats (FBX, glTF, COLLADA). Assimp parses skeletons, meshes, and keyframes and exposes them through a unified API in C++.

Bind Pose
The original, undeformed pose of a skeleton, typically with all joint rotations and translations set to neutral. It serves as the baseline for computing inverse bind transforms used during skinning.

Blend Factor
A floating-point value between 0.0 and 1.0 that determines how much influence each of two inputs has when interpolating or blending between poses or animations.

Blend Space / Blend Tree
A structure used to interpolate between multiple animations based on one or more parameters (e.g., speed or direction). A 1D blend space may interpolate between walk and run, while a 2D space can handle strafe directions.

Bone / Joint
An individual transform node in a character skeleton. Bones influence specific parts of a mesh and are typically organized in a hierarchy where each bone inherits transformation from its parent.

Bone Index and Weight
Used in skinning to associate a vertex with one or more bones. The index identifies the influencing joint, and the weight determines how much influence that joint has on the vertex.

Forward Kinematics (FK)

A method of computing the position and orientation of a bone by applying transformations starting from the root and proceeding through each child. It's the standard approach for pose evaluation from animation data.

GLM (OpenGL Mathematics Library)

A header-only C++ library designed to mirror GLSL syntax and behavior. It provides data types like `vec3`, `mat4`, and `quat`, along with functions for linear algebra operations, interpolation, and transformations.

GLSL (OpenGL Shading Language)

The language used to write shaders that run on the GPU. In animation, GLSL is commonly used in the vertex shader to perform GPU skinning using bone matrices.

GPU Skinning

A technique where mesh deformation due to skeletal movement is calculated on the GPU. This offloads computation from the CPU and improves performance, especially for multiple characters.

IK (Inverse Kinematics)

An algorithm that calculates the rotations and positions of bones to move the end of a joint chain (e.g., a hand or foot) to a specific target. Commonly used for foot placement and weapon aiming.

Keyframe

A recorded transformation (position, rotation, or scale) at a specific point in time for a bone or joint. An animation is composed of multiple keyframes across time for each bone.

Linear Blend Skinning (LBS)

The most common skinning technique in games. It blends the transformed positions of a vertex based on its associated bone matrices and their weights.

Local vs Global Transform

Local Transform: A bone's position and rotation relative to its parent.

Global Transform: The bone's absolute position and orientation in model space, computed by applying the full parent chain.

Look-At Rotation

A rotation that orients an object to face a specific target. It is computed using the direction vector to the target and an up vector to determine orientation.

Matrix Decomposition

The process of extracting position, scale, and rotation components from a transformation matrix. Used when converting between different animation representations.

Mixamo

An online service that provides rigging and pre-authored animations for humanoid characters. It outputs FBX or glTF files compatible with most game engines and animation tools.

Motion Blending

The interpolation of two or more poses or animations. This allows for smooth transitions between states such as idle, walk, and run, based on speed or input.

Pose

The full set of joint transformations for a skeleton at a given time. A pose can be generated from an animation keyframe or computed procedurally.

Quaternion

A four-dimensional mathematical representation of rotation that avoids gimbal lock and allows smooth interpolation (slerp). Quaternions are widely used in animation systems for joint orientation.

Raycast

A method of projecting a line through space to test for intersections with geometry. Used in animation for detecting terrain height during foot placement.

Skeletal Animation

A character animation system based on bones and joints that drive the deformation of a skinned mesh.

Skinning

The process of transforming mesh vertices based on the bones they are associated with. Vertices are weighted to multiple bones and moved accordingly to deform the mesh.

SLERP (Spherical Linear Interpolation)
An interpolation method used between two quaternions to create smooth rotational transitions. SLERP is preferred over linear interpolation for rotation to maintain constant angular velocity.

State Machine (Animation State Machine)
A structured approach to managing animation transitions. Each state represents a specific animation (e.g., idle, run), and transitions between states are defined based on conditions or inputs.

Transform
A combination of position, rotation, and scale. Often represented as a matrix or a combination of a vector, quaternion, and scalar.

UBO (Uniform Buffer Object)
A buffer object used in OpenGL and Vulkan to pass structured data (such as bone matrices) to shaders efficiently. UBOs are commonly used in skinning to send pose data to the vertex shader.

Vulkan
A low-overhead, cross-platform graphics API designed for high performance and parallelism. Vulkan provides explicit control over GPU resources and is used in animation pipelines for shader-based skinning.

www.ingramcontent.com/pod-product-compliance
Lightning Source LLC
La Vergne TN
LVHW081517050326
832903LV00025B/1527